NEW ILLUSTRATED

BRITISH HISTORY

This is a Starfire Book
First published in 2001

04 05 03

3 5 7 9 10 8 6 4 2

Starfire is part of
The Foundry Creative Media Company Limited
Crabtree Hall, Crabtree Lane, Fulham, London, SW6 6TY

Visit the Foundry website: www.foundry.co.uk

ISBN 1 84451 0 61 1

A copy of the CIP data for this book is available from the British Library

Printed in China

SPECIAL THANKS TO EVERYONE INVOLVED WITH THIS PROJECT:
Anna Amari, Frances Banfield, Lucy Bradbury, Roger Buckley, Helen Courtney, Claire Dashwood, Giskin Day, Karen Fitzpatrick, Vicky Garrard, Phil Hempell, George Keyes, Lesley Malkin, Geoffrey Meadon, Sonya Newland, Colin Rudderham, Mel Shaw, Andrea Simmonds, Graham Stride, Helen Tovey, Helen Wall, Sharon Weiss, Nick Wells.

NEW ILLUSTRATED

BRITISH HISTORY

Gerard Cheshire, David Harding, Lucinda Hawksley,
Brenda Ralph Lewis, Jon Sutherland, Helen Tovey

GENERAL EDITOR - PROFESSOR ERIC EVANS

SELECT
EDITIONS

CONTENTS

THEMES

Each A–Z entry is tagged by themes which can be followed as threads throughout the book

Culture **Politics** **Royalty** **War**
Industry **Religion** **Society**

INTRODUCTION

BRITISH HISTORY is an endlessly fascinating subject which can be studied on several levels. Firstly, there is the story of the emergence of a nation in the ninth and tenth centuries from divided and frequently warring local kingdoms. Anglo-Saxon England appeared stable and usually prosperous, until the Norman Conquest of 1066 instituted not only a political but a social revolution, witnessing, as it did, the brutal replacement of one stable landed elite by another, foreign one. Norman and its successor, Angevin rule, proved immensely durable. In various guises, it would survive for more than 400 years; 1066 was to be the last occasion of a successful invasion by a foreign power.

It is possible, but nowadays rather unfashionable, to present the history of post-conquest Britain in terms of general success and increasing influence. Thus, the civil wars of the mid-fifteenth century were ended by the Battle of Bosworth in 1485 which installed a new Tudor dynasty. The Tudors gave the English more efficient government and, with the removal of papal influence from the state during the reign of Henry VIII, a new and increasingly self-confident independence. Passing rapidly over the troubled, short reigns of Edward VI and Mary I, we can dwell on the shrewd and, when necessary, consummately ruthless rule of Elizabeth I, the so-called Virgin Queen, who consolidated a viable Protestant rule in England and saw off an invasion threat from the immensely powerful Philip II of Spain in 1588. Elizabeth also used Parliament when needed, whom she flattered that she was consulting for its advice (when really she wanted its money). The seventeenth century witnessed titantic struggles between the Stuart monarchy and propertied Englishmen represented in Parliament. This century saw civil wars, a brief and troubled republic, the restoration of the monarchy and then monarchical wings decisively clipped by the bloodless and so-called 'Glorious Revolution' of 1688. Since that date, no year has passed without a session of Parliament and monarchs have had to acknowledge clear and defined limits to their power.

The eighteenth and nineteenth centuries witnessed the gradual emergence of a genuine parliamentary government and a reduced (but never a derisory) role for the monarchy. Britain could present itself as the most 'enlightened' nation in Europe and was certainly, by the end of the eighteenth century, the richest. Success in the Revolutionary and Napoleonic Wars saw Britain, from 1815, established as unchallengeably the most powerful nation in the world. The long reign of Victoria (1837–1901) can be represented as the apogee of British power and influence. British leaders felt that they could offer huge benefits to the world. Britain seemed to provide a stable, progressive parliamentary government in which power changed hands peacefully as decided by a large, if still all-male electorate. A constitutional monarch of immense prestige, Victoria was a Queen-Empress from 1876 and was related, by the 1880s, to virtually every other royal house in Europe. A peaceful reign, Britain fought only one brief European war in the century from 1815–1914, which naturally she won. Economic prosperity was aided by a beneficent Empire, grounded in the need for trade, but always ready to educate subject races into the advantages of Protestant religion and a close association with the mother country. Whatever the rest of the world may have thought, British self-confidence and certainty of its own superiority appeared

impregnable. The golden and diamond jubilees of Victoria's accession in 1887 and 1897 were occasions of lavish and triumphal imperial self-congratulation.

Those who picture British history over a millennium as a natural progression, have more trouble with the twentieth century. Two cataclysmic world wars were both won, but at an enormous, unsustainable cost. These wars (in which British colonies and Commonwealth associates played an important part) witnessed the beginnings of the end of Empire. Although British withdrawal from its colonial possessions from the late 1940s to the late 1970s was, in general, a relatively dignified and peaceful affair, it proved difficult to answer the shrewd, and cutting, accusation of the far-from-hostile American critic, Dean Ascheson, that by the 1960s, Britain had lost an empire and failed to find a role. Assimilation with a wider European framework has proved a problematic and controversial affair and no substitute for ruling an empire on which the sun never set. Few would argue that the British have been either eager or successful Europeans since entering the Common Market in 1973. Europe, as a political issue, had brought the Conservatives (once the most successful, democratic political party in the western world) to a pitiful, bickering rump by the beginning of the twenty-first century. Whether New Labour, its successor (however temporarily), as 'the natural party of government', owes anything at all to its roots a century before as a Labour party of, and for, working people and 'the left-out millions', is a matter of high dispute.

Nowadays, though, few want to present British history in this linear way. 'Dominant narratives' are out of fashion. There is no agreement on which events or developments are most important. More historians are now interested in looking at the past from different perspectives. Some have made careers looking at history in a 'bottom up' way and trying to reconstruct the lives, struggles and cultures of those who lacked power and, frequently, the literacy to leave written records of their own. Social history, the dominant perspective of the 1960s and 1970s, has been transformed into cultural history, from the 1980s, with a greater emphasis on shifting perspectives and multiple identities. What it is to be English, let alone British, has been the subject of fierce contention. Certainly, British history can no longer be presented as 'southern English, centrist, moderated by occasional, apologetic glances north and west'. The secure certainties of an imperial power have given way to an anguished introspection, not only about identity, but the nature of history itself.

This volume does not aim to answer deep, philosophical questions about the nature of the subject History, still less probe the future to discern where it is heading. Its aim is less ambitious but, arguably, more satisfying. It gives readers brief, succinct answers to questions about the leading figures, movements and developments in British history over almost two millennia. From this rich assortment of factual information, readers can be led into further and deeper enquiry. If this book proves either a secure starting point for detailed later investigation, or merely the reliable answer to a particular historical query which has puzzled the reader, it will have served its purpose.

PROFESSOR ERIC EVANS

ABDICATION CRISIS (1936)

Furore surrounding the relationship between King Edward VIII and the twice-divorced American Wallis Simpson. The king abdicated on 11 December 1936 after it had been made clear by prime minister Stanley Baldwin and others that Mrs Simpson would not be acceptable as queen. He resigned his throne rather than give her up.

➠ ***Edward VIII, Wallis Simpson***

ABERDEEN GEORGE HAMILTON GORDON, LORD (1784–1860)

British prime minister (1852–55). Aberdeen held the positions of foreign secretary under the Duke of Wellington and Robert Peel. He became Tory prime minister in 1852, but criticism of his management of the crisis in the Crimea forced his resignation three years later.

➠ ***Robert Peel, Duke of Wellington***

ABERFAN DISASTER (1966)

On 21 October 1966 a slag heap at Aberfan in Wales collapsed under its own weight, burying the Pantglas school situated below in two million tons of rock, coal and mud. The disaster left 116 children and 28 adults dead.

ABOLITIONISTS (18TH CENTURY)

Group of eighteenth-century philanthropists who campaigned for the abolition of the slave trade. The Abolition Society was formed in 1787 and Abolitionists travelled around to ports investigating the conditions on slave ships and interviewing captains and crews. The slave trade was finally banned in Britain in 1807.

The settlement of America and other newly discovered lands by Europeans in the sixteenth century coincided with trade routes opening up between Europe and Africa. Trade triangles were established in which ships would carry goods from the colonies to Europe then sail to Africa and buy a cargo of slaves. The slaves would be sold at a profit in the colonies and the process would begin again. In the eighteenth century a group of philanthropists in Britain began a campaign to stop the exploitation of African negroes and other races, but the high profits resulting from slave labour meant they had a fight on their hands. The English evangelist William Wilberforce was instrumental in the abolition of slavery in British dominions by forcing the Abolition Bill through Parliament.

➠ ***William Wilberforce***

ABSOLUTISM

Total and unquestioning acceptance of royal commands, or total obedience to the will of a monarch, whose person and policies are regarded as perfect and unassailable. Absolutism is a result of ascribing divinity to a ruler, making him or her tantamount to God's representative in the business of government.

➠ ***Charles I, James I of England and VI of Scotland***

ACT OF SETTLEMENT (1701)

Act of Parliament passed in 1701, decreeing that Queen Anne should be succeeded by Sophia, Electress of Hanover, a Protestant descendant of James I. Other provisions of the Act were that sovereigns must be members of the Church of England, could not dismiss judges except at Parliament's request or pardon ministers already impeached by Parliament.

➠ ***Queen Anne, Hanoverian Dynasty, Test Act***

ACT OF TOLERATION (1689)

Legislation passed immediately after the Glorious Revolution which allowed religious dissenters to worship in their own meeting houses under licence from the bishop. Ministers were nevertheless intended to subscribe to most of the Thirty-Nine Articles which defined the faith of the Church of England. Thus, although this Act has been seen as a turning point in the history of religious toleration, and although it encouraged the growth of a large number of Dissenting places of worship, its impact can easily be exaggerated. Catholics and Unitarians were excluded from its provisions.

➠ ***Church of England, Church of Scotland, Church of Wales, Enlightenment, Glorious Revolution, Mary II, William III***

ACT OF UNION (1707)

Act that saw England and Scotland unite politically. The Act reflected English dominance and the loss of Scottish political independence. It created one Parliament covering the two countries, with the Scottish Parliament disappearing. Scotland was represented by 45 MPs and 16 peers in the new Parliament. It retained its own laws and religious identity. The Act had its seeds in the seventeenth century when the two countries' Parliaments claimed precedent over each other. Queen Anne was the first monarch of the Union. She paved the way for the Act by agreeing to the succession of the Hanoverian dynasty after none of her children lived to adulthood.

➜ ***Act of Settlement, Queen Anne***

ADAM, ROBERT (1728–92)

Scottish architect. Robert Adam was one of the Adams Brothers, with his architect siblings, William, John and James. Robert studied at Edinburgh University, then travelled through Italy to study the buildings there. The brothers then established an architecture practice in London. In 1762 Robert became sole architect to the king; he resigned after six years in office to become an MP The Adams style, particularly in interiors, has become an enduring characteristic of British architecture.

ADELAIDE, QUEEN (1792–1849)

Born Adelaide of Saxe-Meiningen. Wife of William IV. They married in 1818 in the 'rush to the altar' by George III's sons with the intention of providing heirs to the throne after the death of Princess Charlotte, the Prince Regent's daughter. Two daughters were born to William and Adelaide, but both died in infancy.

➜ ***William IV***

ABOVE Queen Anne receiving the Act of Union

AFGHAN WARS (1839–42, 1878, 1919)

Three wars between Afghanistan and Britain caused by the threat of increasing Russian influence in British India. The First Afghan War began when the Afghan ruler Dost Mohammed refused an alliance with Britain (1838). Britain invaded and replaced Dost Mohammed with Shah Suja; two years later the British envoy in Kabul was murdered and Akbar Khan, Dost Mohammed's military leader, demanded British withdrawal. Britain complied but were attacked by the Afghans along their route. A British force arrived at the Khyber Pass, defeating the Afghans twice before burning Kabul. Dost Mohammed was reinstated in 1842.

In 1878 a Russian mission arrived in Kabul, sparking off the Second Afghan War, which saw the British regain control of Afghanistan. In 1879 the British envoy was murdered and the Afghan ruler, Amir Yakoub Khan, dethroned. At Maiwand and Kandahar the British again asserted their control of the country.

The Third Afghan War took place between May and August 1919, after Afghan forces invaded British India. The outcome was inconclusive, but Afghanistan gained full independence by terms of the peace treaty.

AGINCOURT, BATTLE OF (1415)

Battle fought on 25 October 1415 during the Hundred Years' War, in which a small and battle-weary force of Englishmen under the leadership of Henry V defeated a superior French army.

Following the English capture of Harfleur, Henry V's army was retreating back towards Calais, severely weakened by hunger and disease, planning to return to England. The 25,000-strong French army under the Constable of France, Charles d'Albret, intercepted the smaller 6,000-man English force. An English request for a truce was rejected and they deployed on a narrow front in driving rain. The French troops, mainly heavily armoured cavalry, thundered towards the more mobile English archers and quickly became immobile in the mud. Hundreds were slaughtered. The English advanced, dispatched the stricken cavalry and successfully attacked the French infantry. Over 500 members of the French nobility were killed, including d'Albret, amongst their 5,000 dead. English losses numbered only about 200 men. After the battle England dominated most of France until the middle of the fifteenth century.

➡ ***Henry V, Hundred Years' War***

AGRICULTURAL REVOLUTION (18TH CENTURY)

Name given to the advances in agricultural technology during the eighteenth century. The era saw a wave of industrial inventions that improved the efficiency of farming crops and set agriculture on a new path.

The Agricultural Revolution began in earnest with an invention thought up by English agriculturalist Jethro Tull (1674–1741). In around 1701 he built a machine that he called a 'seed drill', which was designed to solve the problems inherent with sowing seed by hand. The seed drill, which was pulled by horses, inserted seed into the soil in even rows across a tilled field. Hand sowing had always resulted in a random distribution of seed over the field with the additional problem of the seed remaining on the surface, less likely to germinate and vulnerable to hungry birds. Tull's machine changed this and made it possible to weed and harvest the crop with far less wastage. Before long various other machines were seen out in the fields, each designed for performing a different agricultural task: ploughing, tilling, scything and threshing. Improvements in efficiency, combined with various changes in farming management all contributed to the revolution in agriculture.

➡ ***Industrial Revolution***

AIDAN, ST (c. AD 600–51)

Saint and founder of Lindisfarne monastery. Aidan was born in Ireland and then became a monk on the isle of Iona. He went on to establish the monastery on Lindisfarne (Holy Island), convert the vast and prestigious kingdom of Northumbria and become its bishop. He and his missionaries worked under the monarchs Oswald and Oswy. Bede records Aidan's piety and preaching skills. He died on 31 August, subsequently his feast day.

➡ ***Celtic Christianity, Lindisfarne Gospels***

ABOVE Henry V fighting the French during the Battle of Agincourt
FAR RIGHT Philotas being threatened by pikes before Alexander

AIX-LA-CHAPELLE, TREATY OF (1748)

Treaty which ended the War of the Austrian Succession in 1748. It awarded Silesia and Glatz to Prussia and gave Parma, Piacenza and Guastalla to the Spanish. Great Britain continued to have control of slave transportation to Spanish America and important trade agreements with the Spanish colonies. Significantly, the treaty also recognised Protestant succession in England. Prussia emerged as a major European power and the Hapsburgs began to look to the east in order to develop their state.

➠ *War of the Austrian Succession*

ALBAN, ST (AD 3RD CENTURY)

First British Christian martyr. Bede records that Alban was a Roman soldier who, on sheltering a fugitive priest, consequently converted to Christianity. They exchanged clothes and Alban was martyred in his place sometime between AD 209 and AD 304. By AD 429 a church had been established on the site of his martyrdom and later the abbey of St Albans was built there. His martyrdom was typical of the periodic Roman persecution of Christians.

ALBERT, PRINCE (1819–61)

Prince of Saxe-Coburg-Gotha, Germany. Husband of Queen Victoria, whom he married in 1840. Albert was made prince consort by the queen in 1857. Although not greatly liked in England, Albert performed sterling services to the British monarchy and to British cultural life. A brilliant man, whose talents bordered on genius, Prince Albert actively promoted science and the arts, notably with the Great Exhibition of 1851, which he masterminded. He was influential in the establishment of museums at Kensington in London, where many exhibits were later housed. Albert was also a strong influence in foreign affairs. A somewhat prudish man, he helped Victoria create a royal family image of moral family life and respectability. Albert introduced the German-style Christmas to Britain. Victoria, by whom he had four sons and five daughters, adored Prince Albert and was shattered by his early death, probably from typhoid, at the age of 42.

➠ *Edward VII, Great Exhibition, Queen Victoria*

ALCUIN (c. AD 732–804)

Innovator, educator and cleric, but not a saint. Alcuin lived in York for 50 years before becoming the pre-eminent scholar at Charlemagne's court at Aachen in AD 781. His formative influence in Western Europe was his development of the Frankish liturgy and his introduction of Humanist thought. Despite being only a deacon he retains his place in history: his legacy of approximately 300 Latin letters remain a valuable contemporary source.

ALEXANDER I (c. 1080–1124)

King of Scotland (1107–24). A younger son of Malcolm III. Alexander succeeded his brother Edgar as king of Scotland in 1107. He possibly acquired the nickname 'Alexander the Fierce' for his brutality in suppressing an uprising in Moray. Alexander built several castles in Scotland, including Stirling Castle. Among many important reforms, Alexander introduced the first sheriffs into Scotland as Guardians of the King's Peace. Alexander died at Stirling Castle and was buried in Dunfermline Abbey.

➠ *Malcolm III*

ALEXANDER II (1198–1249)

King of Scotland (1214–49). Although known as 'The Peaceful', Alexander ruled with an iron fist; he once displayed the severed head of a rebel leader at his court as a warning to others. When the English barons rose up against King John, Alexander supported them and was one of the signatories of the Magna Carta (1215). The lords of Argyll rebelled against Alexander in 1249, but he died of a fever while preparing for battle against them.

➠ *King John, Magna Carta*

ALEXANDER III (1241–86)

King of Scotland (1249–86), son of Alexander II. Alexander III was seven years old when he succeeded his father. Scotland was peaceful and prosperous during his reign, hence Alexander's nickname 'The Glorious'. Alexander set the boundaries of Scotland after purchasing the Western Isles from Norway in 1266. His personal life was tragic: his wife Margaret died young, in 1275, followed by three of their four children. Alexander himself died in 1286, when his horse stumbled over a cliff.

ALFRED THE GREAT (c. AD 847–99)

King of Wessex (AD 871–99). The youngest son of Athelwolf, king of Kent and Wessex, Alfred was the last of four brothers to rule Wessex in succession. His reign was marked by successful struggles against the Danish invaders. He is also remembered for his encouragement of learning.

On his accession, Alfred inherited the struggle against the Viking invaders and spent most of his reign battling against them. Alfred finally brought the fighting to an end in AD 878 with the Peace of Wedmore, which granted them the Danelaw, an area comprising about half of England. At his insistence, the Danes' leader, Guthrum, became a Christian. In the subsequent eight years of peace, Alfred fortified several boroughs, including Oxford and Hastings, and refortified London. He reorganised and strengthened the English navy and introduced a code of laws. Anxious to promote learning in his kingdom, Alfred encouraged literacy and the study of Latin. Although he was never king of all England, Alfred, the only English monarch to be termed 'The Great' was acknowledged as its overlord.

➠ *Anglo-Saxon Chronicle, Athelstan, Edward the Elder*

ABOVE Alfred the Great fighting off the Vikings
RIGHT The investment of Yorktown

ALLIES, THE (1941)

Term describing the nations that opposed the Axis Forces of Germany, Italy and Japan during World War II. In the first two years of the war this referred to the British Commonwealth and Western European states. Both the USSR and the USA were neutral. The Japanese attack on Pearl Harbor in 1941 brought the Americans into the war on the side of the Allies. Eisenhower favoured the Europe-first approach, and so the combined efforts of the United States, Canada, Great Britain, the USSR and France turned on Germany before facing the Japanese threat in the East.

➠ *World War II*

AMERICAN REVOLUTION (1775–83)

Conflict between Great Britain and members of the 13 British-owned colonies in North America. The revolution (or American War of Independence) eventually resulted in the British losing these colonies and the setting up of an independent United States.

Following the Treaty of Paris, which had brought the Seven Years' War to an end in 1763, Britain found itself in possession of vast territories. In order to recoup the costs of the long conflict, harsh economic and financial measures brought intolerable burdens to the 13 British

colonies. The Sugar Act was introduced in 1764 and the Stamp Act in 1765. The Townshend Duties further increased burdens on commodities such as glass, tea and paper. In 1774 the first American Congress passed the Declaration of Rights. In April the following year General Gage, aiming to seize rebel munitions and agitators in Lexington, sparked off the first battle. On 15 June 1775 George Washington was appointed commander-in-chief and fought the successful action at Bunker Hill. On 1 January 1776, Washington hoisted the colonial flag and on 4 July Congress proclaimed the Declaration of Independence. Now facing General Howe, Washington was forced to undertake a series of battles against veteran British troops. By 1778 the French, under Admiral d'Estaing, had arrived to support the Revolutionaries. The next year saw a series of indecisive battles in the north, but after Cornwallis was defeated by Washington at Camden, the British became entrenched at Yorktown. With the French fleet blockading the harbour, Cornwallis was forced to surrender on 19 October 1781. In 1783 Britain recognised the former colonies as an independent nation and the new American constitution was ratified in 1789.

➨ ***Charles Cornwallis, George III, Battle of Yorktown***

AMRITSAR MASSACRE (1919)

The killing of 379 Indians on 13 April 1919 by British troops in Amritsar, Punjab. A further 1,200 were injured. During World War I over a million Indian soldiers served in the British armed forces. Half of these came from the Punjab. Once the war was over, Britain introduced the Rowlatt Acts, which extended wartime emergency measures into peacetime. Those killed at Amritsar were protesting against these Acts. General Reginald Dyer led a force of 50 soldiers who fired 1,650 rounds of ammunition into a crowd of 10,000 unarmed people. The issue resurfaced in October 1997 when on a state visit to India, the queen resisted calls to apologise to India for the massacre.

ANDREW, ST (d. c. AD 60)

One of the 12 Apostles and patron saint of Scotland. A fisherman follower of John the Baptist until Jesus called him and Peter to become 'fishers of men'. The earliest record of his crucifixion is the fourth century, and it was not until the Middle Ages that it is recorded as an X-shape cross, as in the Scots flag. His relics travelled the Mediterranean, but Pope Paul VI finally returned his head to Patras, the place of his death, in 1964. His feast day is 30 November.

ANGEVIN DYNASTY (1154–1485)

Alternative name for the more commonly called Plantagenet dynasty, which ruled England from the accession of Henry II in 1154 to the death of Richard III in 1485. Both the names Angevin, the more correct, and Plantagenet derived from Count Geoffrey of Anjou, father of Henry II. Geoffrey is said to have acquired the nickname of Plantagenet from the *planta genista*, a stick of broom he habitually wore in his hat.

➨ ***Plantagenet dynasty***

ANGLICANISM

Pre-eminent branch of Protestantism in England, being the doctrine of the established Church of England. The seeds of Anglicanism were sown with the Break with Rome and the Reformation. Charles I and William Laud implemented High Anglicanism, which was intolerant and particularly unacceptable in Scotland. After the Restoration, Charles II made the Church of England the established Church and the whole spectrum of Anglicanism, from Anglo-Catholicism to Evangelical Puritanism, developed. This variety continues to this day.

Break with Rome, Charles I, Elizabeth I, William Laud, Protestantism, Reformation

ANGLO-DUTCH WARS (1652–54, 1664–67, 1672–74, 1780–84)

Series of wars between the English and the Dutch over control of the seas and expansion of empire. The wars saw control of the seas change hands several times throughout the seventeenth and eighteenth centuries. By the conclusion the final war, England had regained control.

As the English and the Dutch were the two leading maritime trading nations in the world in the second half of the seventeenth century, their intense commercial rivalry soon became a reason for armed conflict. Between 1650 and 1652 the British passed three Navigation Acts that effectively excluded the Dutch from their trade. The first war culminated in English control of the seas by the summer of 1653, severely damaging Dutch business. Luckily for the Dutch, the Stadtholderless Dutch Republic managed to regain control. The second war began when Charles II declared war on the Dutch on 4 March 1665. A plague broke out in England in 1667, forcing them to scale down the conflict. However, when the third war broke out in 1672 England gained the upper hand until naval defeat and public opinion forced them to quit the war in 1674. The final war culminated in Dutch defeat off Ostend in June 1784, having been sparked off by Dutch trading with the rebellious American colonies, despite England being allied to the Dutch for 100 years after the Dutch king, William of Orange, had become king of England. The Dutch fleet was completely destroyed with a loss of over 2,000 men.

ANGLO-IRISH AGREEMENT (1985)

Agreement signed in 1985 by the British and Irish governments to increase the level of co-operation between the two countries. It was signed by prime minister Margaret Thatcher and the taoiseach Garret Fitzgerald. The agreement sought to limit terrorism and was a sign of the greater trust developing between London and Dublin. Contentiously, it gave Dublin a greater say in affairs in Northern Ireland. The agreement proved deeply unpopular with unionists who accused the British government of paving the way for control of the North by the Republic and the 'No Surrender' which reasserted the loyalists' position was launched.

Margaret Thatcher

ANGLO-SAXON CHRONICLE (AD 891)

Record of life during the Anglo-Saxon period begun in the reign of Alfred the Great. With the withdrawal of Roman legions in AD 410, Britain began its turbulent rebirth. During the fifth, sixth and seventh centuries Britain was subjected to waves of invasion from various peoples of Germanic origin. They included the Jutes, Angles and Saxons. Their descendants became known as Anglo-Saxons. The *Anglo-Saxon Chronicle* gave a year-by-year account of life in England from the Roman

LEFT The English and Dutch fight for control of the seas
RIGHT A page from the Anglo-Saxon Chronicle

invasion and continued right through to the twelfth century. Although some parts are less detailed than others, the *Chronicle* remains the most valuable source of information about the early history of Britain to date.

➡ ***Alfred the Great, Anglo-Saxons***

ANGLO-SAXONS (5TH–11TH CENTURIES)

Name given to the descendants of the Jutes, Angles and Saxons who invaded the British Isles between the fifth and seventh centuries. Once they had settles into their respective kingdoms they were subject to further threats of invasion from overseas, but it was the Normans who finally overthrew the Anglo-Saxons in 1066.

England was occupied by the Romans from AD 43–410. As a part of the Roman Empire England was introduced to a period of order, albeit under the thumb of a suppressive regime. When the Roman Empire crumbled and withdrew its legions in AD 410 England found itself lacking an infrastructure. In this state it was vulnerable to invasion by new peoples from the European mainland. Soon tribes from the Germanic region of mid-northern Europe were launching waves of invasion against the Britons. From the fifth to the seventh century Britain was occupied by these conquering populations, who included the Jutes, Angles and Saxons. Eventually Britain became divided into kingdoms as the nation separated into Germanic factions. The kingdoms included Wessex (the kingdom of the West Saxons), Essex (the kingdom of the East Saxons), and Sussex (the kingdom of the South Saxons). The Angles claimed the kingdoms of East Anglia, Mercia and Northumbria, while the Jutes had Kent and South Hampshire. As there were seven principal kingdoms they were collectively referred to as the Heptarchy. Now described as the Anglo-Saxon kingdoms, they covered the area that now comprises England and lowland Scotland.

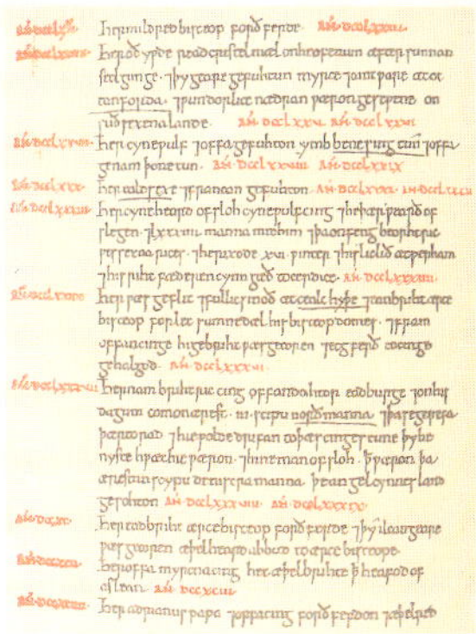

The Anglo-Saxons had to defend their kingdoms from yet more invading forces. The Danes or Vikings – Norsemen originating from Scandinavia – landed on British shores attempting to take control of the island. The Anglo-Saxons united under the overlordship of Wessex, successfully defending southern England from occupation. However, the Danes seized control of a large area of north-eastern territory which became known as the Danelaw. Finally, in 1066, the Anglo-Saxon reign came to an end when the Normans invaded England under William the Conqueror.

The Anglo-Saxons left behind some valuable contributions to British culture. Not least the Anglo-Saxon or Old English language, which was the foundation for modern English. They also bequeathed intricate and decorative manuscripts and pieces of early Christian religious artwork.

➡ ***Alfred the Great, Anglo-Saxon Chronicle, Danelaw, Norman Dynasty, Vikings***

ANNE OF CLEVES (1515–57)

Fourth wife of Henry VIII, whose marriage to him in 1540 was arranged for political reasons. Henry took a dislike to Anne at first sight and refused to consummate the marriage. They were divorced after six months. Anne remained in England. She was the last survivor among Henry's six wives.

➡ ***Henry VIII***

ANNE, QUEEN (1665–1714)

Queen of England (1702–14). Younger daughter of James II. Anne inherited the throne after the deaths of the joint monarchs Mary II and William of Orange. The most notable event of her reign was the Act of Union, which saw England and Scotland united politically.

With her elder sister Mary, the future Mary II, Anne's importance rested on her Protestant faith at a time when her father was attempting to restore Roman Catholicism in England in 1685–88. Parliament was determined to have a Protestant monarchy, and James II was deposed and forced into exile. Anne became heir presumptive to the throne, after Mary and Mary's husband, William III. Anne married Prince George of Denmark in 1683. Though a political marriage designed to cement Anglo-Danish relations, it was a very happy one. It was, however, blighted by the deaths or miscarriage of all 17 of their children. Anne became queen on the death of William III in 1702, with no heir of her own. The premature death in 1701 of her last surviving child, William of Gloucester, prompted Parliament to pass the Act of Succession in which the throne passed to the Electors of Hanover.

Queen Anne has often been presented as weak-willed, suggestible and stupid. This may derive from her long associations with her favourites, the strong-minded Sarah, Duchess of Marlborough and Sarah's ambitious successor, Abigail Masham. Recent research has recast Anne as tough, assertive and politically aware. She regularly attended meetings of the Cabinet and debates in the House of Lords, and frequently conferred with her ministers, showing a firm grasp of affairs. She avoided becoming the 'captive' of any political group. Despite chronic ill-health, due mainly to her frequent pregnancies, Anne was definitely the queen in command.

Act of Succession, Act of Union, John Churchill, James II, Mary II, William III

ANSELM, ST (c. 1033–1109)

Archbishop of Canterbury and player in the investiture controversy. Born in Lombardy, Anselm's intellectual, pious career continued on the continent until William II appointed him Archbishop of Canterbury in 1093. Then arose the investiture controversy. The Council of Rockingham was called to decide whether it was a monarchical or papal right to grant an ecclesiastical position: the bishops backed the king. Anselm left for Europe and wrote his key work, *Cur Deus Homo*? ('Why Did God Become Man?'). Henry I recalled Anselm but in 1103–06 the controversy re-emerged and Anselm again went into exile. In 1163 Becket submitted Anselm's life for canonisation.

Thomas Becket, Henry I, William II

ANTONINE WALL (AD 142)

Barrier constructed to mark the northern frontier of the Roman territory in England. The wall was built in AD 142 under the orders of the emperor Antonius Pius and ran between the rivers Clyde and Forth. It was intended to keep out marauders from the north. It was guarded for some 60 years.

Hadrian's Wall

ARBROATH, DECLARATION OF (1320)

Declaration of Scottish independence. The Declaration of Arbroath in 1320 asserted Scotland's independence following Robert Bruce's victory over the English at Bannockburn in 1314. Composed by the Scottish parliament in Arbroath Abbey and sent to the pope in Avignon. After one further invasion in 1320 the English signed a 13-year truce.

Robert Bruce, Edward II

ARCHBISHOP OF CANTERBURY

Primate of the Church of England. An archbishop has episcopal authority over his diocese, as does a bishop, but he also has jurisdiction over the other bishops in a province. The title of Archbishop of Canterbury first emerged in the seventh century. It is primarily due to

BOTTOM RIGHT The second day of the Battle of Arnhem Bridge
FAR RIGHT King Arthur and Queen Guinevere leaving a banquet

St Augustine's landing in Kent that Canterbury, rather than London, developed as the principal see in England. Significant archbishops have included martyrs and dictators, notably Thomas Becket and William Laud.

➤ ***St Augustine, Thomas Becket, William Laud***

ARKWRIGHT, RICHARD (1732–92)

English inventor. In 1768 Richard Arkwright contrived a machine for spinning the new material cotton. He called his device a 'spinning frame'. It was just one of various pioneering introductions he made to the textiles industry during his lifetime. Three years after perfecting the spinning frame he set up a spinning factory in which the machinery was driven by water power. Two years before his death he installed a steam engine in his Nottingham factory.

➤ ***Industrial Revolution***

ARNHEM, BATTLE OF (1944)

The largest paratrooper action in history. On 17 September 1944, in an attempt to outflank the Siegfried Line, two American and one British airborne divisions were dropped to secure the bridges from Nijmegen to Arnhem. The intention was to capture the valuable Ruhr region – the industrial heartland of the Axis forces. With orders to hold the bridges until land forces arrived, the airborne troops withstood vicious German counter-attacks. Bad weather and the slow progress of the ground troops led to defeat at Arnhem itself and the overall plan, Operation Market Garden, was only partially successful.

➤ ***Allies, World War II***

ARRAS, BATTLES OF (1914–18)

Series of battles in World War I. In the first battle of the campaign German troops occupied the town of Arras from September 1–18, losing it to French forces. The 1915 battle saw 113,000 French deaths with similar German losses. In April and May 1917 Sir Douglas Haig cleared the Germans from the Vimy Ridge. In March 1918, 15 German divisions attacked Arras; they were beaten back with huge losses. On 26 August 1918 British and Canadian forces attacked east Arras, and despite German counter-attack, captured nearly 19,000 prisoners and 2,000 guns.

➤ ***World War I***

ARTHUR, KING (c. AD 6TH CENTURY)

Legendary British king, first made famous by Geoffrey of Monmouth in his *Historia Regum Brittaniae* (History of the Kings of Britain,1136). The real-life 'King Arthur' was possibly a Romano-British chieftain called Artorius or Ambrosius Aurelianus, who used Roman military methods to fight Anglo-Saxon invaders. The romances of King Arthur, Queen Guinevere, their court at Camelot, the Round Table, the magician Merlin and the quest for the Holy Grail developed by the thirteenth century. Arthur was said to have been killed at the battle of Mount Badon (*c.* AD 539). His tomb was supposedly discovered by monks at Glastonbury Abbey in 1190.

➤ ***Glastonbury Tor***

ARTS AND CRAFTS MOVEMENT (LATE 19TH CENTURY)

English artistic movement. Two formative exponents of the movement were William Morris and John Ruskin. The Arts and Crafts Movement began as a reaction to the effects of the Industrial Revolution. By the end of the nineteenth century, the majority of furniture sold in Britain was mass-produced in factories. Many critics complained that it had lost its beauty and craftsmanship through the methods of mass-production. Arts and Crafts devotees wanted a return to artistic expertise and hand-made goods. The movement also saw a reaction against the excessively ornate style typical of the Victorian era. The movement took its name from the Arts and Crafts Exhibition Society, which was set up in 1887 to exhibit the work of artisans. Among the founding members of the exhibition were William Morris and the designer Walter Crane.

➡ ***Industrial Revolution, William Morris***

ASCOT (1711)

Horse racing ground. Royal Ascot Racecourse is in close proximity to Windsor Castle. Although there are race meetings held here throughout the racing season, it is Royal Ascot (in June) for which the course is most famed. The very first horse race to be held at this course was suggested by Queen Anne and took place in 1711.

➡ ***Windsor Castle***

ASKE, ROBERT [1500–37]

Leader of the uprising known as the Pilgrimage of Grace in 1536–37. In 1532 Henry VIII broke with the Catholic Church, declaring himself head of the new Church of England. His policies, including the Dissolution of the Monasteries led to rebellion, particularly in the northern counties. Robert Aske, a barrister from a good Yorskshire family, was the key player in the most significant of these, the Pilgrimage of Grace. Despite efforts at conciliation, Henry failed to fulfill his promises and Aske and other leaders were executed.

➡ ***Henry VIII, Pilgrimage of Grace***

ASQUITH, HERBERT HENRY (1852–1928)

British prime minister (1908–16). Asquith was leader of the Liberal Party in its last period of dominance in British politics. He first became an MP in 1886 and prime minister in 1908. It was a time of great turbulence. He curbed the powers of the House of Lords, was challenged by the suffragette movement, and granted Home Rule for Ireland in 1914, though this was delayed. Asquith was ousted by David Lloyd George in December 1916, as his wartime coalition government was considered weak.

➡ ***Home Rule, House of Lords, David Lloyd George***

ATHELSTAN (C. AD 895–939)

King of the English. A grandson of Alfred the Great, Athelstan exercised authority over the Viking monarchs of the north, the king of Scotland and the Welsh princes. Athelstan was best known for his victory at Branunburgh (AD 937) against the combined army of the kings of Dublin, Strathclyde and Scotland.

➡ ***Alfred the Great, Edward the Elder***

ATREBATES (C. 50 BC)

Celtic tribe. The Atrebates lived in south-central England, from 50 BC under the leadership of Commius, who followed an anti-Roman policy. His son and successor Tincommius, however, was more amenable to Roman rule and was made a client-king in around 15 BC.

LEFT Ascot in 1822
CENTRE The teaching of St Augustine

ATLEE, CLEMENT (1883–1967)

British prime minister (1945–51). Atlee was the first Labour prime minister to hold a majority in the House of Commons. Much of the work of his government set the tone for British social and economic policy up until the election of Margaret Thatcher. Labour introduced the National Health Service, and a heavy policy of nationalisation of the major industries. He granted independence to India. But Britain was a country exhausted and impoverished by war, forcing the government to introduce austerity measures. Many within the Labour Party, especially on the left of the party, criticised Atlee for being too cautious in his policies.

➡ ***Labour Party***

AUGUSTINE, ST (d. c. AD 604)

First Archbishop of Canterbury. Pope Gregory I chose Augustine to convert the predominantly pagan population of southern England. In AD 597 they landed on the Isle of Thanet, Kent. King Ethelbert welcomed them and on Christmas Day 1,000 of his subjects were converted. Gregory ordered that 12 suffragan bishops be appointed and Augustine effectively assigned himself first Archbishop of Canterbury. Augustine's feast day is 26 May in England and Wales.

➡ ***Archbishop of Canterbury, Celtic Christianity, Ethelbert***

AUSTRIAN SUCCESSION, WAR OF (1740–48)

Series of battles over rights to leadership of the Hapsburg Empire. Much of Europe was drawn into the conflict, which dragged on for eight years. Peace was finally concluded with the Treaty of Aix-la-Chapelle in 1748.

The war began after the accession of Maria Theresa as ruler of the Hapsburg Empire. Charles Albert, the elector of Bavaria, claimed the throne, as did Philip V of Spain and Augustus III of Poland and Saxony and Frederick II of Prussia claimed part of Silesia. Frederick allied with France, Spain, Bavaria and Saxony and defeated Maria's Austrians at Mollwitz in 1741. The Prussians agreed a truce in exchange for most of Silesia but the armistice was broken. The English had been at war with Spain since 1739 and allied with Austria to defeat the French at Dettingen in 1743. Following the English defeat at Fontenoy, George II suggested a peace compromise that would lead to the Treaty of Aix-la-Chapelle. Maria Theresa's troops were defeated at Hohenfriedburg and Kesselsdorf, forcing her to sign the Treaty of Dresden with Prussia in December 1745. However, throughout 1746–48, the war continued in Northern Italy, the Low Countries and North America, and peace was not restored until the treaty was signed in 1748. By then Maria Theresa had secured an alliance with Russia but the other states – Austria, Great Britain, Holland and Sardinia against France and Spain – were weary of the war.

➡ ***Treaty of Aix-la-Chapelle, Battle of Dettingen, George II***

AVEBURY (c. 2600 BC)

Ancient stone circles in southwest England. Avebury is the largest known 'stone circle' in the world. It is composed of an outer ring and two inner circles, with the tallest stones are over 20 ft in height. Thirty-six stones are still standing, but there are believed to have been at least four times as many in previous centuries. As with Stonehenge, Avebury's exact origins are a mystery, but it is known to have been a sacred site.

➡ ***Stonehenge***

BABINGTON, ANTHONY (1561–86)

Leader in a plot to assassinate Elizabeth I in 1586. Twenty-five year old Babington was a supporter of the Catholic Mary Stuart. He planned to mobilise English Catholics with the help of a Spanish invasion. Supporters of the queen intercepted a letter detailing his plans. Babington was subsequently tried and executed.

➤ ***Elizabeth I, Mary, Queen of Scots***

BACON, FRANCIS (1561–1626)

Lawyer, statesman and philosopher in the Elizabethan Age. Bacon, born in 1561, was originally a lawyer who worked his way up to the post of Attorney General by 1613. By 1618 he had been appointed Lord Chancellor, but was impeached in 1621 on charges of corruption. A friend of Thomas Hobbes, Bacon's works include *Essays, The Advancement of Learning and Novum Organum* and were influential in the Humanist tradition for more than a century.

➤ ***Elizabeth I***

BACON, ROGER (*c.* 1220–92)

English Franciscan polymath. Initially Bacon was influenced by Aristotle. Among many inventions, Bacon proposed flying machines with flapping wings, and studied the rainbow using lenses. In 1257, whilst very ill, Bacon entered the Franciscan order. They disapproved of his teeming ideas so Bacon produced his great work, *Opus Maius*, in secret. Bacon was imprisoned by the Franciscans between 1277 and 1279.

➤ ***Franciscan Order***

BADEN-POWELL, LORD ROBERT STEPHENSON SMYTH (1857–1941)

British soldier and founder of the Boy Scouts. Baden-Powell joined the 13th Hussars in India in 1876 and between 1888 and 1895 served in India, Afghanistan, Zululand and Ashanti. During the British campaign in Matabeleland (1896–97) he was Chief Staff Officer. After Mafeking (October 1899–May 1900) he was promoted to Major General. He organised the South African Constabulary and became Inspector General of Cavalry in 1903. He was knighted in 1909 and founded the Boy Scouts and Girl Guides.

➤ ***Boer War, World War I***

BAIRD, JOHN LOGIE (1888–1946)

Scottish inventor, amongst those credited with creating television. In 1925 Baird transmitted his first television picture, but his claims were disbelieved by the newspapers. He gave his first demonstration of television in 1926 and in 1928 transmitted a signal between London and New York. His main rival was Marconi, whose television service the BBC adopted in 1936.

➤ ***British Broadcasting Corporation***

BALACLAVA, BATTLE OF (1854)

Battle between 30,000 Russians under Prince Mentschikov and the British under Lord Raglan, 25 October 1854. The Russians drove the Turks from their redoubts at Kadikoi and entered the valley of Balaclava, where they were driven back by the heavy cavalry brigade under General Scarlett. Although particularly famous for Lord Cardigan's Charge of the Light

Brigade, it was the Highland Brigade who distinguished themselves when they repulsed the Russian cavalry. British losses were slight except for the Light Brigade.

➤ ***Charge of the Light Brigade, Crimean War***

BALDWIN, STANLEY (1867–1947)

Three times British prime minister (1923–24, 1924–29,1935–37). Baldwin was a Conservative who became an MP in 1908. He first became prime minister in 1923, succeeding Bonar Law. The Conservatives had lost their majority by the beginning of 1924 but were returned to power by the end of the year. Baldwin was prime minister at the time of the 1926 General Strike, introducing retaliatory legislation against the unions a year later. He was defeated in the next election in 1929, but returned to power in 1935. Baldwin was prime minister during the abdication crisis, when he forbade Edward VIII from marrying Mrs Simpson.

➤ ***General Strike***

BALFOUR, ARTHUR JAMES, 1ST EARL (1848–1930)

British prime minister (1902–05). Balfour was elected as a Conservative MP in 1874 and became secretary for Ireland and later first lord of the treasury. He is best known for his pioneering Education Acts. In 1915 he joined the coalition government as First Lord of the Admiralty and in 1917 issued the Balfour Declaration, which demanded a national home for the Jews in Palestine.

BALLIOL, EDWARD (d. 1364)

Intermittent king of Scotland (1332, 1333–34, 1335–36). Son of John Balliol. A rival of Robert Bruce's family, Edward was crowned on 24 September 1332 but was deposed the following December by rebellious Scots nobles. Balliol's hold on his crown was always precarious. He resigned all his lands to his overlord, Edward III of England, in 1336. Balliol never married and the claims of his family to the Scottish throne ended with his death.

➤ ***Edward III, John Balliol, Robert Bruce***

BALLIOL, JOHN (c. 1250–1313)

King of Scotland. John Balliol was crowned king in 1292 and recognised Edward I of England as his overlord a month later. Balliol rebelled against Edward's control in 1296 and joined the English king's enemy, King Philippe IV of France. Balliol was defeated by the English, stripped of his royal authority and imprisoned in the Tower of London. Released in 1299, John Balliol spent the years until his death on his estates in France.

➤ ***Edward I, Edward Balliol***

TOP LEFT John Logie Baird demonstrating his new invention, the television
BOTTOM LEFT The Battle of Balaclava

BALMORAL (1852)

Scottish castle, the Highland home of Queen Victoria. In 1852 the queen bought the land (10,000 acres) from the Earl of Fife. The castle was built shortly afterwards, paid for by Prince Albert. It became the queen's favourite home and started a fashion in England for all things Scottish. The castle, on the banks of the River Dee, was constructed from Scottish granite. Its tallest tower is over 30 m (100 ft) high. Queen Elizabeth, the Queen Mother lived here.

➤ ***Elizabeth Bowes-Lyon, Queen Victoria***

BANK OF ENGLAND

During the reign of William III (1688–1702) Parliament decided to set up the Bank of England. In 1694 the bank was founded as a tool for dealing with the burgeoning trade between the British Empire and the rest of the world, and to deal with the English national economy. National debt, public sector borrowing, monetary policy and foreign-exchange rates all fell within its remit. It also began supervising the overall English banking system.

➤ ***William III***

BANNOCKBURN, BATTLE OF (1314)

A battle between the Scots and English, 24 June 1314, during the Scottish War of Independence. A 40,000-strong Scottish army under the command of Robert Bruce, king of Scotland intercepted Edward II's 60,000 troops marching to the relief of Stirling Castle. The English launched a mass attack but these troops blundered into concealed pits and were slaughtered by the Scots. The English lost 10,000 men and Scottish independence was won. The battle remains the most celebrated victory of the Scots over the English to this day.

➡ ***Robert Bruce, Edward II***

BAREBONES PARLIAMENT (1653)

Seventeenth-century political assembly during the 11 years that England was a republic after the Civil War. The Lord Protector Oliver Cromwell convened the Barebones Parliament in July 1653. Named after one of its members, it consisted of 140 men, mostly chosen by Cromwell himself. The parliament was dissolved in December of the same year because of the deep ideological split between members.

➡ ***English Civil War, Oliver Cromwell***

BARONS' WARS (1263–67)

Series of rebellions against Henry III, led by Simon de Montfort. Following Henry III's attempts to amend the Magna Carta, which had been adopted by the nobles in 1258 to curb his excesses, Louis XIV of France arbitrated the dispute. In 1263 he decided in favour of the king and the nobles resorted to arms. Henry's troops were defeated at the Battle of Lewes in 1264 and de Montfort, the Earl of Leicester, became virtual ruler. He summoned parliament in 1265 but on 4 August Henry's troops were led by his son, later Edward I and defeated the barons at the Battle of Evesham, where de Montfort was killed.

➡ ***Henry III, King John, Magna Carta, Simon de Montfort***

BATH SPA (c. AD 43)

Roman settlement in the west of England. The city of Bath originated as a Roman spa town. Its Roman name was *Aquae Sulis*, meaning 'waters of Sul'. Sul was then the British goddess of wisdom. The settlement was established and largely built within 20 years of the Roman invasion in AD 43. The natural, hot springs were used for therapeutic bathing by the Romans. Bath became a fashionable spa town again during the eighteenth century.

➡ ***Roman Empire***

BAYEUX TAPESTRY (c. 11TH CENTURY)

Long strip of embroidered linen (not actually a tapestry). The Bayeux Tapestry depicts the events that led to the Norman Conquest: the defeat of England's king, Harold, by the William the Conqueror of Normandy (later William I of England). It was made in the French town of Bayeux and commissioned by a half-brother of William.

➡ ***Norman Conquest, William I***

BAYEUX, BISHOP ODO OF (c. 1036–97)

Half brother of William I (the Conqueror). Bishop of Bayeux (1049). Odo fought at the Battle of Hastings (1066) and was rewarded with Dover Castle and the earldom of Kent. Odo rebelled against William II in 1088 and was permanently exiled to Normandy. He died during the First Crusade.

➡ ***William I, William II***

BEAKER PEOPLE (c. 2700 BC)

A group of early settlers in the British Isles. At a time during the transition from the late Neolithic to the early Bronze Age – around 2700 to 1700 BC – a culture arose that swept across the greater part of Europe. Beaker people probably originated from the Iberian peninsula. They made distinctive waisted drinking vessels, called bell-beakers, from earthenware clay. These beakers are instantly recognisable when found by archeologists, but it is now believed that the Beaker culture spread farther than the Beaker people themselves.

BEATLES, THE (1960s)

English pop band. The Beatles, Paul McCartney, John Lennon, George Harrison and Ringo Starr, came from Liverpool. They had their first hit in 1962 with 'Love Me Do'. In 1963, they reached number one in the UK with 'Please Please Me'. In 1964, the Beatles became the first UK band to take America by storm; in doing so they changed the face of international music forever. The 'Mersey Sound' became popular throughout the world and the songwriting duo of Lennon and McCartney created an entirely new brand of music. The last single before their acrimonious split in 1970 was 'Let It Be'.

BEATON, DAVID (c. 1494–1546)

Scottish cardinal. Beaton had a tumultuous career. In 1539 he became Archbishop of St Andrews, then in 1544 papal legate and consequently quasi-ruler of Scotland. He encouraged the persecution of Protestants: George Wisheart, for example, was burnt at the stake under Beaton's orders. In turn, avenging Scottish nobles murdered him.

➠ ***Church of Scotland***

BOTTOM LEFT A scene from the Bayeaux Tapestry, probably the most celebrated example of tapestries

BEAUFORT, LADY MARGARET (1443–1509)

Mother of Henry VII, her only child. Margaret was descended from Edward III of England through Edward's third surviving son, John of Gaunt, Duke of Lancaster. She was married to Edmund Tudor, Earl of Richmond, who died three months before she gave birth to Henry in 1457.

➠ ***Henry VII, John of Gaunt, Wars of the Roses***

BECKET, THOMAS À (c. 1118–70)

Archbishop of Canterbury, martyr and English saint. Becket's rise was meteoric, becoming firstly archdeacon of Canterbury, then chancellor, then Archbishop of Canterbury (1162). On being appointed archbishop he now miraculously cast off his flashy clothes and adopted the austerity of the Gregorian reforms, thus sowing the seed of conflict between himself and Henry. The reforms concerned jurisdiction over clerical trials and Henry opposed Becket, who fled to France (1164–70). Henry then confiscated Becket's diocesan lands, but in 1170 agreed to the restoration of his land and position, much to the general population's approval and consequently Henry's aggravation. Apparently four knights took Henry's request to be rid of the 'meddlesome priest' literally: on 29 December, his feast day since 1173, he was slain in Canterbury Cathedral, and remains a heroic martyr to his ideals.

Canterbury Cathedral, Henry II

BEDE, THE VENERABLE (c. 673–735)

English religious writer and historian. Bede lived in what is now county Durham. Orphaned at the age of seven, he was consequently looked after by a religious order. At 19 he became a deacon and was a priest by 30. He knew Latin, Greek and possibly Hebrew. His works include *De Orthographia, De Natura Rerum* and the most famous *Ecclesiastical History of the English Nation* – written in Latin, this was first translated into English by Alfred the Great.

Alfred the Great

BELGAE

Tribe of Ancient Britain. During the Roman occupation of Western Europe there remained an enclave of territory known as Gaul. This area contained various tribes of Celtic-speaking people and comprised much of what is now France. The Belgae who gave their name to the Roman province Belgica and ultimately Belgium.

BELL, ALEXANDER GRAHAM (1847–1922)

Scottish-born US inventor. In 1876 the world was introduced to a revolutionary device for transmitting speech from one place to another via electrical signals through a wire. Alexander Graham Bell had perfected

LEFT Thomas á Beckett depicted in stained glass at Canterbury Cathedral
FAR RIGHT Alexander Graham Bell inaugurates the New York - Chigaco telephone on 18 October 1892

the telephone by assembling together the necessary components, begun in part by other scientists. Bell's inventive genius was to realise the potential in scientific developments around him and then turn his ideas into working devices with practical applications.

BENEDICTINE ORDER

Educational monastic order, influential in northern and western Europe, from Charlemagne's reign until the twelfth century. Whilst the Benedictine, Lanfranc, was Archbishop of Canterbury extensive church reform was carried out in England.

➧ ***Archbishop Lanfranc***

BENTHAM, JEREMY (1748–1832)

English philosopher. During the Industrial Revolution in Britain the dramatic changes to the social infrastructure caused people to think about the consequences of their actions. Reacting to the plight of the working class, philosopher Jeremy Bentham published his *Principles of Morals and Legislation* in 1789. He outlined his theory (now known as utilitarianism) that a regime is ethically right only if it aims to achieve 'the greatest happiness for the greatest number' of the population.

BERWICK, SIEGE OF (1333)

Siege during the war between Edward III and the Scots. After the death of Robert Bruce, Edward Balliol laid claim to the Scottish throne. He was a friend and ally of Edward III; the latter decided to set an example and punish the Scots for forcing his friend to flee. On 12 April 1333 Edward laid siege to Berwick Castle. With an army of 13,000 Scots about to arrive Edward hung his hostages and marched to face a Scottish army to the south.

➧ ***David II, Edward III, Battle of Halidon Hill***

BERWICK, TREATIES OF (1357 AND 1586)

Series of agreements between Scotland and England. As a border town, Berwick-upon-Tweed has changed hands between England and Scotland a total of 13 times. Perhaps the most significant treaties include one in 1357 when David II, king of Scotland, agreed that should he have no male heir, then the heirs to the English throne should succeed that of Scotland. In 1560, two years after Elizabeth I became queen, Protestant Reformers north and south of the border signed a treaty to expel French Catholics from Scotland. This was the turning point in the religious conflict between the two countries. In 1586 Elizabeth I and James VI of Scotland signed another Treaty of Berwick, acknowledging that James VI was heir to the English throne. In signing this treaty with his cousin, James succeeded Elizabeth in 1603 as James I, the first Stuart king of England, uniting the two countries.

➧ ***David II, Elizabeth I, James VI***

BETJEMAN, JOHN (1906–84)

English poet. Betjeman also worked as a teacher, journalist, broadcaster and expert critic of architecture. His first volume of poetry was published in 1931. Among his most famous works are: 'A Subaltern's Love Song', 'Myfanwy', 'Slough' and his autobiography, *Summoned by Bells*. He became Poet Laureate in 1972.

➧ ***Poet Laureate***

BISHOPS' WARS (1639 AND 1640)

Two brief campaigns involving the Scots against Charles I. Charles attempted to strengthen control of the Scottish Church by the English bishops with the imposition of the English *Book of Common Prayer* in 1637. In 1638 the Scots pledged themselves in the National Covenant to restore Presbyterianism. The General Assembly of Scottish Churches abolished the bishop's power and the first war ended by the Pacification of Berwick without a single battle having been fought. Charles conceded that the Scots had a right to a Free Church assembly and parliament. Charles managed to raise another army but was unable to prevent the Scots from invading England and occupying Northumberland and Durham, largely due to the refusal of his Short Parliament to grant him money to fight the war. A peace treaty was signed in October 1640 at Ripon and Charles promised to pay the Scots an indemnity that necessitated his calling a Long Parliament.

➧ ***Charles I, William Laud, Long Parliament, National Covenant, Short Parliament***

BLACK DEATH (1348)

Form of the Plague. Just as Europe was finding its feet after the Dark Ages it suffered a catastrophic setback in the form of disease. Originating in Asia the bubonic plague took hold rapidly in Europe, spread by fleas carried on rats that flourished in the overcrowded medieval towns. So called because it causes buboes or boils to erupt under the skin, bubonic plague reached Britain in 1348, killing almost half of the population in a few months. The epidemic had such a profound effect on the infrastructure of Europe that it became known as the Black Death. A second plague struck in 1665.

➧ ***Plague***

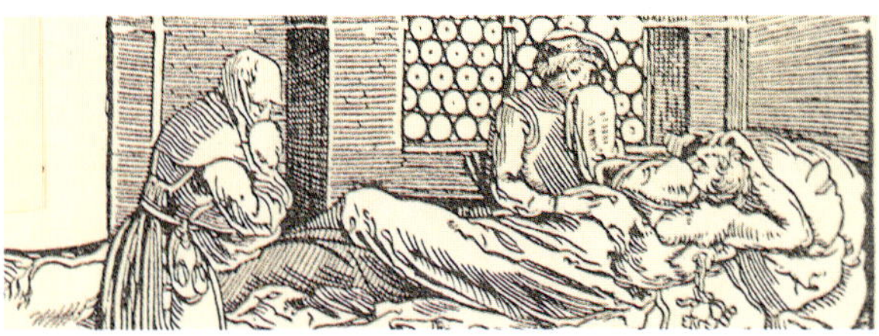

BLAIR, TONY (b. 1953)

British prime minister (1997–). Blair, a former barrister, led Labour in May 1997 to its most comprehensive election victory, ending 18 years of Conservative rule. It won 418 seats, the highest ever recorded by Labour, and took its largest share of votes

since the 1960s. At 44, Blair was the youngest prime minister since Lord Liverpool in 1812. In power he has maintained a centrist approach which many commentators claim is why Labour were elected in the first place. His style is often described as 'presidential' and he is accused of relying too heavily on 'spin' to get across Labour's political message. A fluent French speaker, Blair has committed British troops to action in Kosovo and Sierra Leone. He has introduced a Scottish Parliament, Welsh Assembly, maintained the peace process in Northern Ireland and partially reformed the House of Lords. Leader of the Labour Party since 1994, Blair is credited with re-inventing the party, re-branding it 'New Labour' and making it more voter attractive.

➧ ***Labour Party***

LEFT A victim of the Black Death
RIGHT St Paul's Cathedral survives the Blitz

BLENHEIM PALACE (1705)

English stately home, constructed between 1705 and 1722. The land and sufficient money to build on it were given to the Duke of Marlborough by Queen Anne. The palace, which was designed by John Vanbrugh, is named after Marlborough's great military victory, the Battle of Blenheim (1704), fought in Germany against the French and Bavarians. The magnificent grounds, which encompass over 2,000 acres, were landscaped by Capability Brown. Winston Churchill (a descendant of the duke) was born in Blenheim Palace.

➠ ***Capability Brown, John Churchill, Winston Churchill, John Vanbrugh***

BLENHEIM, BATTLE OF (1704)

Famous victory of John Churchill, 1st Duke of Marlborough and Eugene of Savoy in the War of the Spanish Succession, fought 13 August 1704. 52,000 English and Austrian troops faced a 60,000-strong French army drawn up behind the Nebel River, near Blenheim. Whilst Eugene mounted a strong diversionary attack, Marlborough advanced across the river and swept Tallard's French army into the Danube. Tallard was taken prisoner, along with 13,000 men. The allies lost 12,000 and the French 18,000. The battle saved Vienna from the French and finally dispelled the myth that the French army was irresistible. Marlborough and Eugene were considered perfect partners.

➠ ***John Churchill, War of the Spanish Succession***

BLITZ, THE (1940–41)

Series of intense air raids against British civilian targets during World War II. In order to prepare the way for a German invasion of Great Britain, initially German air attacks were focused on British shipping and then Royal Air Force airfields. Then, in September 1940, the Germans shifted their emphasis to attacks on London and other major cities, with the intention of breaking the British spirit. From 7 September London was attacked on 57 consecutive nights. The air attacks continued until May 1941, by which time they were largely centred on London. The winter of 1940–41 saw the greatest ferocity of attacks and during March and April 1941 nearly 10,000 German sorties were flown, although the Germans had largely switched to night-bombing attacks. Facing mounting casualties, German air operations began to decline, despite notable devastation to Coventry, London and Liverpool.

➠ ***World War II***

BLOODAXE, ERIK (d. AD 954)

King of Jorvik (Viking York). Erik, last Scandinavian king of Jorvik, was the son of King Harold Hairfair of Norway. Expelled from Norway in AD 947, Erik dominated Jorvik, where he offered protection against Saxon attacks. Erik was driven from Jorvik by Eadred, king of the English, but he regained his power there in AD 952. He was probably thrown out again in AD 954 and was killed at Stainmore while fleeing to the Viking kingdom of Dublin. Erik was a typical warrior of his time and was described as 'hot-headed, harsh, unfriendly and silent ... he ruled from York ... under the helmet of his terror'.

Eadred

BLOODY ASSIZES (1685)

Circuit of courts in the West Country to try those implicated in the unsuccessful Monmouth Rebellion. This was a short-lived rebellion that began in Lyme Regis against James II by the Duke of Monmouth, who believed he was the rightful king. After the rebellion was suppressed, the king established the assizes, led by Judge Jeffreys, the lord chief justice. He dealt savagely with anyone involved. Over 300 rebels were hung, drawn and quartered. Jeffreys was rewarded with the position of lord chancellor. After James II was eventually overthrown, Jeffreys was arrested and died in the Tower of London.

James II, Monmouth's Rebellion

BLOODY SUNDAY (1972)

Name given to the day in which 13 unarmed protestors were killed in the Bogside, Derry (30 January 1972) after British soldiers opened fire on civilians protesting against internment. Another man later died from illness attributed to the shooting. Internment without trial had been brought in the previous year. The killings exacerbated the tense situation in Northern Ireland: the British Embassy in Dublin was burned down and violence escalated in the following years. In 1998, the Labour government ordered a new inquiry into the events of Bloody Sunday.

Northern Ireland

BODLEY, THOMAS (1543–1613)

English scholar, after whom the Bodleian Library in Oxford is named. Bodley was proficient in ancient Greek and Hebrew and worked as a lecturer in Greek at Oxford University. He also travelled widely in order to learn modern languages; this led to him being given the distinguished role of foreign diplomat. After marrying a wealthy heiress, Bodley used much of his wife's money to create the now-famous library that bears his name.

Oxford University

BOER WAR (1899–1902)

Series of conflicts between the Transvaal and the Orange Free State in South Africa and Great Britain. Throughout the nineteenth century ill feeling had mounted between the Dutch Afrikaaners – or Boers – and British settlers. The Boers had already migrated north to avoid becoming subject to the British colony of the Cape of Good Hope. Gradually the new Boer republics were annexed by Great Britain and when gold brought thousands of British miners to the area, it seemed clear that the Boers and the British were on a collision course. Paul Kruger, the president of the South African Republic, demanded the withdrawal of the British troops from the Transvaal borders in October 1899. This was not forthcoming and although the Boers were initially successful in trapping British forces at Ladysmith, Natal, Mafeking and Kimberley, fresh British troops soon arrived

ABOVE During the Boer war, the 91st Highlanders advance over the veldt
FAR RIGHT Bostonians disguised as native Americans throw tea overboard in protest over taxation

and the main Boer army under Piet Cronje was forced to surrender in February 1900. Following further defeats, President Kruger fled to Europe but the peace was short-lived. New guerrilla warfare erupted, led by Louis Botha and Jan Christiaan Smuts, and continued until peace negotiations began on 23 March 1902, culminating in the signing of the Treaty of Vereeniging on 31 May. During this guerrilla period the British were under the command of Lord Kitchener and followed a policy of laying Boer lands to waste and putting civilians into concentration camps. The British suffered around 28,000 losses during the war but the Boers, although only losing 4,000 men, had lost 20,000 civilians from disease and starvation.

Robert Baden-Powell, Lord Kitchener

BOLEYN, ANNE (c. 1507–36)

Second wife of Henry VIII. Anne was a lady-in-waiting to Henry's first wife, Catherine of Aragon, when she first caught the king's eye.

Henry was desperate to have a male heir, something Catherine had failed to provide. His efforts to divorce Catherine and marry Anne precipitated the English Reformation (1532–36). Anne, already pregnant, married Henry in 1533. Her child was a daughter, the future Elizabeth I. Henry had already tired of the bad-tempered, demanding Anne and on 1536, after she miscarried of a son, she was accused of adultery and incest. Anne was executed on 19 May.

Catherine of Aragon, Dissolution of the Monasteries, Elizabeth I, Henry VIII

BOLINGBROKE, HENRY ST JOHN, VISCOUNT (1678–1751)

British politician. Bolingbroke served as foreign secretary and secretary of war, during which time he helped to negotiate the Treaty of Utrecht. He was a Jacobite sympathiser and his involvement in the plans to place James Edward Stuart on the throne led to his dismissal from government in 1714.

James Edward Stuart

'BONNIE PRINCE CHARLIE' (1720–88)

Charles Edward Stuart, also known as the 'Young Pretender'. Charles was the grandson of the Catholic James II and son of James, the 'Old Pretender'. In 1745, Charles raised the second Jacobite Rebellion in the Highlands of Scotland in a bid to regain the Stuart throne in England. The Jacobites were defeated at Culloden in 1746, and Charles became a fugitive. He returned to France, but was expelled by Louis XV. He died in Rome, possibly of alcoholism, in 1788.

Battle of Culloden, Jacobite Rebellion, James II, James Edward Stuart

BOSTON TEA PARTY (1773)

Rebellion in North American colonies against British imposition of taxes. The British decided to impose new forms of taxation on their colonists. In 1773 the East India Tea Company delivered a cargo of tea to the harbour at Boston, Massachusetts. In protest at having to pay 'tea tax' before they could unload the cargo a party of Bostonians took matters into their own hands. They disguised themselves as native Americans and boarded the ship in the darkness of night. The tea was then thrown overboard into the ocean. The event became known as the Boston Tea Party.

American Revolution, George III

BOSWORTH, BATTLE OF (1485)

Decisive battle that brought an end to the War of the Roses. The protracted fight for the English throne between the houses of York and Lancaster came to a bitter end in Leicestershire on 21 August 1485. Richard III's troops took up position on Ambien Hill but unknown to him two of his allies, Lord Stanley and Henry Percy, had agreed to support the rebel Henry Tudor. At the crucial moment they turned on their king and Richard's army was routed. Richard preferred death to capture and fell on the field of battle, leaving Henry Tudor to become Henry VII.

➡ ***Henry VII, Richard III, Wars of the Roses***

BOTHWELL, JAMES HEPBURN, EARL OF (1535–78)

Third husband of Mary Queen of Scots. Although a Protestant, Bothwell opposed any alliance with England. He was involved in the murder of Mary's second husband, Lord Darnley, in 1567 and soon afterwards he divorced his wife and married Mary who made him the Duke of Orkney. Opponents of the marriage forced Mary to abdicate in favour of her son James VI. Bothwell fled to Denmark where he was captured and imprisoned until his death in 1578.

➡ ***Lord Darnley, Mary Queen of Scots,***

BOUDICCA, QUEEN (d. c. AD 61)

Queen consort of Iceni tribe. Wife of Prastagus. Also known as Boadicea. She raised a rebellion against the Romans in AD 60, after they had tried to incorporate her late husband's kingdom into their province of Britannia. Boudicca, who resisted the takeover, was flogged and her two daughters were raped. Personally led by Boudicca, the Iceni captured and destroyed the Roman colonies at Colchester and London before their defeat. Boudicca died soon afterwards; it is likely that she committed suicide.

➡ ***Roman Invasion***

BOUVINES, BATTLE OF (1214)

Decisive victory (27 July 1214) by the French king, Philip II, over the Holy Roman Emperor Otto IV, King John of England and Ferdinand of Portugal. The two armies collided south-east of Lille with the French recording a major triumph that propelled France into European dominance and resulted in the downfall of King John.

➡ ***King John***

BOWES-LYON, ELIZABETH (b. 1900)

Queen consort of England. Ninth of 10 children and youngest daughter of the Earl and Countess of Strathmore. Elizabeth has lived to become the oldest-ever member of the British royal family. Elizabeth married Albert, Duke of York, second son of George V and the future George VI in 1923. A woman of great charm and beauty, Elizabeth was a favourite with her somewhat irascible father-in-law. She became queen unexpectedly, when her husband was obliged to accept the Crown after his brother, Edward VIII, abdicated in 1936. At that juncture,

Elizabeth was considered too dull and provincial to be queen consort, but she rose magnificently to the challenge. Her finest hour came after 1939, when she and the king became the much-admired social leaders of the country during World War II. Widowed at 51, Elizabeth went on to become a greatly loved queen mother and lived to celebrate her 100th birthday in 2000.

➡ *Edward VIII, Elizabeth II, George VI*

BOYNE, BATTLE OF THE (1690)

Key battle (1 July 1690) that secured the throne for William III over the exiled James II. Intent on preventing the former king of England, James II, from regaining the throne, the new king, William of Orange, recently crowned William III, moved swiftly to intercept the exile and his troops. James was resting with his 21,000 men on the banks of the River Boyne when the 35,000-strong loyalist army attacked him. James's troops were soundly beaten, losing over 1,500 men to William's 500. James returned to exile in France and William's position was secured by this prompt action. Since 1795, Protestant Orangemen have celebrated the victory.

➡ *James II, William III*

BREAK WITH ROME (1532)

Henry VIII's self-appointment as Supreme Head of the Church of England. His request for the annullment of his marriage denied, Henry decided to remove himself from papal authority. His break with Rome provided an opener for the emergent Protestant ideas to take hold in England.

➡ *Dissolution of the Monasteries, Henry VIII, Reformation*

BOTTOM FAR LEFT Boudicca, Queen of the Iceni
BELOW William III at the Battle of the Boyne

BREAKSPEAR, NICHOLAS (1100–59)

Also known as Adrian IV: the only English pope to date. Born in Abbots Langley, in 1152 Breakspear successfully reorganised the Church hierarchy in Scandinavia, before being elected pope in 1154. He rowed with the Sicilian Frederick Barbarossa and introduced the bill, *Laudabiliter*, that allegedly granted Ireland to Henry II.

BREDA, DECLARATION OF (1660)

Declaration, made on 4 April 1660, that led to the restoration of the monarchy in England. Crowned as king of Scotland in 1649, Charles II led a failed invasion of England in 1651. Repelled by the forces of Cromwell he lived for nine years in exile. Following Cromwell's death in 1658, Charles was asked to return if he made concessions, including a pardon for those who fought against the Crown during the Civil War and greater religious liberty, both outlined in the declaration.

➡ *Charles II, Restoration*

BRETWALDA

Saxon word meaning 'overlord'. During the rule of the Anglo-Saxons in Britain there was much infighting between the Angles, Saxons and Jutes. The struggle for supreme power saw the boundaries of the kingdoms move about. Eventually, in AD 825, the kingdoms fell under the overlordship of Wessex, the ruler of which was known as the 'bretwalda'.

➡ *Anglo-Saxons*

BRIDGEWATER, FRANCIS EGERTON, 3RD DUKE OF (1736–1803)

English pioneer of canal construction. With the onset of the Industrial Revolution in England it became vital that materials and fuel could be shipped from one place to another efficiently. In 1762 work began on the Bridgwater Canal, the brainchild of Francis Egerton 3rd Duke of Bridgewater. The canal ran from Liverpool to Worsley via Manchester and was engineered by James Brindley (1716–72). It included an aqueduct spanning the Irwell Valley. The Bridgewater began a mania for canals across Britain.

➡ *Canals*

BRIGANTES

Tribe of ancient Britain. The Brigantes was one of the largest tribes, occupying most of what is now England. Their main settlements were first at Isurium (present-day Aldborough) and later at Eboracum (present-day York).

BRIGHTON PAVILION (1815)

English stately building, designed by John Nash. The Royal Pavilion at Brighton was built for the Prince Regent (later George IV), who made the seaside town highly fashionable by his patronage. The pavilion

was hugely expensive and derided by opponents of the Regent for its extravagant architecture. The style was actually inspired by the Moghul palaces of India and looks strikingly unusual alongside the rest of the town's buildings. The Pavilion is one of Brighton's most popular tourist attractions.

Beau Brummel, George IV

BRITISH BROADCASTING CORPORATION (BBC) (1927)

Radio and television broadcasting company. The BBC came out of the British Broadcasting Company, founded in 1922. The BBC was set up in 1927 and given broadcasting monopoly (which ended in the 1950s with the advent of commercial television and radio). The corporation was financed by licence fees from radio owners and money from the government. In 1936, the BBC started the world's first television service. Today the BBC's World Service broadcasts across the globe.

BRITAIN, BATTLE OF (1940)

Germany's air war against Britain as a prelude to invasion. In July 1940, Hitler ordered Goering's Luftwaffe to seize control of the Channel and destroy the Royal Air Force. He had 3,000 aircraft at his disposal against about 600 RAF fighters. In early August the attacks centred on the Channel ports and airfields. On 15 August 1940 German aircraft hit targets further north.

In the crucial two-week period from 24 August to 6 September, the RAF lost 25 per cent of its pilots, the Germans twice as many. On 7 September the Germans launched the first of their daylight air raids, huge loses forced a switch to night attacks. By 12 October, with losses mounting, Hitler abandoned Operation Sealion, his invasion plan, and the hitherto invincible German armed forces had suffered their first defeat. The Battle of Britain gave rise to Winston Churchill's famous statement to the nation: 'Never in the field of human conflict was so much owed by so many to so few.'

Winston Churchill, World War II

ABOVE German ground crew refuel and rearm a light-bomber

BRITISH EMPIRE (17TH–20TH CENTURIES)

Land and territory ruled over by Britain from around 1600 to the 1930s. At its height, after World War I, the empire covered over 25 per cent of the world's population and area. It lasted three-and-a-half centuries – almost as long as the Roman Empire.

North America, Asia, Africa, the Caribbean and Australia were the areas affected by Britain's expansion as a world power during the seventeenth to twentieth centuries. By the time Britain began its process of colonisation, Spain and Portugal, two of the imperial powers of the fifteenth and sixteenth centuries, had colonised much of South America. Britain was concerned with opening up new trade routes rather than being driven by the religious zeal that marked the imperial concerns of other countries. At first Britain's empire found its wealth from the slave trade but by the time this was made illegal in 1807, it had grown sufficiently for Britain to rely on other forms of commerce.

Initially colonisation began in North America, in New England, Maryland and Virginia. A settlement in Jamestown, Virginia in 1607 can be viewed as the beginning of the continental British Empire. Its rule of Ireland from the twelfth century, it is argued, was the original starting point. Canada became part of the Empire after British forces were victorious in the Seven Years' War with France between 1756–63.

The first great setback for the seemingly invincible Empire was its defeat by American forces during the American Revolution in 1776. This led to the loss of 13 American state colonies and the establishment of the United States of America. Despite this, the Empire continued to expand in other corners of the globe. The Napoleonic wars saw Britain claim French territory in the Caribbean. But it was the Victorian age that saw the largest expansion; this was the time of the European Scramble for Africa. Britain took control of Kenya in 1888 and Uganda in 1890.There was also a scramble for territory in Asia, with Britain taking control of Hong Kong in 1841. By this time its reach had extended to the South Pacific. A year earlier, Britain had staked its claim to New Zealand.

London formerly ruled India, at the very centre of the Empire, from 1877, but its influence had been strong there since the formation of the East India Company in 1600. The company had effectively ruled India until violent protests in 1857.

In most of their dominions, notably in Australia, Canada, New Zealand and South Africa, the British allowed some forms of autonomous government. But with British power diminishing in the time between the two World Wars, and the changing times leading to resistance to its rule across the globe, the Empire eventually became the Commonwealth, a union that exists today.

➠ ***Commonwealth, Seven Years' War, Queen Victoria***

BELOW British Empire troops

THE JEWEL IN THE CROWN

The Empire was at its height during the reign of Queen Victoria and of all the dominions under the control of Great Britain, it was India that was the jewel in the crown.

In the early seventeenth century Britain and France set up rival trading posts in India, a situation which eventually led to the Seven Years' War and British victory. The British East India Company gained control of many territories in the area over the succeeding years and after the Indian Mutiny of 1857 control of these areas transferred from the East India Company to the Crown. In 1876, Queen Victoria assumed the title Empress of India. The extent and wealth of this dominion surpassed all others.

Conflicts soon began to arise between the areas of India under British control and those under the jurisdiction of native rulers and by 1919 Indian nationalism was a force to be reckoned with. By the time the world had undergone another devastating World War the sun had all but set on the Great British Empire and India was granted full independence in 1947.

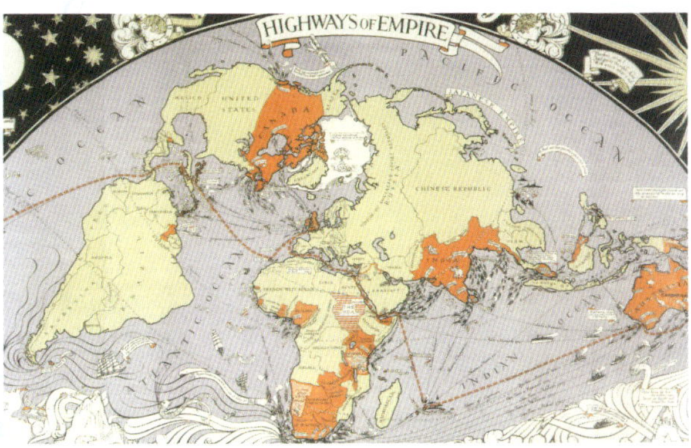

TIMELINE

1607 First colony established at Jamestown (Virginia) in North America

1623 English colony established at St Kitts in the Caribbean

1655 England seizes control of Jamaica, formerly owned by Spain

1713 Britain gains Acadia, Newfoundland and territory owned by the Hudson's Bay Company in Canada, from France, by the Treaty of Utrecht

1732 Establishment of colony in Georgia brings total British colonies in North America to 13

1781 American War of Independence sees the loss of all 13 North American colonies

1788 Penal colonies established at Botany Bay and Sydney, Australia

1799 Malta becomes part of the Empire

1806 Dutch colony at the Cape in South Africa cedes to the British

1840 Britain gains New Zealand through the Treaty of Waitangi

1842 Treaty of Nanjing cedes Hong Kong to the British

1843 Britain seizes the province of Natal in South Africa

1867 Canada becomes a dominion of Britain through the British North America Act

1880 Beginning of the Scramble for Africa, which sees Britain gain territories in South Africa

1882 British rule established in Egypt

1901 Australia becomes a Commonwealth

1929 End of the Boer Wars; Britain gains control of Boer Republics in South Africa

1947 India gains independence

1962 Independence of the Gold Coast begins return of African colonies to independence

1997 Hong Kong returned to China

BUY EMPIRE GOODS FROM HOME AND OVERSEAS

BRITISH EXPEDITIONARY FORCE (BEF)

British standing army that went to France at the beginning of World War I and World War II. The Haldane Reforms of 1908 recognised that Britain's treaty obligations required larger units of the British army to be trained and organised so that they could be mobilised as an expeditionary force. In 1914 the BEF consisted of six infantry divisions and one cavalry division. Of these all except two went to France at the beginning of the war. The BEF again went to France in 1939 but was brought back to England via Dunkirk in 1940 when France fell in the May offensive.

➡ ***Kitchener's Army, World War I, World War II***

BRITTEN, BENJAMIN (1913–76)

English composer. Edward Benjamin Britten was born in Suffolk. He was only four years old when he wrote his first musical composition and began studying music in earnest aged 11. He attended the Royal College of Music from 1930 and became successful as a composer of theme tunes for the radio and film industries. His most famous works include the operas *Billy Budd*, *Peter Grimes* and *Gloriana*, written on the occasion of the coronation of Queen Elizabeth II.

➡ ***Elizabeth II***

BROOKE, RUPERT (1887–1915)

English poet. Brooke's first book of poems was published in 1911, the year he travelled through Europe. In 1913, following a nervous breakdown, he visited North America, Canada and the Pacific. He enlisted as soon as war broke out, but died of blood poisoning while in Turkey. Brooke's youth, good looks and patriotic poetry made him a symbol of Britain's lost generation. His works include 'The Soldier', 'The Old Vicarage, Grantchester' and *Lithuania* (a play).

➡ ***World War I***

BROWN, LANCELOT 'CAPABILITY' (1715–83)

English landscape gardener, who also worked as an architect. Lancelot 'Capability' Brown is the most famous landscape gardener Britain has ever known. He developed a distinct method of design that came to be known as the 'English Style'; his work can be seen at some of Britain's most prominent buildings, including Blenheim Palace and Hampton Court. Brown's nickname came from one of his favourite expressions, that of describing a building as having 'capability' for improvement.

➡ ***Blenheim Palace, Hampton Court Palace***

BRUCE, ROBERT (1274–1329)

King of Scotland as Robert I. Bruce was a claimant to the Scottish throne in 1291, but his rival John Balliol was chosen instead by Edward I of England. Robert Bruce was involved in the uprising headed by William Wallace in 1297–98, but despite this he maintained good relations with Edward. He was, however, simply biding his time until the right moment came to seize the Scots throne, which he did in 1306.

He was crowned Robert I on 25 March 1306 and, having brought the fractious Scots nobility under his control, he finally achieved full power in Scotland in 1308. However, Edward II of England and the pope refused to recognise Robert as king.

RIGHT Robert the Bruce on his deathbed

Recognition came only after Edward's murder in 1327. Robert's greatest achievement was to gain formal recognition for Scotland as a separate and independent kingdom from England (1328). He died in 1329, probably from leprosy.

➜ *John Balliol, Edward I, Edward II, William Wallace*

BRUMMEL, BEAU (1778–1840)

Regency 'dandy'. George Bryan Brummel was distinguished for his fashion sense and renowned for his ready wit while still at Eton. He led the fashion in Regency London and was a favourite of the Prince Regent. In 1816, however, after quarrelling with him, Brummel fled to France, unable to pay a gambling debt. He died there, in poverty.

➜ *George IV*

BRUNEL, ISAMBARD KINGDOM (1806–59)

English pioneering engineer. Of the great nineteenth-century engineers Isambard Kingdom Brunel stands pre-eminent. The son of mass production pioneer Marc Isambard Brunel (1769–1849) he was born with the credentials to go far and he certainly made the most of his 53 years. At the age of just 27 he became the chief engineer for the Great Western Railway and only four years later was building the first of his big ships, the *Great Western*. His achievements also include the steam ships *Great Britain* and *Great Eastern*, Clifton Suspension Bridge and the Thames tunnel project, in partnership with his father.

BUCKINGHAM PALACE (1633)

Official London home of the British monarch. Built in 1633 by Lord Goring and called Buckingham House, it has since been remodelled several times. The house became royal property in 1761, when it was acquired by George III. His son, George IV, turned it into a palace, under the guidance of the architect John Nash. It was unfinished when George died and, in 1830, Nash was dismissed and replaced by Edmund Blore. Queen Victoria was the first monarch to make the palace her official residence. She required Blore to make several changes, including the addition of more nurseries. Marble Arch, which now stands at one end of Hyde Park (a triumphal arch after the battles of Trafalgar and Waterloo) was part of Nash's Buckingham Palace. It was moved during Victoria's reign, however, because it was too narrow for a carriage to pass through. Buckingham Palace is surrounded by St James's Park, Green Park and Hyde Park.

➜ *Hyde Park, St James's Park, Queen Victoria*

BUNKER HILL, BATTLE OF (1775)

First major battle of the American Revolution (17 June 1775). In an attempt to force the British to evacuate Boston, some 1,200 rebel troops, led by Colonel William Prescott, occupied and fortified Breed's Hill on 16 June. Preceded by a naval bombardment, 2,200 British troops, under General Howe, launched three successive and costly assaults on the hills. By now another 300 rebels had joined them and although the British eventually captured both hills, they suffered 1,000 casualties. The rebels lost 400. During the battle British shells hit Charlestown, burning it to the ground.

American Revolution

BURHS (AD 9TH CENTURY)

Fortified towns in Anglo-Saxon Britain. The suffix 'borough' to a place name is a reference to the place originating as an Anglo-Saxon 'burh'. During the reign of Alfred the Great a network of defended enclosures was constructed to safeguard people, goods and livestock from the marauding Danes, with whom the Britons were warring. The king decreed that no village should lie farther than 20 miles from one of these bolt holes.

Alfred the Great

BURKE, EDMUND (1729–97)

Irish philosopher and politician whose influence is felt on British political life today. Burke's work, which stressed freedom, strong support for tradition, and saw political power as a trust, has been a big influence on the modern Conservative Party. A supporter of responsible aristocratic government, Burke opposed the French Revolution in his major work, *Reflections on the French Revolution*. He also opposed British policy towards America, Ireland and India as well as freedom for Parliament from the influence of the king.

George III, William Pitt the Elder

BURNS, ROBERT (1759–96)

Scottish poet. Burns was the son of an impoverished Ayrshire farmer. He wrote his first poems while working as a farm labourer. They were published in 1786, making him suddenly famous. With the money he made he bought a farm for himself and his wife Jean Armour – although his best known lover is Mary Campbell, to whom he wrote many poems. Burns' most famous poem is 'Tam O'Shanter'; he also wrote songs, including 'Auld Lang Syne'.

BUTE, JOHN STUART, 3RD EARL OF (1713–92)

British prime minister (1762–63). Prior to becoming prime minister, Bute was the future George III's tutor and friend. His first experience of high office was when he was invited into the Cabinet in 1760. Two years later he succeeded Thomas Pelham-Holmes, Duke of Newcastle into the post of prime minister. His term of office was short and rancorous. Bute was responsible for ending British involvement in the Seven Years' War that saw Britain joining forces with Prussia and Hanover against Austria, France, Russia, Saxony and Sweden. The war established Britain as a major colonial power but Bute attracted criticism and resigned as prime minister in April 1763

George III

BYRD, WILLIAM (1543–1623)

Elizabethan musician. Byrd and his collaborator Thomas Tallis were key figures in the rise of the arts at the court of Elizabeth I. At the age of 20, Byrd became organist at Lincoln Cathedral and went on to hold the monopoly over music printing, with Tallis.

Elizabeth I, Thomas Tallis

BYRON, LORD (1788–1824)

British poet, associate of Shelley, known for his wild lifestyle. He published his first poetry volume in 1807, and gained fame with *Childe Harold's Pilgrimage* (1812). Byron travelled widely and spent years living in Italy after a scandalous separation from his wife in 1816. Always an idealist, Byron espoused the Greek cause of liberation from Turkey. While commanding a section of the Greek army he died of rheumatic fever. His body is buried in Westminster Abbey, but his heart is buried in Greece.

BELOW Byron ponders the Greek Coastline

CABAL, THE (1670S)

Advisory group to Charles II in the early 1670s, which has been viewed as the precursor to the modern Cabinet. Made up of nobleman, the Cabal took its name from the initials of the surnames of its members, Clifford, Arlington, Buckingham, Ashley and Lauderdale. Unlike the Cabinet, the Cabal had no formal power or status. It advised the king on matters such as foreign affairs.

Charles II

CABOT, JOHN (c. 1450–98)

Italian navigator. John Cabot (Giovanni Caboto) chose England's patronage, under the commission of Henry VII to fund his voyages of exploration. He and his sons based themselves at Bristol and set about constructing a ship called the *Matthew*. Christopher Columbus had already discovered the Americas in 1492 and Cabot arrived at the other side of the Atlantic Ocean in 1497. Coming ashore at Cape Breton Island he became the first European to reach mainland America.

CADE, JACK (d. 1450)

English leader of the Kentish rebellion. In 1450 Henry VI's misgovernment of England, most notably high taxes and corruption at court, gave rise to the Kentish rebellion, an uprising against the royal forces at Sevenoaks. The leader of the rebellion was a landowner named Jack Cade, who ultimately died for his cause. In 1453 the king lapsed into insanity and the country descended into civil war between the houses of York and Lancaster.

Henry VI

CAESAR, JULIUS (100–44 BC)

Roman emperor. Caesar first set foot in Britain in 55 BC, during his conquest of Gaul, intending to prevent the Celts from sending aid to them. He remained only a few weeks before bad weather forced him to retreat. The following year he returned with greater forces and engaged in successful battle against the tribes of ancient Briton. Although neither of these expeditions were planned as invasions, he gained promises from the tribes that they would not interefere in his conquest of Gaul. It was left to the Emperor Claudius, nearly 100 years later, to begin the Roman occupation of the British Isles.

Emperor Claudius, Roman Invasion

CALCUTTA, BLACK HOLE OF (1746)

Airless cell in Fort William, Calcutta. On 20 June 1746 Siraj-ud-Dawlah, the Nawab of Bengal, took the fort from the British East India Company and imprisoned 146 Britons, locking them up in the dungeon overnight. Accounts vary but it is believed that only 23 were found alive the following morning. Other accounts say that 64 were held and 21 survived. Contemporary Indian historians claim that the incident never took place. There was great outrage at the time and the British exacted harsh retributions.

Robert Clive, Battle of Plassey

CALLAGHAN, JAMES (b. 1912)

British prime minister (1976–79). Callaghan's leadership came during a turbulent period in British political history. He led a government that went to the International Monetary Fund for a loan and oversaw the 'Winter of Discontent' in 1979 where wholesale worker dissatisfaction led to widespread strikes. Given a vote of no confidence by the House of Commons,

Callaghan went to the polls and was defeated by Margaret Thatcher, heralding an 18-year period of domination for the Conservative Party.

➜ ***Margaret Thatcher***

LEFT Silver Denarius showing Julius Caesar
BELOW LEFT Jean Calvin

CALVINISM

Theology developed by John Calvin. Calvinism was a specific branch of Puritanism that linked theology with church organisation: its key idea was Presbyterianism. Calvin studied in Geneva and came to believe in predestination and its relation to the works of the individual. After Calvin's death Calvinism became increasingly intolerant: his successors upheld that Jesus died only for certain souls (the elect).

➜ ***Presbyterianism, Puritanism***

CAMBRIDGE UNIVERSITY (12TH CENTURY)

English university. As Europe emerged from the Dark Ages knowledge began to be perceived as a form of power, giving rise to the first seats of learning that we now know as universities. One of the first European universities was established at Cambridge sometime in the 1100s. It now comprises many separate colleges; the oldest is Peterhouse, founded in 1284. Each college is managed as a separate establishment with its own independent corporation, but all general matters of university business are dealt with under a common university banner. Many eminent men and women have received their continued education at Cambridge University.

➜ ***Oxford University***

CAMPBELL-BANNERMAN, HENRY (1836–1908)

British prime minister (1905–08). Campbell-Bannerman served as chief secretary for Ireland (1884–85) and war minister (1886, 1892–95). He was strongly opposed to the wars in South Africa and during his time as prime minister the colonies there were granted self-government.

CANALS

Man-made waterway orginally intended to facilitate transportation of goods to industrial towns. The fundamental feature of any canal is that it comprises sections of level waterway, making them extremely efficient transport routes for bulk materials, because the effort required to move a cargo over still water is relatively little compared with other methods. The first major canal to be constructed in Britain was the Bridgewater Canal. It became a key player in the burgeoning Industrial Revolution because it enabled the transportation of large quantities of coal from collieries in Worsley to factories in Manchester. In turn, manufactured goods could be cheaply moved to Liverpool docks and distributed via cargo ship. The Bridgewater Canal was a significant feat of engineering skill, conducted by James Brindley (1716–72) on behalf of the 3rd Duke of Bridgewater. This pioneering work enabled the eventual construction of a waterway network some 4,000 km (2,500 miles) in length and spanning the greater part of Britain.

➜ ***Duke of Bridgewater***

CANNING, GEORGE (1770–1827)

British prime minister (1827). Seen as a progressive Tory, Canning's short term in office was marked by attacks from colleagues that undermined his power. Canning had been an MP since 1794. As foreign secretary 1807–09, Canning quarrelled with a Cabinet colleague war secretary Robert Stewart, Viscount Castlereagh. The feud was so bitter it ended up as a duel one morning on Putney Heath. Both men survived, but the loathing between them continued as Canning was kept out of office until 1816 because of his jealousy of the Viscount. He only re-entered the Cabinet after Castlereagh's suicide in 1822.

➡ *Viscount Castlereagh*

CANTERBURY CATHEDRAL (6TH CENTURY)

Cathedral of the primal see of England. Established by St Augustine at the end of the sixth century, Canterbury has remained the Christian headquarters of England ever since. The existing cathedral dates from 1070–89, although it has been added to several times. The site of Becket's murder, the cathedral houses his shrine and consequently receives many pilgrims. In the sixteenth century the large crypt was granted to the Huguenots and a weekly service is still held in French.

➡ *Archbishop of Canterbury, St Augustine, Thomas Becket, Huguenots*

CANUTE, KING (d. 1035)

King of England (1016–35), Denmark (1019–35) and Norway (1028–35). Also known as Cnut or Knut. A Dane by birth, Canute came to England with his father, Sweyn Forkbeard, in 1013. In 1016, Canute defeated Edmund Ironside and conquered England. The Witangemot elected him as king in April 1016. At first Canute behaved like a conqueror, giving English earldoms and estates to his Danish followers. He was, however, careful not to isolate the English nobles and after 1021, two of Canute's three advisers were English. Canute's reign was remarkably peaceful for an age in which rivalry and warfare were common. Canute promoted the laws already extant in England, and also encouraged English trade which was greatly helped by his control of the Baltic sea routes. Canute's sons Harold and Harthacanute succeeded him, but they had none of their father's talents and the crown reverted to the English royal line in 1042.

➡ *Edmund II, Edward the Confessor, Sweyn Forkbeard, Harold Harefoot, Harthacanute*

CAROLINE OF BRUNSWICK, PRINCESS (1768–1821)

Princess of Wales. Prince George (the future George IV) married Caroline in 1795 to 'repay' Parliament for discharging his debts. George took an instant dislike to Caroline, and the couple separated within nine months, after their daughter, Princess Charlotte, was born in 1796. Afterwards, Caroline became notorious for her outlandish conduct and adulterous relationships. She died a few weeks after a failed attempt to attend the coronation of her husband in 1821.

➡ *George IV*

CASTLEREAGH, ROBERT STEWART, VISCOUNT (1769–1822)

British statesman who twice served as war secretary and for 10 years as foreign secretary in the early 1800s. Born in Ulster, Castlereagh was a leading figure in Ireland's union with Great Britain when he served as chief secretary for Ireland at the turn of the nineteenth century.

His greatest triumph was his work as foreign secretary when, at the Congress of Vienna between October 1814 and June 1815 following the Napoleonic Wars, Castlereagh secured British security and trading interests. At home his image was less popular. A dispute over a failed expedition to gain British control of Antwerp led to a duel with his Cabinet colleague, George Canning. He was an unpopular spokesman for the repressive government of Earl Liverpool. He was one of the Cabinet members targeted by the Cato Street Conspiracy in 1820. Castlereagh committed suicide two years later.

➠ ***George Canning, Cato Street Conspiracy***

CATESBY, ROBERT

Instigator of the Gunpowder Plot. Under the Protestant James I Catholics were being persecuted in England. In 1605 Robert Catesby hatched the Gunpowder Plot with fellow Catholic conspirators. The plan was to blow up the king and Parliament. The conspiracy was betrayed by an anonymous letter and the conspirators were caught and executed, Catesby among them.

➠ ***Gunpowder Plot, Guy Fawkes***

CATHERINE HOWARD (1520–42)

Queen of England. Fifth wife of Henry VIII. Catherine married Henry in 1540, after his divorce from Anne of Cleves. She was related to his second wife, Anne Boleyn. Catherine was beautiful and vivacious, but uneducated. Henry, 30 years her senior, was old and sickly by this time. By 1541, there were rumours that Catherine was committing adultery. In 1542, she was found guilty of having pre-marital affairs and was beheaded on 13 February 1542.

➠ ***Anne Boleyn, Henry VIII***

CATHERINE OF ARAGON (1485–1536)

Queen of England. First wife of Henry VIII. Daughter of Ferdinand of Aragon and Isabella of Castile. Catherine's first marriage, to Prince Arthur, heir of Henry VII, lasted only a few months. Catherine married Henry VIII in 1509. Her failure to produce a male heir precipitated Henry's attempts to have the marriage annulled after 1526. He claimed that her previous marriage to his brother made it invalid. Catherine maintained that her marriage to Arthur was unconsummated and that her union with Henry was therefore valid. Despite mistreatment, Catherine always refused to relinquish her title of Queen of England.

➠ ***Anne Boleyn, Henry VIII, Mary I***

LEFT CENTRE Illustrated manuscript showing King Canute
BELOW Catherine of Aragon

CATHERINE OF BRAGANZA (1638–1705)

Queen of England. Wife of Charles II. The daughter of John IV of Portugal, Catherine's marriage brought Charles II possession of Bombay and Tangier, which were great commercial gains for England. Catherine was often at loggerheads with her husband's mistress, the haughty Barbara Villiers. She suffered several miscarriages and failed to give Charles an heir. After he died in 1685, Catherine established a convent at Somerset House. She returned to Portugal in 1692.

⇒ ***Charles II***

CATHOLIC EMANCIPATION (1871)

Movement to gain toleration for Roman Catholics in Britain. After the Reformation, Roman Catholics suffered from persecution then restrictive legislation. Daniel O'Connell ('the Liberator') fought to end this. By the 1770s the Catholic threat was seen to be diminished and various Acts were passed. In 1791 Roman Catholics were granted freedom of worship. O'Connell formed the Catholic Association in 1823 and was elected to Parliament in 1828. He refused to take his seat, however, due to the prerequisite anti-Catholic oath. Finally with Robert Peel's Emancipation Act (1829), English and Irish Catholics were readmitted to Parliament. With the universities' Tests Acts of 1871 emancipation was all but complete.

⇒ ***Daniel O'Connell, Reformation, Roman Catholicism***

CATO STREET CONSPIRACY (1820)

Plot to murder foreign secretary Robert Stewart, Viscount Castlereagh and Cabinet ministers. Castlereagh was foreign secretary in 1820 when the plot was discovered. The plot was hatched at Cato Street, Edgware Road, London, with the intention of overthrowing the established government and replacing it with a provincial government. The conspirators were caught and executed.

⇒ ***Viscount Castlereagh***

CATUVELLAUNI

Tribe of ancient Britain. In 55 BC Julius Caesar crossed the English channel to Britain. The king of the Celtic Catuvellauni tribe, Cassivellaunus, took a lead in resisting Caesar's invasion by allying the Celtic tribes, forcing Caesar to withdraw.

⇒ ***Julius Caesar, Roman Invasion***

CENTRE Cato Street
RIGHT Tapestry Page from St Luke's Gospel from The Lindisfarne Gospels

CAVALIER (17TH CENTURY)

Term originally used to describe a horseman or a mounted knight. This was a nickname used to describe Charles I's 'haughty and dash' mounted troops during the English Civil War, as opposed to the

Parliamentarian Roundheads. The term is French, derived from the Latin word *Caballus*, meaning 'nag'.
⇛ *Charles I, Oliver Cromwell, English Civil War, Roundhead*

CAVALIER PARLIAMENT (1661–1679)

English Parliament during the period of Restoration. During the Interregnum, the period of Republican government between 1649 and 1660, Cromwell sought a Parliament that could balance his, the army's and the legislature's interests. He failed, but three years after his death the Cavalier Parliament was convened, consolidating the restoration of the monarchy.
⇛ *Oliver Cromwell, English Civil War, Interregnum*

CAXTON, WILLIAM (c. 1412–92)

English printer and translator. Born in Kent, at that time a centre of clothmaking, Caxton was apprenticed to a clothmaker and spent much of his adult life working in continental Europe. He first learned printmaking while in Cologne and returned with the skill to London. He printed and published Chaucer's *Canterbury Tales* and Thomas Malory's *Morte d'Arthur*. Caxton also translated many works, from French, Dutch, Latin and Greek. He was patronised by Edward IV and Richard III.
⇛ *Geoffrey Chaucer, Edward IV, Richard III*

CECIL, ROBERT (1563–1612)

Statesman and minister to Elizabeth I. Cecil oversaw the transition from a Tudor to a Stuart monarchy when James I became king in 1603. In 1605, in recognition of his duties, James made him Earl of Salisbury. For the next three years he was the king's chief secretary, then from 1608 he became the lord treasurer. However, his influence with the monarch decreased in later life as James I became increasingly annoyed at his failed attempts to get more money from Parliament.
⇛ *Elizabeth I, Gunpowder Plot, James I*

CELTIC CHRISTIANITY

Early Christian Church in Britain. The mission of St Columba from Ireland to Iona, and then of Aidan at Lindisfarne, converted the north of England. Iona, the Celtic Church's headquarters, was world-renowned in its time as a seat of learning and the birthplace of the *Book of Kells*. The defeat at the Synod of Whitby (AD 663–64) by the Roman branch of the Church in Britain, and the Viking invasions of the late eighth century combined to end the power of the Celtic Church in Britain. Sadly the time of a Church of great integrity and beauty had passed.
⇛ *St Aidan, St Columba,* Book of Kells, Lindisfarne Gospels, *Vikings, Synod of Whitby*

CELTS

Early settlers in the British Isles. The Celts dominated large parts of Europe from the third century BC. In Britain the Celtic culture would be subsumed by the Romans, but their language, religion and art would have a lasting influence on subsequent cultures.

Before the Roman Empire began to engulf the greater part of Europe, the Celts had widely invaded most of the territory. The Celts had begun their expansion from a stronghold in Alpine Europe, although they are thought to have been of Indo-European origin. In 390 BC they sacked Rome and overran a good deal of the Continent. They eventually occupied territory as far west as the Iberian peninsula, as far east as Greece and as far north as the British Isles. Despite their success at conquering new lands, the Celts lacked the communicational and organisational skills to unite their empire in the way that the Romans would. Instead emigrant bands would set off and establish permanent settlements. This meant that vast areas all over Europe were dominated by similar cultures and languages. In fact the Celtic culture left such an indelible mark on Europe that Celtic enclaves survived through the subsequent Roman occupation and into medieval times. Celtic languages even survive today as vestiges of a culture that profoundly influenced a Europe heading toward civilisation. Remarkably, Celtic styles of art and music are also still influencing modern cultures in Europe over 2,000 years later.

➧ *Druids*

CHAMBERLAIN, NEVILLE (1869–1940)

British prime minister (1937–40). Chamberlain is most associated with the policy of appeasement, which used diplomacy and concession rather than force to confront the expansionist policies of Nazi Germany. The most notable example of this was the Munich Agreement (September 1938), which ultimately surrendered Czechoslovakia to Nazi control. Chamberlain committed Britain to war if Hitler's forces invaded Poland, which happened in September 1939. The policy of appeasement was popular at the time, although it had critics – including Winston Churchill. Following disasters early on in the war, Chamberlain resigned amid much criticism. Churchill became prime minister and Chamberlain joined his Cabinet, but he later resigned and died in October 1940.

CHANCELLOR, LORD

British Cabinet post, chief law officer of the government, speaker of the House of Lords and privy councillor. Probably the most powerful lord chancellor in British history was Cardinal Wolsey in the sixteenth century. The position highlights the peculiarity of the British political system. The judiciary and executive (Cabinet) are meant to be separate but the lord chancellor is head of one and sits in the other. In the House of Lords, the lord chancellor sits on the woolsack.

➧ *House of Lords, Thomas Wolsey*

CHANCERY

Long-standing court and administrative department of the British political and legal system. A Chancery division of the High Court still exists to this day. Established after the invasion of William the Conqueror in the eleventh century, the Chancery was increasingly influential between the fourteenth and sixteenth centuries. Because it had jurisdiction over its own activities, the courts officers could sue and be sued within the Chancery.

CHANNEL TUNNEL (1994)

Tunnel linking England and France. Officially opened in 1994, the first contact between the French and English sections of the Channel Tunnel was made in 1990. Boring began in 1987 from points near Dover and Calais some 50 km (31 miles) distant. The 'Chunnel' actually comprises twin rail tunnels and a smaller service tunnel.

CHARGE OF THE LIGHT BRIGADE (1854)

Disastrous cavalry charge led by Lord Cardigan during the Battle of Balaclava. Due to a misunderstanding, the Light Brigade charged the Russians at the head of a valley, were shelled from all sides and forced to retire with heavy losses. The event was immortalised by Tennyson's poem of the same name and General Bosquet's remark 'It's magnificent but its not war'.

⟹ ***Battle of Balaclava, Crimean War***

CHARLES I (1600–49)

King of England and Scotland (1625–49). Second son of the Stuart king James I. Charles's disagreements with Parliament led to his ruling for 11 years without calling it. Eventually Parliament fought back and the English Civil War broke out. In 1649 Charles was summarily tried for treason and executed, and the country became a commonwealth until Charles's son was restored to the throne in 1660.

Charles came to the throne on his father's death in 1625. Like his father, Charles believed strongly in the Divine Right of Kings, under which monarchs were appointed by God and were answerable only to him. This idea collided fatally with the growing powers of Parliament, and a series of quarrels ensued which ended in civil war. The strong Puritan influence in Parliament opposed Charles's preference for the pseudo-Catholic 'high church' Arminian religious practices. Parliament also opposed Charles's favourite, the Duke of Buckingham and impeached him in 1626. Buckingham was assassinated shortly afterwards.

In 1628, Parliament forced Charles to accept the Petition of Right, which outlawed the raising of taxes without their consent. The following year, Charles dissolved Parliament and ruled without it for 11 years. During that time, to acquire finances for the royal treasury, he raised taxes in several ways which were barely legal. The most notorious was Ship Money, which was imposed on ports for the purpose of building ships for the defence of England. Charles aroused further fury by demanding Ship Money from inland towns as well.

In 1642 Charles went in person to Parliament with the intention of arresting five MPs on charges of treason. They escaped before he got there. Civil war was now certain and broke out in August 1642, when the king raised his standard at Nottingham. At first, the fortunes of war swung in the king's favour, but Oliver Cromwell's New Model Army gained the upper hand by 1645, when Charles was heavily defeated at Naseby. After this Parliament never lost the initiative in the war. Charles fled to Scotland, where the dominant religion was Presbyterianism. Charles proved equivocal about setting up a Presbyterian Church in England and the Scots handed him over to Parliament. In 1649, a parliamentary court put Charles on trial in London, charged with treason. He refused to recognise the right of any court to try him and was sentenced to death. The king was publicly beheaded on 30 January 1649. To the end, he clung to his belief in the Divine Right of Kings.

⟹ ***Oliver Cromwell, Eleven Years' Tyranny, English Civil War, Ship Money***

LEFT First Century Battersea Shield

CHARLES II (1630–85)

King of England (1660–85). Son of Charles I. Charles II was restored to the throne in 1660. Charles was a great patron of the arts and his reign was marked by the new Renaissance architecture and a revival of theatre, art and literature. But this was also a time of great social disasters, the plague and the Great Fire of London among them. On his death the throne passed to his brother James II.

His father's quarrel with Parliament and the subsequent civil war meant that Charles II spent his youth in exile. This afforded the prince a royal upbringing that was distinctly different from the sheltered and favoured norm. He was often short of money and frequently feared for his life. He was also free to indulge his sexual prowess and had several mistresses and illegitimate children while in exile in France. When his father was executed in 1649, he became Charles II, but this was purely nominal. Parliament ruled in England and England was now a republic.

In 1651, Charles invaded England with an army in an attempt to win back his birthright. He was crowned king in Scotland, but his forces were badly defeated by the parliamentary army and Charles once again fled to France. With the Restoration in 1660, Charles was determined 'never to go on his travels again' and to make his throne secure. Fortunately, he could rely on a residual guilt over the regicide of his father, which curbed any desire Parliament might have had to challenge the monarch again. Nevertheless, Charles knew when it was wise to yield. In 1673, he gave his assent to the Test Act, which effectively barred Catholics from holding public office, even though he himself had Catholic sympathies. Charles also knew when to stand firm, as he did against efforts to deny the succession of his Catholic brother James. Charles could be devious, too. To get round the need to ask Parliament for money, Charles acquired his own – secret – finances from Louis XIV of France, which enabled him to do without Parliament from 1681 until his death in 1685.

RIGHT Thomas Lydgate and Pilgrims leaving Canterbury from Chaucer's Prologue to Canterbury Tales

➠ ***Charles I, James II, Restoration, Test Acts***

CHARLES PHILIP ARTHUR GEORGE, PRINCE OF WALES (b. 1948)

21st Prince of Wales. Heir to Queen Elizabeth II. Married to Lady Diana Spencer in 1981, the couple separated acrimoniously in 1992. Diana's intense popularity with the British public led to criticism over the way the royal family and Prince Charles in particular treated the princess, but he maintained his dignity throughout a diffucult time for the monarchy and recent years have seen a revival in his own popularity.

Prince Charles was born at Buckingham Palace on 14 November 1948, the first of the four children of Elizabeth II (then Princess Elizabeth) and Prince Philip, Duke of Edinburgh. Charles's additional titles are Earl of Chester, Duke of Cornwall, Duke of Rothesay, Earl of Carrick and Baron of Renfrew, Lord of the Isles and Great Steward of Scotland. He was invested Prince of Wales at Caernarvon Castle on 1 July 1969 and as prince, he inherited the Duchy of Cornwall, reserved for the heir to the throne. In 1971, at Cambridge University, Charles became the first heir to the British Crown to earn a master's degree, and afterwards served in the Royal Navy (1971–76). Charles founded the Prince's Trust, a charitable organisation, while in the Navy. On 29 July 1981, he married Lady Diana Spencer. They had two sons, Prince William, born in 1982 and Prince Henry (Harry) born in 1984. The marriage ran into difficulties, and Charles and Diana separated in 1992. They were divorced in 1996. Prince Charles has been an outspoken critic of modern architecture and is a champion of organic farming.

➠ ***Diana, Princess of Wales; Elizabeth II, Heir to the throne; Wales, Princes of***

CHARLOTTE, QUEEN (1744–1818)

Queen of England. Wife of George III. Born Charlotte of Mecklenburg-Strelitz. Although their marriage was arranged, the king and queen had a very happy relationship and he was devoted to her. She remained loyal to him throughout his bouts of illness. They had 15 children. Queen Charlotte set the pattern for moral royal domestic life that was followed by later royals.

➠ *George III*

CHARTISTS (1838–48)

Democratic movement intended to improve the lot of the working classes in Britain. With the evolution of the working class during the Industrial Revolution, social politics began to play their part more obviously. The working class comprised the vast majority of the population in Britain by the early 1800s, yet they had little influence over their own civil rights because the upper classes held sway. Between 1838 and 1848 Chartism flourished in Britain. It derived its name from the People's Charter, a document based on six fundamental reforms, which included universal male suffrage, annual Parliaments and the secret ballot. However, prosperity began to take hold in Britain generally and the momentum of Chartism was lost due to poor organisation among its leaders.

CHAUCER, GEOFFREY (*c.* 1340–1400)

English poet. Chaucer was born into a wealthy family. As an adult he became a soldier and fought in France, where he was captured. He was ransomed by the king of England who later gave him a diplomatic post. While in this position he visited various European countries. He was the first poet to write in English, rather than Anglo-Norman or Latin. As well as the famous *Canterbury Tales* his works include *The Book of the Duchess* and *Troilus and Criseyde*. Many other works, including *The Romance of the Rose*, have been attributed to him, but authorship is unproven.

CHRISTIANITY

Exists in Britain in several denominations, predominantly Protestant, Roman Catholic and Nonconformist. Consistently the dominant religion of Britain since the end of the Dark Ages, Christianity in Britain is marked for its beautiful cathedrals, the initially political origins of its Reformation and its extraordinarily low rate of church attendance today.

In AD 313 Constantine was converted yet the spread of Christianity throughout Roman Britain remained slow. Christianity in Dark-Age Britain developed along two main strands: the Roman Christianity of Augustine and the Celtic Christianity of Aidan. The Protestant Reformation of the sixteenth century caused the next major religious divide, namely between Protestants and Roman Catholics.

The commercial and religious success of the Middle Ages led to incredible architectural feats in praise of God, namely cathedrals such as Salisbury. Equally, eras of trauma produced unusual sects of Christianity, for example, the Black Death and the Flagellants, or the Commonwealth and the Diggers and the Fifth Monarchy Men. The emergence of modern science with the Renaissance encouraged the secularisation of western Europe and the Industrial Revolution, with its social ills and the consequent rise of social conscience, all encouraged a philanthropic manifestation of Christianity in Britain.

Christianity in Britain has evolved through the centuries causing both harm and harmony in weakness and in strength. Churchgoing, however, has never been at such a low ebb (approximately eight per cent of the population).

➧ ***St Aidan, St Augustine, Black Death, Flagellants, Industrial Revolution, Roman Catholicism, Protestantism, Reformation, Salisbury Cathedral***

CHURCH OF ENGLAND

England's national Church since Henry VIII. After his Break with Rome an independent Church developed in England. This – subsequently Anglican – Church became the established Church of England, rather than simply the Church in England that it had been previously.

After Augustine's and Aidan's conversion of the pagans a form of British Christian scholarship developed that was respected worldwide. The Danish invasions then weakened the Church position in England, leaving it open for William the Conqueror to unite it more closely with Latin ideas.

In the sixteenth century Pope Clement VIII refused to annul Henry's marriage to Catherine of Aragon; consequently Henry removed the Church in England from papal jurisdiction and appointed himself Supreme Head of the Church of England. His largely political action coincided with the continental religious Reformation and Protestant changes began to be made: in 1549 Edward VI introduced the *Book of Common Prayer*. After a temporary, yet violent, Catholic interlude under Mary Tudor, Protestantism and the Church of England resumed under Elizabeth I with the Acts of Supremacy and Uniformity and the Thirty-Nine Articles. She, however, modestly desired to be only 'governor', rather than 'head' of the Church.

During Charles I's controversial reign the Church of England became High Anglican, abetted by William Laud, Archbishop of Canterbury. After an 11-year respite, due to the Commonwealth and extreme Puritanism, Anglicanism revived with Charles II. The Church of England remains the established Church.

➡ ***St Aidan, St Augustine, Catherine of Aragon, Edward VI, Elizabeth I, Henry VIII, William Laud, Mary I, Puritanism, John Wyclif***

CHURCH OF IRELAND

Independent Anglican Church in the Republic and Northern Ireland, administered by archbishops in Armagh and Dublin. Centuries of conflict with England, on account of the power and interference of Canterbury and Anglicanism, ended with the disestablishment of the Church of Ireland and its detachment from England.

LEFT A Roman Catholic service
BOTTOM LEFT The divorce of Henry VIII
BOTTOM RIGHT Papists torture Protestants

After Norse raids easily destroyed the church infrastructure of St Patrick's monastic Church, Canterbury gained a hold. Henry VIII's Irish Supremacy Act of 1537 increased English domination. However, the Dissolution of the Monasteries was only partial in Ireland and the language of the new prayer book – English – was largely unspoken. Despite Ireland remaining predominantly Roman Catholic English Anglican priests were appointed to Church posts there and the 1801 the Act of Union bolstered the Anglicanism of the Church of Ireland. According to the 1861 census less than one-sixth of the population of Ireland belonged to the established Church and therefore by 1869 the Disestablishment of the Irish Church was passed.

➡ ***Church of England, Henry VIII, St Patrick***

CHURCH OF SCOTLAND

National Church of Scotland, but not the established Church. The first church in Scotland was probably established by St Ninian *c.* AD 400. With the settling of Iona, *c.* AD 563, by Columba, religious scholarship in Scotland gained worldwide respect. In 1192 the Church in Scotland became subject only and directly to the pope by a special decree. Interestingly because of this allegiance Scotland initally rejected the Protestant Reformation more vehemently than England had, but by August 1560 the Protestants in Scotland had banned papal authority and adopted John Knox's *Scots Confession.*

For the next century Episcopalians and Presbyterians competed, until William and Mary's backing of Presbyterianism. In 1921 the State and the Church of Scotland became disassociated and attempts to affiliate the churches of Scotland and England in 1959 and 1971 have failed. Its archiepiscopal sees remain St Andrews (established 1472) and Glasgow (established 1492).

➠ ***Saint Columba, Episcopacy, Henry VIII, Iona, John Knox, Presbyterianism, William and Mary***

CHURCH OF WALES

Largely ruled over by the Church of England. The origins of the Church of Wales are usually ascribed to the legendary sixth-century Age of Saints. In the twelfth and thirteenth centuries failure to establish an archbishopric in Wales led to Canterbury's domination. The Church in Wales was continually poorer than the Church in England, not having the same political power, and during the Reformation it received the Bible and Prayer Book in the vernacular only thanks to private initiative. Nonconformism undermined the established Church of Wales in the eighteenth century and finally, in 1920, the Church of Wales became disestablished and therefore distanced from the Church of England.

➠ ***Church of England***

CHURCHILL, JOHN, DUKE OF MARLBOROUGH (1650–1722)

English general, considered one of the greatest military commanders in British history. By 1682 Churchill had become a colonel and received his peerage. Churchill was second-in-command of the forces facing Monmouth's Rebellion in 1685, ending the campaign a major-general. At this time he split with James II, who intended to make Roman Catholicism the state religion. When William of Orange landed in 1688, James promoted him to lieutenant-general, sending Churchill to fight against William. Churchill deserted to William's cause and after his coronation was made privy councillor and Earl of Marlborough. In 1702 he became the first Duke of Marlborough after a succession of victories over the French. He is remembered for winning the battles of Blenheim (1704), Ramillies (1706) and Oudenarde (1708). He fell out of favour in 1711, moving abroad, but regained recognition when George I became king.

➠ ***Blenheim Palace, War of the Spanish Succession***

CHURCHILL, WINSTON (1874–1965)

British prime minister (1940–45, 1951–55). Possibly the most famous of all Britain's modern political leaders. He trained at Sandhurst and fought in India and Sudan at the end of the nineteenth century. Churchill was first elected as an MP in 1901 for the Conservatives but joined the Liberals in 1904. He was First Lord of the Admiralty between 1911–15, but was demoted after a failed expedition to the Dardenelles. During the 1930s he was an implacable opponent of appeasement. By the outbreak of World War II he was again First Lord of the Admiralty, but took over as prime minister in May 1940. Over the next five years he established his reputation as leader, statesman and orator. He popularised the phrase 'Iron Curtain' to describe Soviet expansion in Eastern Europe and was re-elected as prime minister in 1951. He was also the author of several historical works, was given a full state funeral and is the only British leader to have an American warship named after him.

➠ ***World War II***

CISTERCIAN ORDER (1098)

Ascetic monastic order founded in 1098. Dissatisfaction with the Benedictine Order's laxity led to the emergence of the Cistercians. Manual labour and uniformity of between houses were their tenets. In 1120 the first sister house was established and that century was their apogee.

Benedictine Order, Dissolution of the Monasteries, Roman Catholicism

CIVIL LIST (1697)

Money paid each year by Parliament to meet the expenses of the Royal Household. The first Civil List Act was passed in 1697. Initially it covered government expenses, but this stopped in 1831. It was substantially amended by George III in 1761, who gave up revenues from Crown land in return for an annual payment. In recent years the list has been amended after growing criticism of the behaviour of several members of the royal family.

RIGHT McIan. a clan of the Scottish highlands

CLANS

Family groups, especially Scottish. The word 'clan' is derived from the Gaelic clann, meaning 'children', because Scottish clans are characterised by their own ancestry. The prefixes 'Mac' and 'Mc' both indicate that someone is descended from a particular ancestral line, so McCartney means 'son of Cartney'. Originally clan members kept strictly to themselves and there was intense rivalry between clans. Each clan had its own territory to be fiercely defended.

CLARE, RICHARD DE (1130–76)

Second Earl of Pembroke, an Anglo-Norman lord, nicknamed Strongbow. With large estates in Wales, Richard fought in Ireland (1170) for Dermot Mac-Murrough who ruled the province of Leinster. He took Waterford and Dublin, married Dermot's daughter, claiming the throne when Dermot died. He gave Dublin to Henry II (1171) incorporating Ireland into England's dominions.

Henry II

CLARENDON CODE (1661–65)

Four anti-Nonconformist Acts passed by Edward Hyde, 1st Earl of Clarendon. Clarendon did not entirely agree with these intolerant, eponymous, pro-Anglican Acts. The Corporation Act (1661) forbade municipal office to non-communicants of a parish church. The Act of Conformity (1662) similarly provided exclusion from church offices. The Conventicle Act (1662, revised 1667) made public Nonconformist meetings illegal. Finally the Five Mile Act (1665) stipulated that Nonconformist ministers must live at least 5 miles (8 km) outside towns.

➠ ***Charles II, Edward Hyde Clarendon***

CLARENDON, EDWARD HYDE (1609–74)

Statesman, politician. Clarendon was a long-time supporter of the monarchy including through the period of the English Civil War. He served in the Short Parliament in 1640 and Long Parliament from 1640–60. Following failed attempts to reconcile differences between Charles I and Parliament he went into exile in France in 1646. Clarendon became Charles II's closest advisor and helped to negotiate the return of the monarchy. On his return to England he became Lord Chancellor. His downfall was brought about by the Dutch War; he was forced into exile in France, where he died.

➠ ***Charles II, Long Parliament, Short Parliament***

CLAUDIUS, EMPEROR

Roman emperor. Leader of the Roman conquest of Britain. Although Julius Caesar had made forays into the British Isles in 55 BC, it was Claudius who conducted the first campaign of conquest in AD 43. He stayed only for the initial stages of the campaign against the tribes, leaving the remainder of the conquest to his generals.

➠ ***Julius Caesar, Roman Invasion***

CLIVE, ROBERT, BARON OF PLASSEY (1725–74)

Founder of British India. From a humble position as a clerk in the East India Company, Clive was posted to Madras in 1744. After the city's capture by the French he joined the British army in 1747. In 1751, with just 500 men, he captured Arcot and raised the Siege of Trichinopoly. He defended Arcot for 11 weeks. In 1753 he came back to England as a hero, returning to India in 1756 and, recapturing Calcutta, forced the French out of India and defeated Siraj-ud-Dawlah's 50,000 men with less than 3,000 of his own. He was knighted in 1764.

➠ ***Battle of Plassey, Seven Years' War***

COALBROOKDALE

Centre of the Industrial Revolution in Britain. The Industrial Revolution was literally fuelled by coal, which heated the boilers of the steam engines and fired the furnaces. England had vast reserves of coal at that time and Abraham Derby (1678–1717), based at Coalbrookdale on the river Severn, pioneered the use of coke for smelting iron.

Industrial Revolution

COINAGE, DEBASEMENT OF (1540s)

Reduction in standard and content of metal in coins. During the reign of Henry VIII, Britain suffered a monetary depression due to extreme levels of inflation triggered by unprofitable trade with other countries. Henry's solution was to debase the value of coinage. This meant effectively declaring lower denominations of coin worthless apart from their bullion (weight) value. The idea behind debasement was to stimulate sharp rises in the prices for exported goods and so recover the economy of Britain.

Henry VIII

COLERIDGE, SAMUEL TAYLOR (1772–1834)

English Romantic poet; also a philosopher and playwright. An idealist, Coleridge left Cambridge early to join the army. Rescued from a miserable military existence by wealthy friends, he befriended the poet Robert Southey, with whom he dreamed of founding a 'Pantisocratic' community in America. Coleridge's first poems were published in 1794. He met Wordsworth in 1797 and in 1798 they published the joint volume *Lyrical Ballads*, which included Coleridge's masterpiece *The Rime of the Ancient Mariner.* His other works include 'Kubla Khan' and 'Osirio'. Coleridge was married with four children (he is also reputed to have been in love with Wordsworth's sister-in-law, Sara).

Cambridge University, William Wordsworth

COLLEGE OF ARMS (1484)

London-based institution that holds the official records of heraldic entitlements; it is also the body that grants the entitlements. The College of Arms was set up by Richard III. Following Richard's defeat at Bosworth Henry VII succeeded the throne and he created a new set of rules and gave a new building to the corporation. The present-day College of Arms stands on the same site (Queen Victoria Street), although the original building was destroyed in the Great Fire of London. The current building dates from the 1670s.

Great Fire of London, Henry VII, Heraldry, Richard III

COLLINS, MICHAEL (1890–1922)

Irish nationalist leader. Collins first became a member of the Irish republican brotherhood and took an active part in the 1916 Easter Rising. Collins was a founder of the IRA and intelligence director. He died in 1922 at the hands of fundamentalists.

Easter Rising, Home Rule, Sinn Fein

CENTRE LEFT Robert Clive receiving a grant for the Clive fund from the Newab of Bengal
LEFT Ironbridge at Coalbrookdale
ABOVE College of Arms, London

COLUMBA, ST (c. AD 522–97)

Statesman, hermit and missionary to Scotland. Born in County Donegal, Columba carried Christianity from Ireland to Iona. Here he established the most prestigious monastery of the time, from which Aidan was to convert western Scotland. Columba also participated in the council of Druim Cetta, which decided issues of monarchical status within Ireland. He lived his last years on Iona, writing hymns and already being regarded as a saint. His feast day is 9 June.

➠ *Saint Aidan,*

COMMONWEALTH, THE (1931)

Group of independent sovereign states, once formerly part of the British Empire. Some countries remain dependencies of the United Kingdom, but all are voluntary members of the Commonwealth.

By the beginning of the twentieth century the British Empire was in decline, leading to the creation of the Commonwealth. During World War I a representative from the South African imperial war cabinet, Jan Smuts, suggested the British Empire be renamed the 'British Commonwealth of Nations'. In 1931 the name was recognised in the Statute of Westminster. Following World War II many old empire members had developed a growing sense of independent nationhood which led to the name being simplified to the Commonwealth.

The essence of the Commonwealth is that it is an association comprising voluntary members. Many are old members of the British Empire but several have joined subsequent to its creation. There is no charter of constitution for the Commonwealth because it does not operate officially on political or economic grounds. Instead it is run according to traditional and sentimental rules. Members of the Commonwealth benefit from a nepotistic relationship with one another so there are diplomatic advantages to be had from membership. Membership withdrawal does therefore carry some political significance. This happened to Nigeria in 1995, because of its record on human rights abuses, making the country a pariah on the world stage.

➠ *British Empire*

ABOVE Notes and coins of Commonwealth countries

RIGHT Margaret Thatcher, Prime Minister from 1979 to 1990

CONCORDE (1976)

Supersonic aeroplane. In 1976 the Anglo-French Concorde project succeeded in bringing the first and only supersonic airliner into commercial service. Only allowed to reach supersonic speed whilst over oceans and unpopulated territory, due to the sonic 'boom', Concorde continued flying with a clean safety record until one crashed near Paris in 2000.

CONSCRIPTION (1939)

Compulsory military service. Although most of the major powers during World War I had conscripted military service it was not until 1916 that Britain resorted to conscription. Before then they had depended on volunteers. In May 1939 the Conscription Act was brought into force and adopted on 3 September, requiring all males between 18 and 41 to serve compulsory military service. The Emergency Powers Defence Act further reinforced this in May 1940 and extended conscription in order to fully mobilise all the human resources of the country. After the war conscription in the form of National Service continued until the 1950s.

➠ *World War I, World War II*

CONSERVATIVE PARTY (1830S)

British political party. It first emerged in the 1830s and in the twentieth century established itself as one of the two major parties in British politics. The party emerged from the Tory group, which began in the 1860s. The term, Irish for 'outlaw', is still used today to describe the Conservatives.

In the 1830s, the Conservatives allied themselves to the reactionary and repressive government of Lord Liverpool. Under Robert Peel, the party adopted the Tamworth manifesto which accepted reform where necessary, still a tenet of modern-day Conservatism. The party split during the mid-nineteenth century but was united over attempts at giving Ireland Home Rule in the 1880s. In 1912, the Conservatives merged with the Liberal Unionists and became the Conservative and Unionist Party, still its official name. Its domination of British politics began in the 1920s.

Andrew Bonar Law was elected as Conservative prime minister in 1922. Between 1924 and 1929 it was in power under Stanley Baldwin. Tories dominated the national government between 1931–35 and Baldwin became prime minister between 1935–37. He was then succeeded by Neville Chamberlain, who in turn was succeeded by Winston Churchill. Between 1951 and 1964 it had 13 years of unbroken rule under Churchill, Anthony Eden, Harold Macmillan and Alec Douglas-Home. Edward Heath retook power for the Tories in 1970, but was ousted in 1973. During that time he took Britain into the European Economic Community. In 1975, the party elected its first female leader, Margaret Thatcher, who was prime minister from 1979 to 1990. Her brand of confrontational, right-wing Conservatism was at odds with many of her predecessors. After she resigned in 1990 the party was led by John Major until 1997 when it was defeated at the polls.

➧ ***Stanley Baldwin, Neville Chamberlain, Winston Churchill, Alec Douglas-Home, Anthony Eden, Edward Heath, Andrew Bonar Law, John Major, Margaret Thatcher***

CONSTITUTIONAL MONARCHY (1689)

Introduced in 1689, the principle underlying constitutional monarchy is that a monarch reigns, but does not rule. It developed considerably over the years. Monarchs lost the right to make war and their power of veto and choice of when to dissolve Parliament were curtailed. Royal rights to choose ministers and award honours gradually faded with the development of party politics. As compensation for this loss of power, constitutional monarchy raised monarchs above damaging political controversies.

➧ ***Mary II, Hanoverian Dynasty, Parliament, William III***

CONVENTION PARLIAMENT

Two Parliaments convened in the seventeenth century without the summons of the sovereign. The first Parliament was between April and December 1660 and recalled Charles II to the throne. The second was in February 1689. This met after the overthrow of James II.

➧ ***Cavalier Parliament, Oliver Cromwell, English Civil War***

COOPERATIVE PARTY (1917)

Political party. Formed in 1917, it was closely associated with the Labour Party. It emerged from cooperative movement that sought to protect consumers by forming societies that made and sold produce without profit. Socialist Robert Owen pioneered the movement in the nineteenth century with the building of his model community in New Lanark.

➧ ***New Lanark, Robert Owen***

CORN CIRCLES (1980s)

Patterns in cornfields of unknown origin. In the 1980s a wave of complex patterns began to appear in cornfields across the UK, giving rise to the theory that they were the work of alien life forms. Subsequent investigation has revealed that many were elaborate hoaxes, but the UFO theory still has its adherents.

CORN LAWS

Laws introduced to control the import and export of corn. At the end of the Napoleonic Wars in 1815, and during the early stages of the Industrial Revolution, the government of Lord Liverpool introduced the most famous Corn Law. It prohibited the import of any foreign corn until the domestic price reached 80 shillings a quarter – in effect a famine price. This law proved immensely controversial since it was represented as advantaging the landed interest and making the price of bread for the working man much higher than it needed to be. The law was modified in 1828 and 1842 and, after pressure from the largely middle-class Anti-Corn Law League, abolished by the government of Robert Peel in 1846.

CORNWALLIS, CHARLES, 1ST MARQUESS (1738–1805)

General and statesman during the American Revolution. Defeated by Washington at Trenton (26 December 1776) and Princeton (3 January 1777). Cornwallis won victories at Brandywine Creek (September) and Camden (16 August 1780). He was forced to retreat to Yorktown after the bloody battle at Guildford Court House (March 1781) where he was later compelled to surrender on 19 October.

➡ *American Revolution, Battle of Yorktown*

CORPORATION ACT (1661)

Act of Parliament that excluded people from municipal office who refused to take communion in the Church of England. The act was finally repealed in 1828. It formed part of the Clarendon Code that sought to restore the supremacy of the Anglican Church.

➡ *Charles II, Clarendon Code*

COUNCIL OF THE NORTH (16TH AND 17TH CENTURIES)

Political body that administered government policy and law in the sixteenth and seventeenth centuries in the north of England, including Cumberland, Durham, Northumberland and Yorkshire. It was originally

established by Richard III, but dissolved in 1509. Henry VIII's lord chancellor, Cardinal Wolsey, re-established the council in 1525. Twelve years later it became a permanent body. With its close connections to government policy it became identified with the more unpopular edicts passed down from on high at an especially turbulent time in English history. The council was finally abolished by the Long Parliament in 1641.

Henry VIII

COUNTER-REFORMATION (17TH CENTURY)

Roman Catholic retaliation against sixteenth- and seventeenth-century Protestantism. Also called the Catholic Reformation, its origins were in the Roman Inquisition, particularly the Spanish Inquisition, established in 1542 to fight heresy. The Council of Trent (1545–63), was a more self-contemplative attempt to regain religious ground in western Europe and proposed some internal reforms within the Catholic Church. The Catholic mission was primarily fought by a new monastic order, the Jesuits. Apart from during the reign of Mary I their impact in England, Wales and Scotland was limited: Protestantism and Calvinism continued to dominate.

Jesuits, Mary I

COVENANT MARTYRS (17TH CENTURY)

Signatories of seventeenth-century Scottish Presbyterian covenants, persecuted under Charles II. With the Restoration in 1660, Episcopacy was re-established, the oaths of the covenants were deemed unlawful and Archbishop Sharp initiated the use of troops to collect intimidatory fines. The covenanters' rebellions (1666, 1679 and 1685) were fiercely suppressed and 210 covananters were transported.

National Covenant, Restoration

CRAIG, JAMES (1871–1940)

First prime minister of Northern Ireland (1921–40). During his time as leader Craig was a particularly strong defender of Protestants' rights in and domination of Northern Ireland. Craig was an MP from 1906 until 1921. Between 1913 and 1920 he also organised the Ulster Volunteer Force, preparing it for armed confrontation amid Loyalist fears of Home Rule being granted to Northern Ireland.

Home Rule

LEFT The British, including Cornwallis, surrendering to George Washington after the Siege of Yorktown

ABOVE The signing of the covenant in Greyfriars' churchyard, Edinburgh

CRANMER, THOMAS (1489–1556)

Archbishop of Canterbury (1533–56). Cranmer exerted enormous influence on the religious practice of England in the Tudor era and subsequently for years to come. As Archbishop, he declared Henry VIII's marriage to his first wife Catherine of Aragon void and then sanctioned the monarch's marriage to Anne Boleyn. By doing so he also sanctioned England's split from Rome's papal orthodoxy and the Protestant dominance. When Mary I, a devout Catholic, came to the throne in 1553, Cranmer was burned at the stake.

➡ ***Henry VIII, Mary I***

CRÉCY, BATTLE OF (1346)

Major battle (26 August 1346) between the English and French during the Hundred Years' War. When Edward III invaded France for the second time he was blocked in northern France by a 40,000-strong army led by Philip VI and King John of Bohemia. The English deployed their 19,000 men on the slope of a hill. When the French attacked, the English longbowmen decimated them. After 16 assaults the French were left with 1,500 dead. English casualties were negligible.

➡ ***Hundred Years' War***

CRICK, FRANCIS (b. 1916)

British scientist who jointly dicovered the structure of DNA. 1953 was the year that saw science progress into the realm of modern genetics. Much was already known about heredity from breeding experiments with animals and plants, but it took three molecular biologists to finally discover the mechanism responsible for the way genetic information is coded. Francis Crick and American James Watson (b. 1928) determined the structure of DNA (Deoxyribonucleic Acid), helped by the work of Maurice Wilkins (b. 1916).

ABOVE The Battle of Crécy

ABOVE CENTER Corporal Philip Smith winning the Victoria Cross during an assault in the Redem

CRIMEAN WAR (1853–56)

War that began as a quarrel between Russian Orthodox monks and French Catholics over Jerusalem and Nazareth; fought between England, Turkey, France and Sardinia against the Russians. The work of Florence Nightingale in the Crimea revolutionised nursing practice.

Russia occupied Turkish Moldavia and Walachia in July 1853. The Turks declared war and in March 1854 England and France declared war on Russia, followed by Sardinia in January 1855. The allies began by driving the Russians out of Moldavia and Walachia but it was decided that the Russian naval base at Sevastopol presented a threat to security in the region. In September 1854 allied troops landed in the Crimea with the intent of capturing Sevastopol, which was heroically defended until September 1855. Military operations were marked by stubbornness, gallantry and incompetence.

As the allies marched southwards to invest Sevastopol the Russians unsuccessfully tried to prevent the allies from crossing the River Alma. The Russians twice tried to relieve Sevastopol but were beaten at Balaclava and Inkerman. The winter of 1854–55 brought great misery to both the allies and the Russians. The British discovered their supply situation was grossly incapable of supplying the men. Through the work of Florence Nightingale mortality rates of the British wounded at the hospital in Scutari were drastically cut. In early 1856 Sevastopol finally fell and the war was brought to a conclusion by the Peace of Paris. This was the only European war that Britain fought between the ending of the Napoleonic Wars in 1815 and the beginning of the Great War in 1914.

➡ ***Battle of Balaclava, Charge of the Light Brigade, Florence Nightingale***

CROMWELL, OLIVER (1599–1658)

Political leader, statesman and soldier. Lord Protector of England during the Commonwealth. Cromwell's Puritan ideals introduced radical change in England during the Civil War and subsequent Republic. Despite his overthrow of Charles I, Cromwell did not want to be ruler of England, but was attempting to establish a 'society of saints'.

Born in Cambridgeshire and educated at Sidney Sussex College, Cambridge, Cromwell rose from relatively humble beginnings to become the most powerful man in England. He was elected to the Long Parliament for Cambridge City and made his name as a radical. He then proved himself to be a natural military tactician when the Civil War broke out in 1642. Dissatisfied with the way war was being fought he established the New Model Army, which helped to inflict a decisive defeat on the Royalists at Naseby in 1645. Once the royal forces had been subdued and Charles I executed in January 1649, Cromwell set about establishing his position. He ordered the massacres of civilians in Drogheda and Wexford and repelled further Royalist forces from Scotland summoned by Charles II. He established the Long Parliament and Barebones Parliament. The latter being a failure, Cromwell installed himself as Lord Protector. Although increasingly autocratic, a degree of religious tolerance (he allowed the Jews back into Britain, although this was also for commercial reasons) allowed his rule to be, by and large, sanctioned by the country. His death in September 1658, though, revealed the extent to which the political consensus revolved around him. His successor, his eldest son Richard, was deposed within six months.

➡ ***Barebones Parliament, Charles I, Richard Cromwell, English Civil War***

CROMWELL, RICHARD (1626–1712)

Son of Oliver Cromwell, Lord Protector of England (1658–59). Richard, as Oliver Cromwell's eldest son, succeeded his father on his death in 1658. Unlike his father, though, his time in office was short and he was dismissed by the Long Parliament in 1659. He managed to escape to France a year later. However he returned to England 20 years on and lived out his life in seclusion.

➡ ***Oliver Cromwell***

CROMWELL, THOMAS (1485–1540)

Tudor statesman. Cromwell oversaw England's religious separation from Rome in his position as Henry VIII's closest advisor. Cromwell arranged the divorce of the king from Catherine of Aragon in 1533. Subsequently he also dissolved the monasteries and ensured that their wealth was transferred to the Crown in the late 1530s. He had risen to this position from humble origins, beginning his career in the employ of Cardinal Wolsey. His fall from grace occurred after he persuaded Henry VIII to marry Anne of Cleves, whom the ageing king found unattractive. He was executed in 1540 on trumped-up charges of treason.

➧ ***Henry VIII, Thomas Wolsey***

CROWN JEWELS

Jewellery or regalia for royal ceremonial. The Crown Jewels include jewellery used at coronations, comprising St Edward's Crown, the Imperial State Crown, the jewelled Sword of State and the *ampulla*, containing the oil for anointing the monarch. Other crown jewels consist of swords of state, the orb and the sceptre.

➧ ***Tower of London***

CRUSADES (1095–1270)

Military and religious expeditions to the Holy Land initiated by the popes. During this time pilgrimages and relics were in vogue, commercial ventures were undergoing expansion and the Turks were

threatening the Byzantine Church. Thus the popes' crusading calls were welcomed initially. In the First Crusade Jerusalem fell to the Christians in 1099. The Second Crusade was a failure and in 1187 Saladin recaptured Jerusalem. It was in the Third Crusade (1189–92), under the leadership of Richard I, that England played a more prominent role. Despite Richard's victory at Arsuf, which allowed the crusaders to gain Joppa, the Christians failed to recapture Jerusalem and infighting emerged, culminating in Richard's kidnap. By the Fourth Crusade (1198), the crusaders side-tracked and aided Venice's trading ventures, sacking Constantinople in 1204. Consequently the Byzantine and Latin churches were deeply divided.

➧ ***Richard I, Jews***

CRYSTAL PALACE (1851)

Building constructed for for the Great Exhibition (1851). The Crystal Palace was a fantastic building of glass and iron, designed by Joseph Paxton. Two thousand workers were needed to construct it. It stood originally in Hyde Park, but was moved after the exhibition to the area of south-east London now known as Crystal Palace. The building burned down in 1936.

➧ ***Great Exhibition***

LEFT A Crusader Knight
ABOVE The interior of Crystal Palace
RIGHT Cutty Sark

CULLODEN, BATTLE OF (1746)

Last battle (16 April 1746) of the second Jacobite Rebellion. Charles Edward Stuart, the Young Pretender and James II's grandson landed in Scotland in July 1745. Having taken Edinburgh and fought three battles in Scotland and invaded England as far as Derby, he was forced to retreat into north-eastern Scotland. His army of 5,000 Highlanders were cornered at Drummoissie Muir or Culloden Moor and routed by 9,000 British regulars under the Duke of Cumberland, George II's son. Charles fled to France and 1,000 nobles that had supported him were condemned to death. For his atrocities Cumberland was named The Butcher.

➧ ***Bonnie Prince Charlie, Jacobite Rebellion***

CURIA REGIS

Royal court of the Norman and Angevin monarchies. Curia Regis was the period's most important executive and legislative body and it also served as a court for all matters relating to the king. It usually met three times a year, at Easter, Pentecost and Christmas. The court's influence had declined by the thirteenth century, with government expanding and the rise of specialist departments such as the Chancery.

➧ ***Chancery, Privy Council***

CUTTY SARK

Only surviving tea clipper. In the nineteenth century ships were specifically built for transporting cargoes of tea from the colonies to Britain. They were known as tea clippers. The only surviving example is the *Cutty Sark*, now kept at Greenwich, London. She was built in 1869 and her name comes from a Robert Burns poem.

D-DAY (1944)

Allied amphibious and airborne landings in Normandy (6 June 1944). On D-Day British, Canadian and US troops established five bridgeheads on the Cotentin Peninsular in Northern France along a 30-mile stretch. The Americans landed on Omaha and Utah beaches and the Anglo-Canadian forces at Sword, Juno and Gold. Simultaneously, American paratroopers were dropped behind the German lines and numerous small-scale commando raids were launched against key positions in the area. This was all preceded by an intensive naval and airborne bombardment, coupled with extensive sabotage by the French resistance. By midnight the Utah beach troops had penetrated nine miles inland but those at Omaha, where 3,000 Americans had been killed, had only managed one mile. At Gold Arromanches and Bayeux had been taken; Sword had failed to capture Caen and the Canadians at Juno had swept seven miles inland. By 12 June the bridgehead was 80 miles long and 10 deep. The D-Day battle had been won.

➡ ***World War II***

DANELAW (AD 886)

Area of north-east England settled by the Danes in the eleventh century. By the late ninth century Norsemen had managed to secure a good deal of the British territory formerly occupied by the Anglo-Saxons. By the year AD 886 they held most of northern and eastern England, an area known as the Danelaw, and had introduced their own laws, customs and language.

➡ ***Vikings***

DANES

Invaders of Scandinavian origin who plundered and eventually settled in the British Isles. The Dark Ages in Britain were characterised by waves of invasion from foreign forces. The Anglo-Saxons came from the Germanic region of Europe, while Norsemen came from Scandinavia. Norsemen, known as Vikings or Danes, were skilled sailors and efficient warriors. Initially they paid

RIGHT HMS Queen Elizabeth shelling forts during the Dardanelles Campaign
BELOW: Allied landings in Normandy

DANBY, THOMAS OSBORNE, EARL OF (1631–1712)

British politician under Charles II. Danby was chief minister to the king between 1673–78. He was instrumental in instigating the Glorious Revolution in 1689 and his efforts were rewarded as he took up his position again for William III in 1690.

➡ ***Glorious Revolution***

DANEGELD (AD 991)

Money paid by the English in exchange for peace with the Danes during the tenth and eleventh centuries. The money was raised from taxation; the first payment in AD 991 was for £20,000. Several kings used the levy, seeing it as a useful way of raising revenue.

➡ ***Danelaw, Ethelred the Unready, Vikings***

Britain fleeting visits to raid villages, plundering and pillaging as they went. Eventually, though, the Danes secured a foothold in Britain and conquered the Danelaw region of northern and eastern England.

➠ *Vikings*

DARDANELLES CAMPAIGN (1915–16)

Unsuccessful allied invasion of Turkey (25 April 1915–8 January 1916). The campaign was proposed and devised by the British to relieve Turkish pressure on the Russians and to gain control of Istanbul and the Black Sea. Naval operations in February 1915 had failed due to mining. The amphibious landing began in April and was met with heavy Turkish resistance. Hamilton, the British Commander, seemed over-cautious and as a result little headway was made from the beaches. In August the Allies launched another offensive but due to the inspired leadership of Mustafa Kemal this attack also failed. Allied troops were withdrawn in December and January.

➠ *Gallipoli, World War I*

DARNLEY, HENRY STUART, LORD (1546–67)

Son of Malcolm Stuart, Earl of Lennox. Husband of Mary, Queen of Scots. Like Mary, whom he married in 1565, Darnley was descended from Henry VII through Henry's daughter Margaret. The couple were soon estranged, over Mary's refusal to grant Darnley the Crown Matrimonial. He grew extremely jealous and was implicated in the plot by Scots nobles to murder Mary's Italian secretary, David Rizzio in 1566. Rizzio enjoyed Mary's confidence and Darnley suspected him of being her lover. Darnley was himself murdered in 1567. James Hepburn, Earl Bothwell, who married Mary soon afterwards, was thought to have instigated the killing.

➠ *Mary, Queen of Scots*

DARWIN, CHARLES (1809–82)

English scientist. Darwin had a curiosity for the natural sciences and was in the privileged position of being able to choose a career as a naturalist. During a voyage on HMS Beagle (1831–36), visiting South America and the Galapagos Islands a realisation came to him about the way species evolve. Knowing what a furore his theory would cause, he did not reveal it for a further 22 years. By 1858, however, Alfred Wallace (1823–1913) had written to him outlining a similar idea. Darwin was forced to publish his life's work, *On the Origin of Species by Natural Selection or the Preservation of Favoured Traits in the Struggle for Life* was published in 1859.

DAVID I (c. 1085–1153)

King of Scotland (1124–53). An exemplary ruler, who established his independence as sovereign ruler of Scotland, David married Matilda, great-niece of William I of England and drew on his Norman connections to modernise his realm. He brought Norman knights to Scotland, where they established strong lordships, manned castles for the defence of the country and knights for the king's army. David also 'normanised' Scots law and government, and developed the religious and economic life of his kingdom. The Normans were not allowed to be dominant in Scotland: David also promoted the Celtic nobility and included them in the governing élite.

Feudal System, William I

DAVID II (1324–71)

King of Scotland (1329–71). Only son of Robert Bruce, David II became king in 1329 but fled to France when Scotland was invaded in 1332 by Edward Balliol and Edward III of England. While the English king was engaged in war in France, David invaded Scotland, but was defeated and captured by an English army at Neville's Cross in 1346. He was ransomed in 1357. King at last after almost 30 years, David proved a strong ruler. He crushed several revolts by his nobles. However, on his death he had no heir and the Bruce dynasty ended with him.

Edward III, Hundred Years' War, Robert I

DAVID, ST (c. AD 520–600)

Patron saint of Wales. David's mother was St Non and he was born in St Bride's Bay, Pembrokeshire, and educated in Cardigan. He moved the headquarters of Church government from Caeleon to Mynyw, present-day St David's and the cathedral city in western Wales. Pope Calixtus II is said to have canonised David in about 1120, but as with many details relating to his life there is a degree of uncertainty. His feast day is 1 March.

DAVITT, MICHAEL (1846–1906)

Irish nationalist, instrumental in finding the Irish Land League in 1879, which sought land reform in Ireland. Davitt supported the notion of armed struggle against the English and spent several years in prison. During one jail sentence (1882) he was elected as an MP but was unable to take up his seat.

Land League, Charles Parnell

DAVY, HUMPHREY (1778–1829)

English chemist, inventor of the Davy lamp. The transition from eighteenth to nineteenth centuries was a period which saw marked advances in scientific understanding of the chemical world. Humphrey Davy was at the forefront of this field and made some important discoveries. Utilising the invention of electrolysis, he was able to isolate and discover no fewer than seven new elements between 1807–08. He is perhaps best known, though, for inventing the Davy safety lamp for miners.

ABOVE Davy Lamps

TOP RIGHT Protestors in Washington during the Depression

DE VALERA, EAMONN (1882–1975)

Irish prime minister and president (1937–48, 1951–54, 1957–59). De Valera was also president from 1959–73. American-born to a Spanish father and Irish mother, De Valera was an early leader of the Sinn Fein movement. He headed the party's provisional government from 1919 to 1922 but De Valera opposed the terms of the 1921 Anglo-Irish Treaty. In 1926, he created the Fianna Fail party. It won the 1932 election and he was president of the Executive Council of the Irish Free State. He also served in a senior position during the 1916 Easter Rising. He revived the Irish language.

Easter Rising, Irish Free State, Sinn Fein

DECLARATIONS OF INDULGENCE (1662, 1672, 1687 AND 1688)

Series of Acts passed by Charles II and James II to alleviate religious intolerance. Their sympathies were Roman Catholic, but they were willing to attempt to grant religious freedom to Nonconformists and other Puritans. Charles's first declaration (1662) failed: he capitulated to Parliament in return for extra taxes. His second declaration (1672) also had limited success due to his financial dependency on an unwilling Parliament and his association with the Treaty of Dover and Catholic France. James's declaration of 1687 was motivated by his desire to gain Nonconformist supporters to create a new Parliament. His reissued declaration (1688) and its stipulated reading in every parish church was refused by many bishops.

Charles II, Clarendon Code, Treaty of Dover, James II

DEPRESSION

Name given to the years after the 1929 financial crash in which there was a worldwide recession. On 29 October 1929 millions of dollars were wiped off US share values in only a few hours. The Wall Street Crash, as it was dubbed, caused an economic crisis as US overseas investments were recalled. Europe, especially war-torn Germany, was severely affected by this as levels of international trade fell dramatically. Britain, along with other European countries, made a slow recovery over the late 1930s.

DERBY, EDWARD STANLEY, 14TH EARL OF (1799–1869)

British prime minister (1852, 1858–59, 1866–68). First a Whig and then a Tory, Derby was responsible for introducing the bill for abolishing slavery.

DESPENSER, HUGH (1261–1326)

Favourite of King Edward II, together with his son Hugh. The king's favour and the extensive estates he granted them made the Despensers extremely unpopular. Resentful English nobles forced Edward to exile them in 1321. They returned but fell foul of Edward's vengeful queen, Isabella. Both were executed in 1326.

Edward II, Piers Gaveston

DETTINGEN, BATTLE OF (1743)

Battle that took place on 27 June 1743 during the War of the Austrian Succession. The allies, 40,000 strong under George II, found their retreat cut by 60,000 French under de Noailles and 23,000 under de Grammont. George II led a charge that broke the French – the last British monarch to lead his troops into battle.

➧ ***War of the Austrian Succession, George II***

DEVOLUTION (1998)

Tony Blair's Labour government established an elected Scottish Assembly and smaller Welsh Assembly in 1998 after both countries voted for their own Parliaments. The Scottish Parliament, based at Holyrood, controls a budget of around £17 billion and has tax-raising powers. The budget in Wales is £7 billion, but with no tax-raising powers. Some believe the creation of the Parliaments calls into question the existence of the United Kingdom.

➧ ***Scottish Assembly, Welsh Assembly***

DEVONSHIRE, SPENCER HARTINGTON, 8TH DUKE OF (1833–1908)

British politician. Devonshire was leader of the Liberal Unionists from 1886 to 1903. He was primarily responsible for the defeat of Gladstone's 1886 Home Rule Bill.

➧ ***Home Rule***

DIANA, PRINCESS OF WALES (1961–97)

Princess of Wales. Diana, daughter of Earl Spencer, married Prince Charles on 29 July 1981. She achieved phenomenal worldwide popularity as a fashion icon, for her charitable work and as devoted mother to her two sons, William and Harry. Diana became the most photographed woman in the world and attracted intense media interest. The marriage dissolved due to allegations that Charles was having an affair; Diana is also believed to have had an affair. In 1992, she contributed to a book *Diana, Her True Story* by Andrew Morton, which revealed the truth about her so-called 'fairytale' marriage. The book created a scandal and the same year Diana and Charles separated. They divorced four years later. Diana continued her charity work and, among other projects, championed a campaign against anti-personnel mines organised by the Red Cross organisation. In 1997, Diana was in Paris with her friend Dodi Fayed when their car crashed while being pursued by paparazzi. Dodi was killed and Diana, who was severely injured, died a few hours later. Her funeral in London attracted extraordinary public grief. Diana was afterwards buried at the Spencer family home, Althorp House, in Northamptonshire.

➧ ***Prince Charles, Elizabeth II, House of Windsor***

DICKENS, CHARLES (1812–70)

Nineteenth-century English writer and favourite of Queen Victoria. Dickens had a financially unstable childhood, during which his father was imprisoned for debt. Consequently, Dickens, aged 12, was sent out to work, rudely interrupting his education. At the age of 16 he began working as a journalist. Shortly after his 21st birthday he produced *Sketches by Boz*, published as a magazine series: a method of publication he used for most of his works, reaching a much wider audience than novel-readers alone. Dickens' first bestseller, *Pickwick Papers*, was written while he was still in his early twenties. His many later novels include *David Copperfield*, *A Christmas Carol*, *Nicholas Nickleby*, *Oliver Twist* and *A Tale of Two Cities*. An amazingly prolific author, Dickens died aged just 58, in the middle of writing *The Mystery of Edwin Drood*. He is buried in Poets' Corner, Westminster Abbey. Charles Dickens remains one of Britain's best-loved writers, and his works are regularly dramatised in films, on television and on the stage.

➠ ***Queen Victoria***

DISRAELI, BENJAMIN (1804–81)

British prime minister (1868–74, 1874–80), statesman and novelist. Disraeli also served as Chancellor of the Exchequer and was made Earl of Beaconsfield by Queen Victoria, with whom he enjoyed good relations. Born to a Spanish Jew, but baptised a Christian, Disraeli was a Conservative. His career was marked by the introduction of social reforms including the Reform Act of 1867, which doubled the number of people eligible to vote and, when prime minister, he introduced the Public Health Act. On the international stage he made Queen Victoria Empress of India in 1876 and paved the way for British occupation of Cyprus. Disraeli was concerned with controlling Russian expansionism by asserting British power. His great political rival was Benjamin Gladstone. He was seen as a great parliamentary orator. His career as a novelist was also distinguished. His most famous works included *Coningsby and Sybil.* He once remarked that if he wanted to read a good novel then he would write one. In 1880 he lost his last election and decided to retire from politics. He died just one year later.

➠ ***Queen Victoria***

DISSOLUTION OF THE MONASTERIES (1536)

Policy of Henry VIII and Thomas Cromwell during the Protestant Reformation. Having appointed himself Supreme Head of the Church, Henry set about destroying the monasteries in England and Ireland. The dissolution was organised by Thomas Cromwell and provided Henry with about £100,000 per annum, but left between 7,000 and 10,000 monks homeless. The traditional north of England especially resented the dissolution, as demonstrated by the Pilgrimage of Grace. Nevertheless Henry pressed on and chantries were also dissolved. Although his motives were not religious, the dissolution did ensure the long-term survival of the Reformation in England: the nobility and gentry were unwilling to return their newly acquired land to the re-Catholicised Church of Mary Tudor.

➠ ***Thomas Cromwell, Henry VIII, Pilgrimage of Grace***

TOP FAR LEFT George II at the Battle of Dettingen

DIVINE RIGHT OF KINGS

Doctrine of monarchical authority. The divine right was the belief that monarchs received their authority directly from God and were therefore unanswerable to anyone else. Originally a medieval idea, it came to England from Scotland via James I. Both James's and Charles's belief in their divine right was outdated in England and Charles paid the ultimate price for his autocratic attitude.

➧ ***Charles I, James I***

DOMESDAY BOOK (1086)

Survey conducted by William I after the Norman Conquest to establish the extent of Crown lands in England. Following the Battle of Hastings (1066) William I commissioned a survey of England. The purpose of this was to assess the wealth of William's kingdom. Carried out in 1086, the survey covered land tax and other dues owed by the population. It also ascertained the value of lands belonging to the Crown and enabled William to estimate accurately the wealth and power of his vassal barons, who held their lands by feudal tenure on conditions of homage and allegiance to the king. The survey document is known as the *Domesday Book*.

➧ ***William I, Normans, Anglo-Saxons***

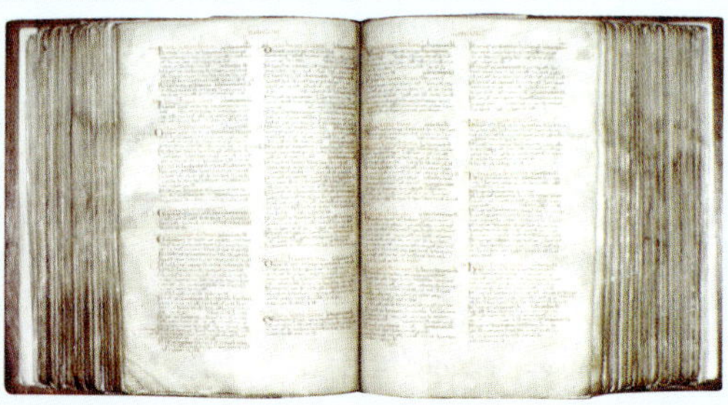

DOMINICAN ORDER (1215)

Mendicant Roman Catholic order, also known as the Black Friars. Established by St Dominic in France, there are also Dominican sisters. From 1278 the order was based on Thomas Aquinas's ideas. The Dominicans' extensive membership aided the implementation of the Inquisition.

➧ ***Roman Catholicism***

DONALD III (c. 1033–99)

King of Scotland (1093–99). Also known as Donald Bane. Donald seized the Scots throne on the death of his brother Malcolm III. Donald was opposed by Duncan II, Malcolm's eldest son and, helped by William II of England, he forced Donald out in 1094. Duncan was himself dislodged soon afterwards, and was killed in battle. Donald retrieved his throne, but not for long. Edgar, another of Malcolm's sons, won the backing of William II in 1097, He defeated and imprisoned Donald, who was blinded on his orders two years later. Possibly as a result, Donald died sometime in around 1099.

➧ ***Duncan II, Edgar, Malcolm III, William II***

DOUGLAS-HOME, ALEC (1903–95)

British prime minister (1963–64). From an aristocratic background, Douglas-Home renounced his title as Earl of Home to become prime minister. He succeeded Harold Macmillan as Conservative party leader. The party was in a weak state when he took over and was still feeling the effects of the Profumo Affair. His government was defeated at the polls by Harold Wilson's Labour Party in 1964. Home also served as Foreign Secretary in Edward Heath's government between 1970 and 1974.

➧ ***Conservative Party, Harold Macmillan***

DOVER, TREATY OF (1670)

Pact between the British and the French to help France conquer Holland. Charles II and Louis XIV negotiated the treaty. The British would gain territory from the pact also. Charles also agreed to convert to Roman Catholicism as part of the deal. Two years after the treaty a third Dutch War began, lasting two years. Peace was finally concluded by the Treaty of Westminster, signed in 1674.

➧ ***Anglo-Dutch Wars, Charles II***

DRAKE, SIR FRANCIS (1540–96)

English explorer. The end of the Medieval period was marked by European exploration of the globe. Francis Drake was one of the pioneers in this field. Drake made a name for himself and became a wealthy man by his activities as a pirate or buccaneer against the Spaniards

in the Caribbean between 1567 and 1572. When Elizabeth I came to the throne she sponsored Drake on a voyage round the world in the *Golden Hind* (1577–80). Drake became mayor of Plymouth (1581) and fought the Spanish Armada (1588), but died of dysentery off the coast of Panama.

➡ ***Elizabeth I, Spanish Armada***

DREADNOUGHT (1906)

First battleship powered by steam turbines. Constructed in just 366 days, HMS *Dreadnought* had 10 12-inch guns, a maximum speed of 21 knots and was a massive 22,000 tons. For Britain battleships were a major component of national power and *Dreadnought* represented the move towards greater armour and increased offensive power, with larger guns and more destructive capability. *Dreadnought* represented a major move forward and all ships of a similar type took this name.

ABOVE Queen Elizabeth I knights Francis Drake
BELOW HMS Dreadnought

DROGHEDA, SIEGE OF (1649)

Siege (3 September 1649) during Cromwell's campaign in Ireland. Oliver Cromwell's 10,000 Parliamentarian troops laid siege to Drogheda, held by The Marquis of Ormonde's 3,000-man garrison. The first assault was repulsed; the town was stormed and the garrison put to the sword. Over 4,000 are reputed to have been killed.

➡ ***Oliver Cromwell***

DRUIDS

Celtic priests. When the Celts took control of Britain they brought with them their heathen religion called Druidism, which involved belief in spirits of the Earth. Druids held that the oak tree was sacred and centred their rituals around great oak trees. They also believed in reincarnation, considering the soul to be immortal. They were responsible for the stone circles and related Neolithic features in the landscape. Druidism was largely stamped out eventually by the invading Romans.

➡ ***Celts***

DRYDEN, JOHN (1631–1700)

English poet, playwright and satirist. Dryden came from a family of Cromwellian supporters, although his own allegiance shifted after the Restoration. Dryden was the first poet to hold the official title of Poet Laureate (awarded in 1668). His poems include 'Annus Mirabilis' (about the Great Fire of London), 'Heroic Stanzas on the Death of Oliver Cromwell' and 'Astraea Redux' (on Charles II's return). His plays include *Marriage à la Mode* and *The Indian Queen*. He is buried in Westminster Abbey.

➠ ***Charles II, Oliver Cromwell, Great Fire of London, Poet Laureate, Restoration***

DUDLEY, LORD GUILDFORD (d.. 1554)

Husband of Lady Jane Grey. Dudley was a son of the Duke of Northumberland who, in 1553 organised his marriage to Lady Jane Grey in an attempt to stop Mary I, a devout Catholic, claiming the throne. The plot failed as Mary became queen and had Dudley executed the following year, along with Lady Jane Grey.

➠ ***Lady Jane Grey***

DUDLEY, ROBERT, EARL OF LEICESTER (1532–88)

Nobleman and confidant of Elizabeth I. Dudley was a favourite of the queen's and, at one time, was thought of as a suitable and possible husband for her. He was the fifth son of the Duke of Northumberland. Dudley became a privy councillor in 1559 and advocated a pro-Protestant foreign policy. He was married twice. When his first wife Amy died, rumour at the time held him responsible for her death. He married again in 1578.

➠ ***Elizabeth I***

DUNBAR, BATTLE OF (1650)

Battle (3 September 1650) during Cromwell's Scottish campaign. David Leslie's 22,000-strong Scottish Royalists faced Cromwell's 11,000 near Dunbar. Foolishly, Leslie left his advantageous position on the heights and marched to meet Cromwell. He was promptly routed, with 3,000 killed and 10,000 taken prisoner. Cromwell's losses were comparatively small.

➠ ***Oliver Cromwell, English Civil War***

DUNCAN I (1001–40)

King of Scotland (1034–40). The 'King Duncan' of Shakespeare's play *Macbeth*. Duncan was possibly appointed as successor by Malcolm II. In 1039 Duncan unsuccessfully attacked Northumbria. Macbeth, king of Moray, challenged him for the throne and Duncan was killed at the Battle of Pitvageny. Subsequently, Macbeth became king of Scotland.

➠ ***Malcolm II, William Shakespeare***

DUNCAN II (c. 1060–94)

King of Scotland (1094). Eldest son of Malcolm III, Duncan was handed over as a hostage after his father submitted to William I of England in 1072. Duncan spent 15 years as a captive, but was freed and made a knight by William in 1087. In 1094 William supported Duncan in his bid to unseat his uncle, the usurper Donald III. Duncan was successful at first, but his uncle hit back and he was forced to dismiss his Norman supporters. Afterwards, Duncan was killed at Mondynes, near Aberdeen, and Donald III was restored to the Scots throne

➠ ***Donald III, William II***

DUNKELD DYNASTY

Scottish royal dynasty. The Scots Dunkeld dynasty was descended from Duncan I, whose two sons, Malcolm III and Donald III ruled after him. Malcolm's son Duncan II ruled briefly after his father. Three other Dunkeld monarchs – Donald MacWilliam, grandson of Duncan II, and MacWilliam's sons Gothred and Donald were killed in attempts to regain the throne. Subsequent Scots kings were descended from Donald III.

➠ ***Donald III, Duncan I, Malcolm III***

DUNKELD, BATTLE OF (1689)

Battle (21 August 1689) during the Jacobite Rebellion. A force of Highlanders under Colonel Canon attempted to dislodge the Cameronian Regiment under Colonel Clelland, who had occupied the house belonging to the Marquis of Athol. Canon was killed in the action and the Highlanders were forced to retire without their leader.

➡ *Jacobites*

DUNKIRK (1940)

Allied evacuation from France (26 May 1940). After the Germans had captured Boulogne and Calais, British withdrawal from France under the code name Operation Dynamo began from Dunkirk at 6.57 p.m. With the French 16th Corps and the British Expeditionary Force holding the perimeter, 338,266 men, including 120,000 French, were brought back to Britain by an armada of 860 small ships of which 240 were sunk. They still left one million allied troops to become prisoners of war.

➡ ***World War II***

DUNSTAN, ST (AD 924–88)

Hermit, noble and Archbishop of Canterbury. A chief adviser to Edmund and Eadred of Wessex, Dunstan's career was marked by his conflict with Edwy, AD 955, regarding Edwy's monarchical laxity. On Edgar's succession Dunstan became Archbishop of Canterbury and an era of major monastic reform and intellectual blossoming occurred.

➡ ***Archbishop of Canterbury, Edwy***

ABOVE The evacuation of Dunkirk, 1940

RIGHT Saint Dunstan

EAST ANGLIA, KINGDOM OF

Province of Ancient Britain. During the era of Anglo-Saxon occupation in Britain the territory was divided into kingdoms. One kingdom was dominated by the Angles and so called East Anglia. It covered an area which roughly corresponds with the modern counties of Norfolk and Suffolk. It used to be geographically isolated by fen land.

➠ *Anglo-Saxons, Sutton Hoo*

EAST INDIA COMPANY (1600)

Company established to secure a monopoly on trade routes between England and the Far East. The East India Company came into being in around 1600 and lasted for 258 years, helping to finance the expansion of the British Empire. Links with India were being forged in Elizabethan times, so it made sense to establish an official trading relationship between the two countries as a way of seeing off competition from other dominant European nations, including France and the Netherlands. In 1784, Tory prime minister William Pitt introduced the India Act, which forced the company to form a committee responsible to Parliament in London, thereby ensuring that the Crown still had a significant say in the rule of India, which by then was virtually run by the East India Company.

➠ *Robert Clive, Seven Years' War*

EASTER RISING (1916)

Uprising in Dublin, Ireland, protesting against British rule. The fighting involved about 3,000 men from organisations opposed to the British, including the Irish Republican Brotherhood and the Citizen Army. Fighting commenced on 24 April when the rebels took up positions in the centre of Dublin. The leaders hoped others would pick up their armed opposition in the country but their hopes proved unfounded. Within a weeks the fighting was over. However, although the uprising proved unsuccessful, the British authorities' repressive response fostered widespread resentment. Fifteen of the leaders were executed. Thousands of others were imprisoned. Politically the uprising increased support for Sinn Fein. At the 1918 General Election, Sinn Fein, which favoured a free Ireland, won most seats. The MPs did not take up their seats in Westminster, however. They boycotted the British Parliament and set up their own illegal assembly in Dublin.

➠ *Home Rule*

EDEN, ANTHONY (1897–1977)

British prime minister (1955–57). Eden took over at Number 10 from Winston Churchill. His term in office was brief, though, dominated by the Suez Crisis of 1956. Egypt had nationalised the canal, prompting an Anglo-French military response. International condemnation was so high they were forced to withdraw. Eden resigned soon after.

➠ *Suez Crisis*

EDGAR THE ATHELING (c. 1052–1125)

Edgar, great-grandson of Ethelred II (the Unready) was proclaimed king of England by the defeated English after William of Normandy's victory at Hastings in 1066. Edgar took part in the subsequent revolts against Norman rule in 1069–70. Reconciled with William in 1074, Edgar became one of his courtiers.

Edmund II, Norman Dynasty, William I

EDGEHILL, BATTLE OF (1642)

First battle of the English Civil War (23–24 October 1642). Indecisively, this battle pitched 14,000 Parliamentarians under the Earl of Essex against a similar number of Royalists led by Charles I. Royalist cavalry broke the Parliamentarians, who lost many men in the disorganised pursuit. Essex abandoned the battlefield and the Royalists marched on London.

Charles I, Oliver Cromwell, English Civil War, Battle of Marston Moor

EDINBURGH CASTLE (c. 7TH CENTURY)

Historic Scottish building. The oldest parts of Edinburgh Castle date back to Edwin of Northumbria, from whom the city takes its name. The first historical mention of the castle as a royal residence is the death of Queen Margaret (1093). She was later canonised and a chapel bearing her name built at the castle. In 1174 the castle was won by Henry II, but passed back to the Scots in 1186. The first Scots Parliament met here in 1215. Edward I took the castle in 1291 and looted many of its treasures. It was won back again in 1313, after which all but St Margaret's Chapel was destroyed by Robert Bruce so the English could never take it again. Despite this, battles continued to rage between the two nations, over the site and subsequent buildings, for centuries. In 1566 James VI (James I of England) was born here. The castle's dungeons were used to house foreign prisoners during the Napoleonic Wars.

Robert Bruce, Edward I, Henry II, James VI of Scotland, Malcolm III, Mary, Queen of Scots, Napoleonic Wars

ABOVE A baggage train is attacked at Edgehill

EDMUND I (c. AD 922–46)

King of England (AD 939–46). Edmund succeeded his brother Athelstan, for whom he had fought at the Battle of Branunburgh (AD 937). At this time, the Vikings were active in the north of England and Olaf Guthfrithsson, king of Dublin forced Edmund to give up control of the area. In AD 942, however, Edmund retrieved the 'Five Boroughs' – Lincoln, Nottingham, Derby, Stamford and Leicester – after the local Anglo-Danish people expressed a preference for a Christian Saxon ruler rather than their Irish-Scandinavian overlords. Edmund also regained Viking York and Northumbria by AD 946, but he was murdered at Pucklechurch in Gloucestershire soon afterwards.

Erik Bloodaxe

EDMUND II (c. 990–1016)

King of England (1013–16). Known as Edmund Ironside. Son of King Ethelred the Unready, Edmund resisted the invasion of England by Canute in 1016. Canute was prevented from capturing London, but Edmund was defeated at Ashingdon in Essex in the autumn of 1016. Canute agreed to share England with Edmund, who would have possession of Wessex. However, Edmund died on 30 November, possibly murdered. Rumours that Edmund was disembowelled have not been positively refuted. Subsequently, Canute was able to take over the whole of England as its king and Edmund's children fled abroad. Edmund's grandson was Edgar the Atheling.

➠ ***Canute, Edgar the Atheling, Kingdom of Wessex***

EDMUND, ST (1175–1240)

Outspoken Archbishop of Canterbury and scholar. Edmund introduced the teaching of Aristotelian philosophy to western Europe and his seminal work, *Speculum Ecclesiae,* was a major contribution to medieval theology. Edmund excommunicated Henry III after clashing with him over Church rights. Henry therefore delayed the referral for his canonisation until 1247. Patron saint of the weather.

➠ ***Henry III***

EDUCATION ACTS (1870, 1902, 1918, 1944)

Series of Acts of Parliament designed to rationalise and improve the education system. Basic literacy and numeracy education were not made available to the working class in Britain until the early nineteenth century. In 1808 the 'British and Foreign Schools Society' was established followed, three years later, by the 'National Society for Promoting the Education of the Poor in the Principles of the Established Church'. Both improved the lot of working-class children considerably and in 1862 the British government made grants available for the education of some children up to 12 years old. Then in 1870 came a breakthrough. Parliament passed the Elementary Education Act (Forster's Act) creating district school boards and provided education to all children as a basic civil right. The Education Act 1902 saw the evolution of county council-run education authorities. The Education Act 1918 raised school leaving age to 14 and secondary schooling was introduced by the 1944 Act. Each Act since has brought new educational benefits.

EDWARD I (1239–1307)

King of England (1272–1307). Son of Henry III. Known as 'Longshanks' because of his height. Edward was the first strong king in England after over 80 years of weak or ineffectual royal rule. During his father's reign, he acquired valuable experience of government and was a notable military leader. He frequently took part in tournaments and went on crusade to the Holy Land in 1270. He defeated the rebellious barons in battle during his father's reign and, as king, he had conquered Wales by 1283 and put down a rebellion by the Welsh princes (1294–95). On his orders, castles were built in Wales to control the population. After 1296 he established English influence in Scotland, whose king became his vassal. The Scots under Robert Bruce rebelled in 1306. The following year Edward marched north with

an army to suppress the rebellion, but died on the way, near Carlisle. Edward I recognised Parliament as a necessary adjunct to his rule, and worked with its members, including the barons, in his tax and legislative reforms. Edward's famous Model Parliament of 1295 included knights of the shire and burgesses for the first time.

Henry III, Model Parliament, Simon de Montfort

EDWARD II (1284–1327)

King of England (1307–27). Son of Edward I. In 1301, he became the first English Prince of Wales. As king, Edward II was a total contrast to his father. Weak, impressionable and petulant, he was uninterested in matters of government. An incompetent military leader, his army was crushed by Robert Bruce at the battle of Bannockburn in 1314. A suspected homosexual, Edward enraged his barons by ruling through greedy and arrogant favourites. Edward refused to discard them and the barons took their revenge. Edward's first favourite, Piers Gaveston, was murdered in 1312. The other two, Hugh Despenser and his son (also Hugh) were executed in 1326. Edward neglected and insulted his French wife, Isabella. Together with her lover, Roger Mortimer, Earl of March, Isabella invaded England from France late in 1326. Edward was forced to abdicate in favour of his son who became Edward III. Edward II was imprisoned in Berkeley Castle, Gloucestershire, where attempts were made to starve him to death so that it would appear that he had died naturally. When this failed, he was murdered on 27 September 1327, with a red-hot poker pushed into his bowels. Edward II was afterwards buried at Gloucester Cathedral.

Battle of Bannockburn, Hugh Despenser, Edward I, Piers Gaveston, Roger Mortimer, Princes of Wales, Robert I

RIGHT Coronation of Edward III
LEFT Edward I seated on his throne

EDWARD III (1312–77)

King of England (1327–77). Son of Edward II. Succeeded on his father's abdication. Edward instituted the Most Noble Order of the Garter in 1348. He spent much of his youth in France with his mother Isabella, who was estranged from his father. He was largely influenced by Isabella and her lover Roger Mortimer, until he took control in 1330. Mortimer was executed and Isabella entered a convent. Edward III took positive steps to include the barons in the processes of government, through Parliament. The strong and well-organised royal systems were able to retain control in England despite the catastrophe of the Black Death (1348–50), which crippled the English economy and killed one-third of the population. Edward organised his court along lines taken from the recently written tales of King Arthur and the Knights of the Round Table and held frequent tournaments which were attended by the greatest knights in Europe. In 1346 he claimed the French throne and precipitated the Hundred Years' War. With his son, Edward, the Black Prince, the king won a great victory over the French at the Battle of Crécy (1346) but the French nevertheless refused to acknowledge him as their overlord. Another victory over the French, at Poitiers in 1356, resulted in the capture and imprisonment of King John II of France. In 1360, at the treaty of Brétigny, Edward was given sovereignty over the former English lands in France, Aquitaine and Calais. In return, he withdrew his claim to the French throne.

Edward II, Edward, the Black Prince, Hundred Years' War, Roger Mortimer

EDWARD IV (1442–83)

King of England (1461–70, 1471–83). Son of Richard, Duke of York. First king of the Plantagenet House of York. His reign was troubled by threats from the deposed Lancastrian king Henry VI, but despite this Edward ruled well and was a popular king.

After his father's death at the battle of Wakefield in 1460, during the Wars of the Roses, Edward IV inherited the Yorkist claim to the throne and was proclaimed king on 4 March 1461. Edward defeated the army of the Lancastrian Henry VI, who fled to Scotland but was afterwards imprisoned in the Tower of London. With the deposed Henry still alive, it was important that Edward rule wisely. This he did by winning the support of his barons and boosting England's foreign trade. Edward became personally rich through his own commercial ventures which meant that the monarchy could avoid financial control by Parliament.

Edward IV was an attractive king – 19 years old, tall, handsome, charming, artistic and approachable. The splendour of his court rivalled that of France. He gained a reputation for frequent love-affairs and in 1464 he secretly married the widow Elizabeth Woodville. His supporter, Richard Neville, Earl of Warwick (known as 'the kingmaker') had been arranging a marriage for the king with a French princess and was infuriated. Warwick switched allegiance and plotted with the French king, Louis XI, to overthrow Edward. Warwick now backed Queen Margaret, wife of Henry VI, in her efforts to regain her husband's crown. When Margaret and Warwick invaded England in 1470, Edward was forced to flee to Burgundy. Henry was restored to his throne, but Edward returned in 1471 and Warwick was killed in the Battle of Barnet. Shortly afterwards, Queen Margaret was beaten at the battle of Tewkesbury and her only son, Edward, was killed. Henry VI was subsequently murdered. Edward remained secure on his throne until his sudden death in 1483.

➡ ***Edward V, Henry VI, Queen Margaret, Richard III Richard Neville,***

EDWARD V (1470–83)

King of England (1483). Son of Edward IV. After his accession in 1483, Edward's uncle, Richard, Duke of Gloucester, removed him from the custody of his mother, Elizabeth Woodville. Together with his brother Richard, Duke of York, he was sent to the Tower of London to await his coronation. Meanwhile, Richard declared the child-king to be illegitimate because his father had been betrothed to Lady Eleanor Butler when he married Elizabeth Woodville. Edward was deposed on 25 June 1483 and Richard became king in his place. Edward and his brother were probably murdered in the Tower about three months later.

➡ ***Richard III, Tower of London, Elizabeth Woodville***

EDWARD VI (1537–53)

King of England (1547–53). Only son of Henry VIII. Edward became king at the age of just nine. He had been brought up and educated as a Protestant and during his brief reign steps were taken to reform the Church of England along Protestant lines: the reforms included the introduction of a new Prayer Book in 1552. Edward himself was a typical Tudor – imperious and demanding, but cautious. He was described by the Venetian ambassador to his court as 'handsome, affable, of becoming stature' and later as 'a likely lad, of quick, ready and well-developed mind'. Tragically, Edward contracted tuberculosis when he was only 15. John Dudley, Duke of Northumberland forced the young king on his deathbed to sign a will disinheriting his half-sisters Mary and Elizabeth, naming Dudley's daughter, Lady Jane Grey, as his heir. Edward died at Greenwich Palace on 6 July 1553.

➡ ***Elizabeth I, Lady Jane Grey, Henry VIII, Mary I***

EDWARD VII (1841–1910)

King of England (1901–10). Son of Queen Victoria and Prince Albert. As Prince of Wales, Edward was subjected to an extremely strict and arduous educational regime, but he was not academically inclined and became a difficult and fractious child. In 1861 he scandalised his moralistic parents by having sexual relations with a girl named Nellie Clifden, who had been acquired for him by sympathetic friends. Prince Albert died shortly afterwards, probably from typhoid. The queen blamed Edward and never truly forgave him, barring him from his proper share in state affairs. In 1863, Edward was married to Princess Alexandra of Denmark in an effort to 'steady' him, but he was an unfaithful husband from the first and soon plunged into a hedonistic lifestyle. He had numerous mistresses and he came close to public scandal on more than one occasion. Edward became king on Victoria's death in 1901 and his years of socialising proved to be an asset as he became a royal ambassador for England, able to converse easily with other monarchs and their ministers. His self-indulgence – excesses of smoking, drinking and women – caught up with him in 1910, when he died after a series of heart attacks.

➡ ***Queen Victoria, Prince Albert***

EDWARD VIII (1894–1972)

King of England (1936). Eldest son of George V and Queen Mary. As Prince of Wales, Edward travelled extensively, but was never happy with his royal role, its restrictions, ceremonial and deference. Edward viewed kingship in a different way from his father: he saw it as less aloof, less ceremonious, requiring more direct contact with his subjects. He rejected the elitist royal social life, preferring the hedonistic, night-clubbing company of the *nouveaux riches* and social climbers. It was in this company, that he met Mrs Wallis Simpson and her husband Ernest in 1931. Edward fell in love with Wallis.

He succeeded the throne after George V's death on 20 January 1936 and intended to marry Wallis and make her his queen. This move was strongly opposed by the British and Commonwealth governments, the Church and his family. Prime minister Stanley Baldwin told him that the now twice-divorced Wallis would not be acceptable as queen of England. Rather than give her up, Edward abdicated on 11 December 1936. His brother took his place as George VI. The Duke and Duchess of Windsor, as Edward and Wallis became, married in 1937 and spent most of their life together abroad. Edward died in Paris in 1972.

➡ ***Abdication Crisis, George V, George VI, Wallis Simpson***

EDWARD, THE BLACK PRINCE (1330–76)

Prince of Wales (1343). Son of Edward III. The Black Prince – so called because of the black armour he wore – earned his military reputation at the Battle of Crécy (1336) and added to it at Poitiers (1356) and Najerá in Spain (1367). He was afterwards regarded as a great chivalric hero.

In 1362 his father made him Prince of Aquitaine, but he was a careless ruler, incompetent with finances, and returned Aquitaine to the king's control in 1372. The Black Prince died before his father, in 1376.

➠ ***Edward III, Hundred Years' War, Richard II***

EDWARD THE CONFESSOR (c. 1005–66)

King of England (1042–66). Known as the 'Confessor' because of his saintliness. After a long exile in France, Edward succeeded the throne in 1042. Often portrayed as a pious weakling, Edward was in fact an astute ruler who reconciled his Anglo-Saxon and Danish nobles and kept his kingdom intact. Edward was childless and the king apparently promised the throne to both his brother-in-law Harold and William of Normandy, thus causing the dispute that would lead to the Norman Conquest. Edward spent much time on the rebuilding of Westminster Abbey, where he was buried in 1066.

➠ ***Harold II, Norman Conquest, Westminster Abbey, William I***

TOP Gilt copper effigy of Edward the Black Prince
RIGHT Kidney Ridge action, El Alamein
ABOVE Henry VI and Edward the Confessor
FAR RIGHT: T. S. ELIOT

EDWARD THE ELDER (c. AD 871–924)

King of Wessex (AD 899–924). Son of Alfred the Great. A worthy successor to his famous father. After AD 910, Edward retrieved much of the Danelaw from Danish rule. Edward was recognised as overlord by the Welsh princes, the Scots kings, and by rulers in the north of England.

➠ ***Alfred the Great, Danelaw***

EDWARD THE MARTYR (c. AD 962–78)

King of the English (AD 975–78). Son of Edgar the Peaceable. Edward was arrogant and soon alienated his council. In AD 978 Edward was visiting his stepmother Elfrida at Corfe Castle when her retainers stabbed him to death. Elfrida was blamed for the murder.

EDWY (c. AD 941–59)

King of the English (AD 955–59). Son of Edmund I. Edwy was headstrong and intransigent and soon clashed with Abbot Dunstan of Glastonbury, whose character was similar. Dunstan was enraged when Edwy disappeared during his coronation and was eventually found romancing a young lady. Edwy banished Dunstan from England in AD 957, but he continued to clash with other members of his council. Edwy died suddenly aged 18; it is possible that he was murdered.

➠ ***Saint Dunstan, Edmund I***

EL ALAMEIN, BATTLES OF (1942)

Two battles (1 July and 23–24 October 1942) in North Africa during World War II. General Auchinleck managed to stop the oncoming German and Italian assault on Egypt. He was replaced by Field Marshall Montgomery who commanded 200,000 men and 1,100 tanks. In October he launched a counter-offensive that claimed nearly 9,000 axis casualties, 30,000 prisoners and a pursuit of 1,500 miles across North Africa to Tunis. The second battle was one of World War II's most decisive.

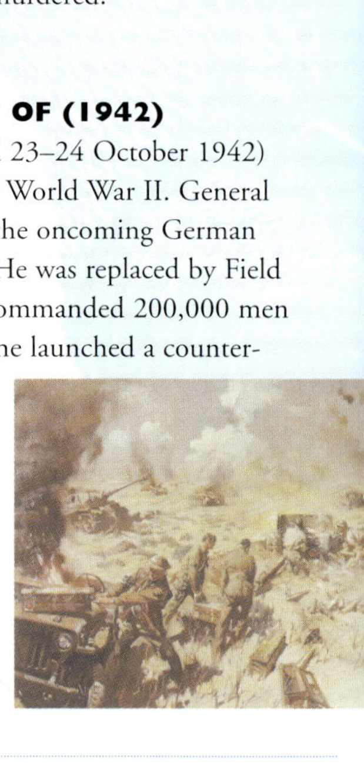

➠ ***Field Marshall Montgomery, World War II***

ELEANOR OF AQUITAINE (c. 1122–1204)

Wife of Henry II. Eleanor married Henry in 1152 and added the duchy of Aquitaine to his possessions. Eleanor resented Henry's infidelities and backed her sons when they rebelled against him. The rebellion failed and Eleanor was imprisoned in 1173. She was not released until after Henry's death in 1189. While his successor, her son Richard I, was abroad on Crusade and in France, Eleanor helped rule England on his behalf.

➠ ***Henry II, King John, Richard I***

ELEVEN YEARS' TYRANNY (1629–40)

Term used to describe the years after which Charles I dissolved Parliament and ruled without its guidance. After a number of confrontations with Parliament, Charles felt that the challenge to his 'divine right' was unforgivable and refused to convene Parliament. Although there was little overt oposition to this during the 11 years, the simmering resentment eventually gave rise to the English Civil War.

➠ ***Charles I, Divine Right of Kings, English Civil War***

ELGAR, EDWARD (1857–1934)

English composer. Elgar began his career as a bandmaster in a lunatic asylum, but soon made a name for himself through his immense talent. He composed orchestral works for events such as the coronation of Edward VII and his 'Pomp and Circumstance' (better known as 'Land of Hope and Glory') has become a second national anthem.

ELIOT, GEORGE (1819–90)

Pen-name of Mary Ann Evans, English novelist. Like the Brontë sisters, Eliot chose to wrote under a pseudonym to assist publication in a male-dominated industry. Her most famous novels include *Middlemarch*, *Silas Marner* and *Daniel Deronda*.

ELIOT, T. S. (1888–1965)

American poet, playwright and critical essayist who moved to England in 1915. Eliot worked as a schoolteacher, a bank clerk, a book reviewer, a book editor and a director of Faber and Faber publishers. His first published poem was 'The Love Song of J. Alfred Prufrock' (1915). His first volume of poetry was published in 1917. He was friends with Ezra Pound and Virginia Woolf. His poetry includes *The Waste Land* and *Old Possum's Book of Practical Cats* (on which the musical *Cats* is based). Amongst his plays are *Murder in the Cathedral* (about Thomas Becket) and *Sweeney Agonistes.* Eliot was awarded the Nobel Prize for Literature in 1948

➠ ***Thomas Becket***

ELIZABETH I (1533–1603)

Queen of England (1558–1603). The last monarch of the Tudor dynasty. Daughter of Henry VIII. Elizabeth has become one of the most famous of English monarchs. She attempted to find a middle road in the question of religion, abhorring the extremes of the previous two reigns and under her the country saw a new flourishing of art and literature. Her reign was marked by conflict with Catholic Spain. She never married and on her death she bequeathed the throne to the Scottish James VI.

Elizabeth's mother, Anne Boleyn, was executed and Elizabeth herself declared illegitimate before she was three years old. During the reign of her half-sister, the Catholic Mary I, Elizabeth was imprisoned in the Tower of London. Elizabeth became queen on Mary's death in 1558, but her right to the throne was not recognised in Europe, where she was still considered illegitimate. While opting for a Protestant Church of England, Elizabeth was tolerant towards Catholics and other dissidents, but despite this she was excommunicated by the pope in 1570 and subsequently her reign was marked by numerous Catholic plots against her life.

Philip II of Spain, her erstwhile brother-in-law, declared war on Elizabeth as soon as she became queen, and the possibility of a Spanish invasion of England was ever-present. Until the invasion attempt transpired in 1588, when the Spanish Armada was decisively defeated, Elizabeth played a dangerous game in which she appeared uninterested in poaching on the Spanish colonies in America while secretly encouraging her seamen, such as Francis Drake, to raid these settlements. Her own equivocal position as monarch and the relative poverty of her realm was cunningly covered up by Elizabeth through the outward magnificence of her court and her own publicity which pictured her as a majestic, almost legendary figure.

Elizabeth never married, although she entertained many suitors. She declared herself married to her kingdom. She had several love affairs, the most serious with Robert Dudley, Earl of Leicester. One motive for Elizabeth remaining the 'Virgin Queen' may have been the interference in England's affairs that was implicit in acquiring a foreign husband. However, her mother's death at the hands of her father may have led her to equate marriage with danger. Elizabeth refused to name her successor until shortly before she died in 1603. Her nearest relative in line for the succession was Mary, Queen of Scots, but she had been the focus of plots against Elizabeth and was executed in 1587. Elizabeth was succeeded by Mary's son, James VI of Scotland, who became James I of England.

➡ ***Anne Boleyn, Francis Drake, Henry VIII, Mary I, Spanish Armada***

RIGHT Queen Elizabeth in robes of the thistle

ELIZABETH II (b. 1926)

Queen of England (1952–). Daughter of George VI. Elizabeth became heir presumptive to the throne after her uncle, Edward VIII, abdicated in 1936. She succeeded the throne after the untimely death of her father in 1952. The half-century in which she has ruled has been one of enormous change for the monarchy, but Elizabeth has remained a dutiful and well-informed queen.

As young girls, Elizabeth and her younger sister Margaret became known as 'The Little Princesses' and they were the darlings of the press and the public. Their relationship with their parents was very loving. Their mother, Queen Elizabeth, later Queen Mother, brought them up to be aware of their royal responsibilities. King George was passionately attached to Elizabeth. It was George who talked of 'Us Four' – the close family unit comprising himself, his wife, Elizabeth and Margaret.

Elizabeth married Lieutenant Philip Mountbatten RN, a distant cousin, in 1947. He became Prince Philip, Duke of Edinburgh. They subsequently had four children. Elizabeth and Philip built up a strong family based image with their four children, but this was badly dented by the scandals later surrounding their heir, Prince Charles, and his wife Diana. As Princess Elizabeth, she publicly dedicated herself to the service of her people. As queen, Elizabeth has proved a non-controversial monarch with a strong sense of duty. She has made frequent state visits overseas and takes part in regular royal ceremonials at home, including most importantly the State Opening of Parliament and the ceremony at the Cenotaph at Whitehall, London, commemorating Britain's war dead. Elizabeth is head of the Commonwealth, which is made up of former territories of the British Empire. In private life, the Queen is an expert on horses.

➡ ***Elizabeth Bowes-Lyon; Charles, Prince of Wales; Edward VIII; George VI***

ENCLOSURE ACTS (1603)

Series of Acts intended to limit depopulation of rural areas because of enclosure of common land. Until the fourteenth century most land was treated as common, where anyone had the right to graze livestock or grow food. Then the wealthy began the practice of enclosure: appropriating common land as private property. Enclosure continued through the fifteenth and sixteenth centuries, causing widespread poverty and homelessness. Populations in rural areas fell with the loss of common land and ultimately led to peasant revolts. The Enclosure Act of 1603 was introduced by government to prevent landowners from depopulating rural areas too much, only to see it sabotaged at local level by the landowners. From 1760 new Enclosure Acts of Parliament were passed to reduce the class of smallholding yeomen to agricultural labourers, thereby denying them a right to own the land they farmed. They were thus forced into the employment of landowners or forced to leave and make a living elsewhere.

ENGLISH CIVIL WAR (1642–48)

War between Parliament and Charles I. The roots of the war lie in Charles's tyrannical attitude and determination to be governed by no man. The subsequent rebellion led to years of battles between Royalist and parliamentary forces, both sides aided intermittently by the Scots. The Parliamentarians eventually won the day and the Commonwealth was established under Oliver Cromwell after the king was executed in 1649. The Republic lasted 11 years until the Restoration of Charles II in 1660.

In 1625 Charles I became king and following in the footsteps of his predecessor, James I, he continued his struggle against Parliament, believing in the Divine Right of Kings (that the monarch was God's representative on Earth and therefore subject to no man's will). His first confrontations with Parliament led him to dissolve it in 1626, but an urgent need for revenue which could legally only be granted by Parliament, forced him to reconvene it two years later. In 1629 he again dissolved Parliament and this time he ruled for 11 years – until there was another financial crisis.

In 1642 Charles tried to have Parliamentary leaders arrested and rejected Parliamentary demands to limit his powers. Parliament and the Royalists were on a collision course. The first battle of the Civil War took place at Edgehill on 12 October, but its outcome was inconclusive.

In September the following year the Scots joined the war, siding with Parliament and with their help Cromwell defeated the Royalists at Marston Moor on 2 July 1644. Throughout 1644–45 Parliament reorganised its army under Puritan influence and thus was born the New Model Army.

On 14 June 1645 Cromwell beat Charles at Naseby and in the following year on 26 March he lost again at Stowe-on-the-Wold. Charles surrendered himself to the Scots on 5 May and was turned over to Parliament in January of the next year. With Presbyterians turning to the Royalist cause and Parliament ordering the army to disband, Charles effected his escape in November and negotiated that the Scots should join his cause. During 1648 Parliament found itself fighting against Scotland, Royalists and Presbyterians in the second Civil War, but Cromwell beat the invading Scots at Preston (17–19 August 1648). The army captured Charles in December and all pro-Royalists were expelled from Parliament.

After his trial Charles was beheaded on 30 January 1649 and the monarchy was abolished. Cromwell then became the head of the new Commonwealth. The monarchy was re-established in 1660 after the death of Cromwell with Charles II taking the crown.

➠ ***Charles I, Oliver Cromwell, Battle of Edgehill, Eleven Years' Tyranny***

LEFT Oliver Cromwell

ABOVE Prince Rupert at the Battle of Edgehill

RIGHT Cromwellian and Royalist troops in the English Civil War

THE NEW MODEL ARMY

The New Model Army was organised by Parliament to replace the private armies of Parliamentarian leaders. In the Self-Denying Ordinance of April 1645, leaders could not take command of armies. The exception was Oliver Cromwell who replaced the original commander, Thomas Fairfax, who himself succeeded The Earl of Essex. The New Model Army was a highly trained, efficient force, well equipped and organised. It became Oliver Cromwell's power base and he used this to great effect against his opponents both in and out of Parliament. Marston Moor (1644), Naseby (1645), Preston (1648) and Worcester (1651) are testaments of the army's efficiency.

TIMELINE

1626 Charles I dissolves Parliament for the first time

1628 The king is forced to reconvene Parliament

1629 Charles dissolves Parliament again and begins the Eleven Years' Tyranny

1634 Charles introduces Ship Money taxation to raise revenue for his campaign against the Scots

12 October 1642 Inconclusive battle at Edgehill between Royalist and parliamentary forces

1643 Parliamentarians and Scots sign the Solemn League and Covenant of allegiance

2 July 1644 Cromwell and his troops defeat the Royalists at Marston Moor

14 June 1645 Parliamentarians defeat Royalists at Naseby

26 March 1646 Another parliamentary victory at Stowe-on-the-Wold

5 May 1646 Charles I throws himself on the mercy of the Scots

January 1647 The Scots hand the king over to the Parliamentarians

November 1647 Charles escapes from captivity and convinces the Scots to join his side

17–19 August 1648 Cromwell defeats the Scots at Preston

December 1648 Charles is captured again and anyone showing Royalist sympathies is expelled from Parliament

January 1649 The king is executed and the monarchy abolished in England

May 1649 The Rump Parliament officially declares England a Commonwealth

3 September 1650 Cromwell defeats the Scots at the Battle of Dunbar

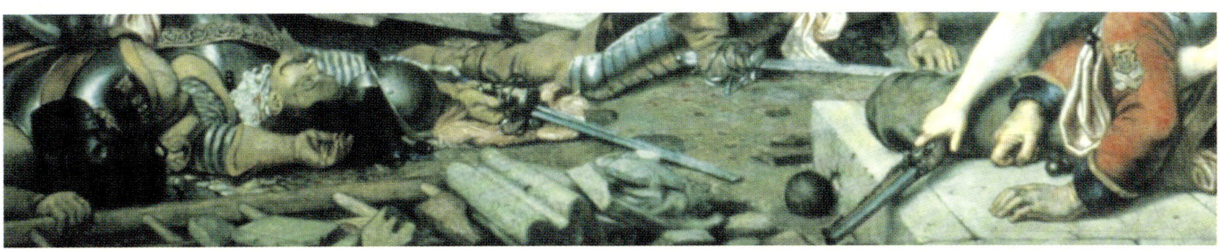

ENLIGHTENMENT (18TH CENTURY)

Name given to the period in the eighteenth century which saw a move towards rational and humanist views. The eighteenth century saw a revolution in many areas, especially in philosophy and science. Britain was at the fore during this period, now known as the Enlightenment. The essence of the Enlightenment was that it believed in liberating the possibilities of rational and scientific knowledge. The social environment was dominated by religion at this time, which was seen by thinkers as an inhibiting agent on the human mind because of superstitious beliefs.

ENTENTE CORDIALE (1904)

British–French diplomatic rapprochement before and during World War I. Both countries used the alliance to draft military plans for use against Germany, whose power both countries feared. The alliance began in 1904 and continued throughout the next decade. They saw the alliance as a way of containing the threat of Germany. The joint plans formed the basis of the Allied strategy when war broke out in 1914.

➠ ***World War I***

EPISCOPACY

Church government by bishops. The Episcopalian Church in Scotland is an independent branch within the Anglican Church and has seven dioceses. Episcopalianism developed out of Protestantism, but was nevertheless opposed to Presbyterianism. The Episcopalians became involved in the Jacobite Rebellions of 1715 and 1745 and therefore their old enemies, the Presbyterians, almost totally banned them. In 1792 these laws were repealed and in 1929 the Episcopalian prayer book was published.

➠ ***Jacobites, Presbyterianism***

FAR RIGHT Ethelred I

RIGHT Scottish Presbyterians worship

ESSEX, KINGDOM OF

Province of Anglo-Saxon Britain. During the height of Anglo-Saxon rule in Britain, England was divided into seven kingdoms, known as the heptarchy. The Saxons claimed rule over the three kingdoms: Essex, Sussex and Wessex. Essex was easily accessible to the Teutonic invaders from mainland Europe, forming part of the East Coast that looks out over the North Sea. It also comprised the north bank of the Thames estuary and had natural harbours at Harwich and Malden. In fact it was at Malden in the year AD 991 that the Saxons were defeated in a battle against the Vikings, who landed there having sailed from Scandinavia.

➠ ***Anglo-Saxons***

ESSEX, ROBERT DEVEREUX, 2ND EARL OF (1566–1601)

Favourite of Elizabeth I. Essex was handsome, extravagant, vain, petulant and lacking in judgment. He was, however, personally brave and fought well in Holland under the leadership of his stepfather, Robert Dudley, Earl of Leicester. Essex was knighted for gallantry in 1586. Elizabeth appointed him Lord Lieutenant of Ireland, but he failed to quell the Irish rebels in Tyrone and instead attempted to negotiate a peace. Elizabeth considered her favourite's conduct 'perilous and contemptible'. Essex returned to England in disgrace. In 1600, he became involved in a plot against Elizabeth and was executed in 1601.

➨ ***Elizabeth I***

ETHELBERT (c. AD 833–65)

King of Kent and Wessex. Ethelbert, already sub-king of Kent, from AD 855, succeeded his brother Ethelbald to the throne of Wessex in AD 860. Soon afterwards, England was invaded by the Vikings, followed by a larger force under Ragnar Lodbrok in AD 865. The Vikings raided along the east coast and despite an agreement with the Saxons, they ravaged east Kent. At the height of this crisis, Ethelbert suddenly died, aged about 32, and was buried at Sherborne Abbey. He was succeeded by his brother Ethelred I.

➨ ***Ethelred I, Kingdom of Wessex***

ETHELRED I (c. AD 837–71)

King of Wessex. On succeeding his brother Ethelbert, Ethelred I had to deal immediately with the Danish raids and invasions of England. In AD 866, Vikings from Dublin attacked and captured York. Mercia sought help from Wessex, but their two armies failed to dislodge the Danes, who now prepared to march south and attack Wessex, plundering the countryside as they went. In AD 871, Ethelred and his younger brother Alfred narrowly escaped being killed in a battle at Ashdown, Wiltshire. Ethelred, however, was seriously wounded in a subsequent battle, at Martin, Hampshire and died some weeks later at Witchampton, near Wimbourne.

➨ ***Alfred the Great, Ethelbert***

ETHELRED II (c. 968–1016)

King of the English (AD 978–1016). Known as 'the Unready' ('noble counsel'). Son of King Edgar. His government was controlled by his mother Elfrida and the powerful Alfthere. Ethelred took over after AD 983 and reversed their policy of reducing the power of the monasteries. Ethelred updated the laws in the Wantage Code of AD 977, which included acceptance of Danish customs. After AD 991, Ethelred faced fresh Danish raids and had to pay the Danegeld several times to keep the invaders at bay. They always returned, however. When Ethelred died in 1016, the problem of the Danish invasions was still unresolved.

➠ ***Danegeld, Edgar***

EUROPEAN UNION (1993)

Community of European nations. On 1 November 1993 the European Union (EU) was formed when the Maastricht Treaty came into force. It was a revamping of the existing European Community (EC), of which Britain had been a member since 1973. The European Union not only embraced the old EC but also comprised two intergovernmental 'pillars'; one responsible for covering 'Common Foreign and Security Policy' (CFSP); the other covering 'Co-operation on Justice and Home Affairs'. In 1995 came the EU statement that it wished to commit to the attainment of a single European currency – monetary union – and that the unit of currency would be the euro. The reason for membership of the European Union is that it theoretically bestows cultural and economic advantages on a country, primarily because it allows a collective to function as a whole on the world stage where markets are dominated and largely controlled by America, Japan and other super rich nations. The EU's aims are therefore to expand European trade, reduce competition, remove restrictive trade practices, and improve the flow of capital and labour within the continent, so that theory is put into practice. Culturally the EU works on a liberal philosophy, seeking to encourage the integration of European peoples.

➠ ***Treaty of Rome***

BELOW The European Parliament Building
RIGHT Simon de Montfort is killed at the Battle of Evesham

EVESHAM, BATTLE OF (1265)

Last battle of the Barons' War (4 August 1265). The baron's troops, some 5,350 under Simon de Montfort, were taken by surprise, believing Prince Edward's 8,000 Royalists were in fact their own reinforcements. De Montfort was killed and his troops scattered, leaving the coast clear for the restoration of Henry III.

➡ ***Barons' Wars, Henry III, Simon de Montfort***

EXCHEQUER (12TH CENTURY)

Financial and accounting office for medieval England. It obtained its name because accounts were calculated by means of counters on a chequered table in its Westminster headquarters. The Exchequer consisted of an Upper Exchequer and Lower Exchequer and was established in the twelfth century. The Lower department dealt with receipts received by government, the Upper Exchequer was also known as Exchequer of Account. Its power waned when the Treasury became the most important central financial department in the time of Elizabeth I.

EXCLUSION BILLS (1679, 1680, 1681)

Three seventeenth-century parliamentary bills introduced to stop James, Duke of York, from succeeding to the throne. The first bill was in 1679; the second in 1680 and the final bill was laid in 1681. The bills were introduced by the Country Party. This was made up of landed MPs who were anti-Catholic and did not have to depend on royal patronage. Its members were prominent anti-Royalists who provided the parliamentary opposition to the Crown. The party was a forerunner of the more widely known Whig party. In turn this party became the Liberal Party in the nineteenth century. Parliament was dissolved after the second reading of the first bill and the House of Lords rejected the second bill. Charles II dissolved Parliament when the third bill was introduced. James II became king in 1685.

➡ ***Charles I, Charles II, Roman Catholicism***

FABIAN SOCIETY (19TH CENTURY)

Moderate left-wing organisation committed to achieving a socialist society through gradual, evolutionary rather than revolutionary means. Its supporters have included the playwright George Bernard Shaw and author H. G. Wells. It was established in the late nineteenth century and continues today. Its influence on the Labour Party has been vast. It helped to establish the party in 1906 and has influenced its policies in the past. Labour prime minister Clement Attlee was a member of the Fabian Society. It is steeped in the cautious, centrist tradition of the British Labour Party.

»» ***Labour Party***

FACTORY ACTS (1802)

Series of Acts to protect the lot of factory workers. The Industrial Revolution caused the urbanisation of Britain. Millions of people migrated to urban environments to find the only work available to them. These people were vulnerable to exploitation by factory owners, knowing that jobs were difficult to come by elsewhere. Eventually empathetic politicians intervened by introducing a series of Factory Acts to make sure that the working class was not abused. Beginning with the Health and Morals of Apprentices Act (1802), employers began having to comply with regulations, facing prosecution for not doing so. Other acts determined the minimum age at which children could legally be expected to begin work and the weekly hours an employee might be expected to put in. Legislation establishing the basic rights of women and children in particular were much needed in the textile mills.

»» ***Industrial Revolution***

ABOVE A Fabian society meeting
RIGHT The Falklands War of 1982
FAR RIGHT Michael Faraday lecturing at the Royal Institution

FAIRFAX, THOMAS, 3RD BARON OF CAMERON (1612–71)

Scottish Parliamentarian general. Fairfax first served in the Parliamentarian army in Yorkshire and became commander-in-chief in 1645 with Oliver Cromwell as his lieutenant general. He helped win the Battle of Naseby and besieged Colchester in 1648. He presided over the trial of Charles I in 1649 but resigned, disagreeing with the death sentence. He resigned his commission in 1650 but came out of retirement in 1659 to lead the commission to visit Charles II at The Hague to ask him to take the British throne.

»» ***English Civil War***

FALKIRK, BATTLE OF (1298)

Battle between the English and Scots (22 July 1298). Intent on ensuring Scottish independence, William Wallace captured many English castles north of the Forth and at the Battle of Stirling Bridge on 11 September 1297 he annihilated an English army crossing a narrow bridge. In 1298 an 8,500-strong English army under Edward I defeated Wallace's 10,000 at Falkirk and forced him into hiding. He fled to France, returned to Scotland, was captured, taken to London, tried for treason and executed.

»» ***Edward I, William Wallace***

FALKLANDS WAR (1982)

War between Argentina and Britain over ownership of the Falkland Islands. The Argentinians took the island in April 1982 and Britain responded in kind. After two months of fighting the Argentinians surrendered.

The Falklands were discovered by the British navigator John Davis in 1592 but the first colony was a French one, established in 1764. The French passed it to the Spanish and after they abandoned it Argentinians settled there in 1820. The British occupied the islands in 1833. Since then, and particularly in 1966, when negotiations began regarding its ownership in the United Nations, the Argentinians have laid claim to the islands.

In early April 1982 Argentinian forces took the islands. A great swell of patriotism seized both Argentina and Great Britain and Margaret Thatcher, the British prime minister, ordered that the islands be retaken. A small force retook the Falkland dependency of South Georgia on 25 April 1982 and, after a series of vicious air and naval actions, British troops landed on East Falkland on 21 May. The force was made up of paratroopers, Ghurkhas, Royal Marines and British regulars. Marching west and southwest, British troops pushed the Argentinian conscript army back to their entrenchments in the capital Fort Stanley. After strategic hills overlooking the town had been taken the Argentinians were forced to surrender on 14 June. Over 650 Argentines were killed and 250 British servicemen lost their lives, as well as suffering serious warship and aircraft losses. The Falklands became a separate British dependent territory in 1985 but it was not until 1990 that diplomatic links between the two countries were re-established. The Argentinians have not renounced their claims over the islands.

➧ ***Margaret Thatcher***

FARADAY, MICHAEL (1791–1867)

English chemist and physicist. Michael Faraday is generally regarded as the 'father of electricity'. In fact he was one of many scientists of his era for whom electricity was a central fascination. In 1821 he began his own experiments with electromagnetism, resulting in the invention of a device for generating electricity, the dynamo. He then built an apparatus which converted electrical energy into motive force, the very first prototype model of an electric motor.

FAWKES, GUY (1570–1606)

Co-conspirator in the Gunpowder Plot to blow up the Houses of Parliament on 5 November 1605. His deed is remembered in Britain every year on Guy Fawkes Night, on 5 November. Fawkes was a staunch Roman Catholic and joined a group of three other conspirators. He was executed in 1606 after he betrayed his fellow conspirators under torture.

➧ ***Gunpowder Plot, James I***

FENIAN MOVEMENT (1858)

Irish underground society, forerunner to Sinn Fein. The movement was based in America. It was founded in 1858 and was an Irish-American group. There were many from Irish stock in America and they had the sympathy and money to consider it worth while attempting to establish an independent Irish republic, as Ireland was a part of the United Kingdom at that time. Various uprisings (1866–70) failed, however.

➧ ***Sinn Fein***

FEUDAL SYSTEM

Social hierarchy in the Middle Ages. When the Normans took control of Britain under William I they introduced the feudal system as a means of structuring society. The feudal system was based on land ownership and extended over much of medieval Europe because it was a logical way of assessing power. The king owned large areas of Crown land across the country. This put him at the very top of a hierarchical triangle which extended downwards from him. Beneath the king were other members of royalty, then nobility, lesser gentry, free tenants, villeins and serfs. These groups were linked by legal duties and obligations.

➠ **Domesday Book, *William I***

FIELD OF THE CLOTH OF GOLD (1520)

Meeting near Calais between Henry VIII and Francis I of France. It was meant to be an attempt at demonstrating the good relationship between the two countries, though both nations and leaders were suspicious of each other. It was also an extravagant party. Over 4,000 people and 2,000 horses travelled with Henry VIII and a further 1,000 with his wife Catherine of Aragon across the Channel. The cost to the Crown has been put at £15,000.

➠ ***Henry VIII***

FLAGELLANTS (14TH CENTURY)

Fourteenth-century sadomaschistic religious sect. Many people regarded the Black Death as punishment from God. In the aftermath minority sects grew up. Possibly the most disturbed were the Flagellants, who would walk the streets each whipping the back of the person in front in an attempt to purge them of their sins.

Black Death

FLEMING ALEXANDER (1881–1955)

Scottish bacteriologist. Fleming began his ground-breaking work in 1922. While studying an antibacterial enzyme he chanced upon an unusual mould culture which led to his discovery of the antibiotic penicillin.

FLODDEN, BATTLE OF (1513)

Battle (9 September 1513) of the Anglo-Scottish Wars. When Henry VIII refused to cease his wars against France, James IV of Scotland invaded England at the head of 100,000 men. By the time his army reached Northumberland desertions had reduced his army to about 30,000. It was here that the English army, under the command of the Earl of Surrey, faced him. James's position on top of a hill was turned, claiming 10,000 Scots dead, including the king himself, the Archbishop of St Andrew, 12 earls and hundreds of leaders of Scottish clans. English losses were about 4,000.

Henry VIII, James IV

FORKBEARD, SWEYN (c. AD 960–1014)

King of Denmark and England (1013–14). Sweyn first raided England in AD 993 and returned each year on fresh raiding expeditions. In 1013, having obtained the submission of Wessex, Sweyn marched to London and was recognised as king of England. Sweyn Forkbeard died six weeks later after a fall from his horse.

Canute, Kingdom of Wessex

ABOVE LEFT Peasants rebel against the feudal system
BELOW LEFT A meeting at the Field of the Cloth of Gold near Guines, France

FREDERICK, PRINCE OF WALES (1707–51)

Prince of Wales. Son of George II, with whom he quarrelled violently. At Leicester House, Frederick's court, separate from his father's, became a meeting place for opponents of Robert Walpole, the king's chief minister. The influence of the Leicester House group in Parliament faded quickly after Frederick suddenly died.

George II, George III, Robert Walpole

FREE CHURCH OF SCOTLAND (1843)

Organised by the First General Assembly of the Free Church of Scotland. These evangelical dissenters from the Church of Scotland were led by Thomas Chalmers. They raised funds for ministers, schools and charitable work in the age of victorian philanthropy. In 1929 the Free Church and the Church of Scotland reunited.

Church of Scotland

FRENCH, FIELD MARSHALL SIR JOHN DENTON PINKSTONE (1852–1925)

British commander at the beginning of World War I. A distinguished cavalry commander during the Boer War, French relieved Kimberley and occupied Bloemfontein. He served as chief of the Imperial general staff in 1912 but resigned in 1914 in opposition to troops in Northern Ireland. He was supreme commander of British troops on the Western Front in 1914 and at the first Battle of Ieper stopped the German thrust towards Calais. He resigned in December 1915 following criticism about the huge numbers of casualties suffered under his command.

Boer War, World War I

FRY, ELIZABETH (1780–1845)

English prison reformer. The philanthropic Quaker Elizabeth Fry took pity on the plight of female prisoners. She formed an association in 1817 to improve their conditions of imprisonment and, with her brother, compiled a report on prison reform in 1819.

LEFT Gallipoli landing from HMS Clyde
FAR RIGHT TOP Improvised transport during the General Strike

GALLIPOLI (1915–16)

Allied land invasion of Turkey (25 April 1915–10 January 1916). Initially 145,000 men were landed on the Gallipoli Peninsular, but due to indecision and incompetence, little progress was made. By the time the troops were withdrawn the British had lost 205,000, the French 47,000 and the Turks around 300,000. Despite the fiasco, the Turks were sufficiently weakened to allow the British to take Palestine in 1917 and for the Germans to cancel their planned offensive in France in 1915.

➠ *World War I*

GANDHI, MAHATMA (1869–1948)

Indian spiritual and nationalist leader. Mahatma Gandhi's real name was Mohandas Karamchand Gandhi. Mahatma means 'great soul' in Hindi. Throughout his life Gandhi was a champion of the poor and disenfranchised through non-violence. He moved to South Africa in 1893 where he developed his policy of peaceful non-co-operation, or 'satyagraha', with the authorities in the struggle against racial discrimination. A lawyer, he moved back to India in 1914 and became leader of the Indian National Congress. Frequently imprisoned by the British, Gandhi visited London in 1931 for the Round Table Conferences to determine India's political future. His message to the British was for them to leave India. Gandhi's simple style of dress won him many friends but his lack of formality apparently annoyed Winston Churchill. After World War II he was a central figure in negotiations for Indian independence. He was assassinated by a Hindu extremist who opposed Gandhi's support between Hindus and Muslims.

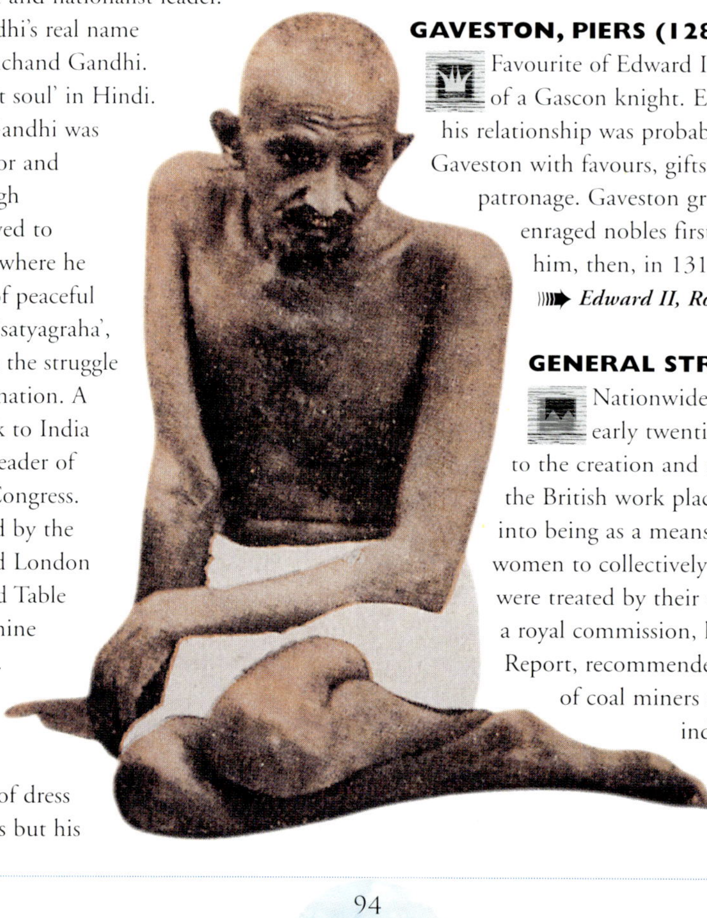

GARTER, ORDER OF THE (1344)

Highest order of English knighthood. Edward III was responsible for creating the Order of the Garter in around 1344. Legend has it that whilst dancing with the Countess of Salisbury a garter dropped from her leg and the king placed it on his own leg in a moment of merriment. He then said 'shame to be him who thinks evil of it' in French, which became the motto of the order.

GAVESTON, PIERS (1284–1312)

Favourite of Edward II. Gaveston was the son of a Gascon knight. Edward II, with whom his relationship was probably homosexual, showered Gaveston with favours, gifts and power over royal patronage. Gaveston grew arrogant and the enraged nobles first forced Edward to exile him, then, in 1312, had him murdered.

➠ *Edward II, Roger Mortimer*

GENERAL STRIKE (1926)

Nationwide workers' strike. The early twentieth century was witness to the creation and rise of trades' unions in the British work place. Trades' unions came into being as a means for working men and women to collectively influence the way they were treated by their employers. In 1926 a royal commission, known as the Samuel Report, recommended a cut in the wages of coal miners as a means of making the industry more competitively buoyant on the world stage. The Trade Union Congress

(TUC) responded by calling a nationwide workers strike known as the General Strike. The mine owners also demanded that their employees work longer hours and sympathies ran so high that over two million people boycotted work across the country. The country coped with the standstill for nine days before all but the miners returned to work. The miners continued their lone strike for almost seven months, but ultimately without success.

GEORGE I (1660–1727)

King of England (1714–27). The first monarch of the Hanoverian dynasty, George was not popular amongst his subjects. He endured a difficult relationship with his son and spent much time abroad in his old electorate. He was succeeded by George II.

George succeeded to the throne after the death of Queen Anne, the last Stuart monarch, by right of his descent from James I and under the provisions of the Act of Succession (1701). At the time, he was Elector of Hanover. Unable to speak English, he communicated with his ministers in England in French, relying on his son, George Augustus, the future George II, to translate for him. Before long, however, George ceased to attend cabinet meetings and his chief minister, Robert Walpole, chaired them instead. This prompted the rise of Walpole as the first prime minister but reduced the king's control over affairs.

George was divorced from his wife, Sophea Dorothea, 20 years before he became king. She was imprisoned for life for adultery in 1694. George never remarried, but brought his German mistresses with him to England. There were bitter quarrels between the king and his son, George Augustus, who had revered his mother. The rather mulish and pompous King George, who made no secret of his dislike of England, was not particularly popular with his subjects. He was no intellectual, but loved music and patronised the work of the composer George Frederick Handel.

The system of government in England was very different from Hanover, where as Elector, George was an absolute monarch. He never got used to the constitutional monarchy under which he reigned – but did not rule – in England, and had to work in conjunction with, and largely under the control of, Parliament. George attempted to manipulate the system by setting off the Whig and Tory parties in Parliament against each other. Robert Walpole, however, allied himself with the estranged George Augustus, who acted as his father's regent during the king's numerous visits to Hanover. The king was also opposed by the Leicester House Set, a separate court set up by George Augustus, which included Walpole. This opposition was too great for the king and to his fury, he was obliged to reconcile with Walpole. George I died on his way to Hanover in 1727 and was buried there.

➡ ***George II, George Frederick Handel, Robert Walpole***

GEORGE II (1683–1760)

King of England (1727–60). Essentially a soldier, George II became the last English king to lead his troops in battle during the War of the Spanish Succession. He had a loving relationship with his wife, Caroline, who was a beneficial influence, and worked well with his prime minister Robert Walpole. He was succeeded by his son George III.

After 1701, George was prepared for a future role as king with studies in the English language, government and lifestyle. He became a naturalised British citizen in 1705. He was irreconcilably opposed to his father over the latter's treatment of his mother. A consummate soldier, George Augustus – as he then was – fought at the battle of Oudenarde in 1708 during the War of the Spanish Succession and later, in 1743, at Dettingen, became the last king of England to fight in battle.

George Augustus married Princess Caroline of Anspach in 1705. She proved to be a strong and beneficial influence on him. However, backed by Caroline, George II quarrelled with his son and heir, Frederick, Prince of Wales in exactly the same way as he had done with his own father. Like his father, George II was limited in his powers in England which was frustrating for a man who liked to be seen to be in control. However, it was the clever Caroline who largely guided policy behind the scenes, in league with Robert Walpole: the two of them succeeded in giving the king the impression that the policies Walpole proposed were his own. Walpole had a strong influence in his own right and was able to hold the king back from involving England in several European wars. However, Caroline died in 1737, to her husband's extreme distress, and Walpole fell from power in 1742. The king was unable to find a congenial replacement and was forced to turn to William Pitt, a supporter of his estranged son Prince Frederick.

On the personal level, George II was more popular in England than his father, being less decidedly 'German' and showing more interest in his kingdom. George found constitutional monarchy restrictive, nevertheless, and was glad to visit his Electorate of Hanover where he could get away from 'that damned House of Commons'. Britain's importance vastly increased during George's long reign and by the time he died in 1760, he was ruler of an appreciable overseas empire.

➠ ***George I, George III, Robert Walpole***

GEORGE III (1738–1820)

King of England (1760–1820). Son of Frederick, Prince of Wales, grandson and successor to George II. George III was the first Hanoverian monarch to be born and educated in England. His great interest in farming and botany earned him the nickname of 'Farmer George'. King George was stubborn and his political judgment was poor, but he was very religious and very moral.

One of his first acts as king was to issue a proclamation against immorality. George III's only lapse seems to have been his rumoured marriage in 1757 to a shoemaker's daughter, Hannah Lightfoot. King George married Charlotte of Mecklenburg-Strelitz in 1761 and together they had 15 children.

George III wanted to retrieve some of the control Parliament had taken away under the system of constitutional monarchy and chose prime ministers he believed would support him in this aim.

The first was John Stuart, Earl of Bute, a royal family friend, but he was incompetent and unpopular and was forced to resign in 1763. The strain of insults and libels against the king himself caused him to have a nervous breakdown in 1765. Criticism of George continued and rose to unprecedented heights when the repressive policies of prime minister Frederick, Lord North's administration towards the American colonies, which were fully backed by the king, prompted the Revolution and War of Independence (1775–83). After the colonies won their independence, the king and Lord North were vilified more than ever before. Lord North resigned in 1781.

George was implacably opposed to the emancipation of Roman Catholics, as were many of his Protestant subjects, and when his prime minister, William Pitt the Younger, attempted to introduce a Catholic Emancipation Act in 1801, he was forced to resign. George suffered personal and family troubles. His heir, Prince George, the future Prince Regent and George IV, was a wastrel and libertine who built up huge debts. In 1788, George had his first attack of madness, which has since been ascribed to the blood disease porphyria. He recovered in 1789, the madness returned in 1810. George, now blind as well as mad, spent the rest of his life a prisoner in Windsor Castle while his son, the Prince of Wales, ruled in his place as Prince Regent. George III died in 1820.

➡ ***Queen Charlotte, Frederick, Prince of Wales, George IV, William Pitt the Younger***

GEORGE IV (1762–1830)

King of England (1821–30). Son of George III. Both as Prince of Wales and king, George IV was uninterested in his royal duties and preferred the pleasures of high society social life. He was a reprehensible character, giving his father a great deal of grief, with his libertine ways, his monumental debts and his many mistresses. In 1785, George married a widow, Maria Fitzherbert. Although he took more mistresses after the marriage, Mrs Fitzherbert was the abiding love of his life. The marriage was, however, illegal because it contravened the provisions of the Royal Marriage Act of 1772. In 1795, George was forced to marry his first cousin, Princess Caroline of Brunswick. This came about because Parliament had agreed to pay his debts provided he took a legal wife. The marriage was a disaster. The prince felt sick the first time he saw Caroline and asked for a brandy. Caroline thought the prince was too fat and, though he had been handsome in his youth, she found him unattractive. The marriage was consummated and a daughter, Princess Charlotte, was born nine months later, but the couple separated soon afterwards and lived apart until Caroline's death in 1821. They were never divorced, but there was continual warfare between them as the prince attempted to keep Caroline out of England and tried to use Parliament to indict her for her many adulteries. Caroline managed to survive her husband's moves against her.

When his father went mad in 1810, George became Prince Regent, but his powers were limited by Parliament. The Prince Regent's extravagance and taste for lavish entertaining did not, however, decrease. It was at this time that the Royal Pavilion in Brighton, a mock-oriental minor palace, was created for the prince by John Nash. The Prince Regent became George IV on the death of his father in 1820. His coronation in 1821 was the most lavish ever known. His daughter and only child, Princess Charlotte, had died in childbirth in 1817.
He was succeeded by his brother William IV.

➡ ***Brighton Pavilion, George III, Royal Marriages Act***

RIGHT A cartoon faturing George IV under 'the horrors of digestion'

GEORGE V (1865–1936)

King of England (1911–36). Second son and successor of Edward VII. When his elder brother, Prince Albert Victor (Eddy) died in 1892, Prince George became his father's heir and was obliged to resign from the Royal Navy. George was a very keen and knowledgeable philatelist and created the Royal Postage Stamp Collection, which is now classed as a national treasure. He married Albert Victor's bereaved fianceé, Princess May of Teck, in 1893. They had six children. George V came to the throne in 1910 in a time of political crisis: the House of Lords was resisting the Liberal government's plans for higher income tax to create old age pensions and the king was asked to create enough new peers to get the measure passed. This proved uneccessary, but the king resented being brought into party politics. Nevertheless, behind the scenes, King George supported political moves, such as the Irish Home Rule Bill and he repeatedly warned his first cousin, Kaiser Wilhelm II of Germany, against his warlike policies. In public, the King and his wife, now Queen Mary, preferred their role as exemplars of royal social leadership, which placed them above political controversies. Their style was somewhat aloof and distant, but they became very popular and highly respected. Both the king and queen were personally very shy, but they unfailingly performed their duty as public figures. George V was the first English monarch to be crowned Emperor of India in Delhi, in 1911, which had not been the case with his two predecessors, Queen Victoria and Edward VII. King George was a model royal leader of the nation during World War I, but the post-War years were saddened by his estrangement from his son and heir, who became King Edward VIII on his father's death in 1936.

Edward VII, Edward VIII, George VI, Victoria, World War I

GEORGE VI (1895–1952)

King of England (1936–52). Albert, Duke of York, who succeeded his brother Edward VIII after the latter's abdication in 1936, never expected to become king – nor was he trained for it. A nervous man, George struggled all his life against his stammer and at the abdication, is said to have panicked at the prospect before him. As Prince Albert, he had served in World War I and was present at the Battle of Jutland in 1916, but a stomach ulcer forced his retirement from active service. Subsequently, he became known as the 'Industrial Duke' for his interest in British industry. In 1923, the duke married Lady Elizabeth Bowes-Lyon, who became his staunch helper and support as his queen. Despite his drawbacks, George VI became a highly respected king. He was both dutiful and devoted to his people. His ability to manage the pressures of kingship were doubted before World War II began in 1939, but he proved all doubters wrong by his courageous conduct. The king and queen became the social leaders of Britain at war and remained in London, where Buckingham Palace was bombed several times in air raids. The royal couple toured England constantly, travelling by special train, and were there to comfort victims of air raids in London and other cities. The strain on the king was, however, considerable and by 1945, when the war ended, he had aged noticeably and his health began to deteriorate. He had always smoked heavily and in 1951, he underwent an operation for lung cancer. He appeared to recover, but sent his heir, Princess Elizabeth and her husband Prince

TOP RIGHT St George and the Dragon
RIGHT Hundreds camp out each year at the Glastonbury Festival

Philip on a tour of East Africa which he had been meant to undertake. The King died suddenly on 6 February 1952 and Elizabeth, now Queen, had to be recalled.

Elizabeth Bowes-Lyon, Edward VIII, Elizabeth II, World War II

GEORGE, ST (c. 3RD CENTURY)

Christian martyr and patron saint of England. Legends about him date from the sixth century. Most famous is his slaying of a dragon in order to rescue a maiden. By the eighth century he was revered in England, then Edward III appointed him patron saint of the Order of the Garter. Finally he became England's patron saint.

GIBBONS, ORLANDO (1538–1625)

English composer. Gibbons was a choirboy at King's College, Cambridge and later the organist at Westminster Abbey. He was a favourite of the young Charles I and played in his court. Gibbons wrote over 40 pieces of church music, mainly anthems and madrigals. He also wrote music for the viol and virginal.

Charles I, Westminster Abbey

GIBRALTAR

British colony in the Mediterranean. 'The Rock of Gibraltar' as it is commonly known, first passed into British control in 1704. Three separate treaties in the eighteenth century gave approval to British rule. However, the Spanish government still maintains that Gibraltar, which borders the southern coast of Spain is part of its sovereign territory. The countries, although allies and both members of the European Union, are still in dispute over Gibraltar.

GLADSTONE, WILLIAM (1809–98)

British prime minister (1868–74, 1880–85 and 1892–94). In total Gladstone was an MP for 62 years, from 1832 until 1895 with only year in between when he did not serve in Parliament. Prior to becoming prime minister he held junior office and was Chancellor of the Exchequer in the 1850s and 1860s. As leader of the Liberal party, Gladstone tried unsuccessfully to forge a political solution in Ireland. He also introduced an education act that provided schooling for all children in England and Wales aged between five and 13. During his second term in office he introduced the third Reform Act which gave the power of vote to farm workers. In his final term in office he again concentrated on the issue of Ireland and tried to force through, unsuccessfully, Home Rule for Ireland. Although a bill got through the House of Commons, it was defeated in the House of Lords, prompting Gladstone's resignation. Queen Victoria once famously said of him: 'He speaks to me as if I was a public meeting.' He died of cancer in 1898.

Queen Victoria

GLASTONBURY FESTIVAL (1970)

Music festival. It was set up by farmer Michael Eavis, who held the festival on his land, in Glastonbury, southwest England, in 1970 – the audience numbered 1,500. By the late 90s it was attracting up to 100,000 people. Originally a hippy festival, Glastonbury became a general music festival – one of the biggest events on the musical calendar.

GLASTONBURY TOR

Sacred hill in south-west England, traditionally in the legendary Isle of Avalon. The Tor stands on the leylines – geographical lines that connect ancient sacred sites – and is one of several rumoured burial sites of King Arthur. On it stands St Michael's Chapel, an important early Christian church. Glastonbury Tor was a sacred Celtic site and has many ancient rituals associated with it. Archeological evidence has found links to sacred rituals dating back to 500 BC.

➔ *King Arthur*

GLENDOWER, OWEN (1354–1416)

Landowner and symbol of the struggle for Welsh independence from England. Glendower (or Owain Glyndwr in Welsh) styled himself as the Prince of Wales and sought to forge an alliance with the French to throw off English rule. A dispute over land in 1400 in North Wales sparked off a 15-year revolt against Henry IV. One of his policies was to create a Welsh university and church. Although the revolt was ultimately unsuccessful, Glendower became a national hero.

➔ *Henry IV*

GLORIOUS REVOLUTION (1688–89)

Name given to the deposition of the Catholic James II in 1688 and the accession in his place of his son-in-law and daughter as the joint monarchs William III and Mary II. Also known as the Bloodless Revolution because it took place without violence. James's policy of re-Catholicising his kingdom after his accession to the throne in 1685 was unacceptable to the Protestant Parliament. However, in 1649, James's father, Charles I, had been publicly executed after the Civil War with Parliament, and MPs were loath to repeat the exercise. Instead, James was encouraged to flee into exile in France. James's first attempt to get out of England, in disguise, was thwarted by fishermen who captured him off Sheerness in Kent and returned him to London. Parliament, greatly embarrassed, arranged for James to escape again and this time, he reached France safely.

➔ *Queen Anne, Charles II, Mary II, William III*

GODERICH, FREDERICK JOHN ROBINSON, VISCOUNT (1782–1859)

British prime minister (1827–28). Goderich became Chancellor of the Exchequer in 1823. In 1927 the serving prime minister George Canning granted him his peerage; Goderich succeeded him the same year, but he was unable to control the warring Tories and Whigs and resigned the following year.

➔ *George Canning*

GOOD FRIDAY AGREEMENT (1998)

Political agreement that paved the way for a directly elected Northern Irish assembly. The agreement formed part of the peace process that had made faltering progress from the beginning of the 1990s. Although this process had been challenged intermittently, especially through the Omagh bombing in the summer of 1998, the Assembly was still elected with Ulster Unionist David Trimble becoming First Minister. The Assembly has been suspended mainly over rows on arms decommissioning, however it has since reconvened.

➔ *Northern Ireland*

GORDON RIOTS (1780)

Anti-Catholic riots in London, led by Lord George Gordon. Gordon made himself head of the Protestant Association, which aimed to abolish the Catholic Relief Act of 1778. He and his supporters marched on Parliament, carrying their petition against the tyranny of Catholicism. That June rioting was quashed by 12,000 troops, resulting in 700 fatalites and 25 executions.

➔ *Catholic Emancipation*

GRAFTON, AUGUSTUS HENRY, 3RD DUKE OF (1735–1811)

British prime minister (1767–70). Descended from Charles II and his mistress Barbara Villiers, Grafton came to notice as first lord of the treasury in

ABOVE Glastonbury Tor
RIGHT The Great Exhibition at Crystal Palace

1766. He was neither popular or successful as prime minister and his attitude towards the American Revolution forced his resignation.

GRAND ALLIANCE (1689)

Name given to a political and strategic alliance formed amongst major European powers; Austria, England, the Netherlands, Spain and a number of German states aimed at checking French expansionism under Louis XIV. The alliance ultimately proved ineffective as war raged in Europe throughout this period until almost the year 1700. A further 'grand alliance' was formed in 1701, this time between Austria, England and the Netherlands aimed at preventing the all-powerful union of the French and Spanish Crowns. This was organised by William III of England. Portugal and Prussia eventually joined the alliance. This all ultimately led to the War of the Spanish Succession between 1701 and 1714, provoked by the childless death of Charles II of Spain.

➞ *William III*

GREAT EXHIBITION (1851)

Exhibition to show the greatness of the British Empire. The Great Exhibition of 1851 was a special project of Queen Victoria's husband, Prince Albert. It was held in the Crystal Palace in Hyde Park between May and October 1851. The brainchild of Henry Cole (later to become Chairman of the Society of Arts), the exhibition was intended to exonerate the glorious achievements of Britain and its Empire. It was held at the height of the Industrial Revolution with exhibits brought from all over Britain and her colonies, including new inventions, works of art and jewels. The Koh-i-Noor diamond was among the treasures on display. People came from all over Britain, as well as all over the world, to visit the Crystal Palace – in total, over six million people flocked to Hyde Park during the five months of the exhibition. The hundreds of thousands of pounds raised by the exhibition went towards building museums in the South Kensington area of London

➞ *Prince Albert, Crystal Palace*

GREAT FIRE OF LONDON (1666)

Fire that destroyed many of London's finest buildings. Between 1665–66 England suffered its second major epidemic of bubonic plague. The Great Plague killed around a fifth of the population of London because rats were abundant on the filthy streets. On 2 September 1666 a fire began at a bakery in Pudding Lane. Most of the city's buildings were made of timber and a prevailing wind quickly carried the fire to other properties. The Great Fire of London burned for four days. It consumed 13,000 houses over an area of 400 acres, but the disaster had at least cleansed the city of plague carrying rats.

➞ *Black Death, Charles II, Christopher Wren*

GREAT REFORM ACT (1832)

Three separate parliamentary acts throughout the 1800s which gave the vote to millions more within Britain. The first act in 1832 was initially defeated sparking riots throughout the country. Only on the intervention of William IV did the act become law. It got rid of the 'Rotten Boroughs' and gave more areas the chance of electing their own MP to Parliament. Although the act increased the number of those who could vote by 50%, this still only extended the franchise to the middle class. The second Reform Act of 1867, under Disraeli, gave almost a million more people the vote, doubling the country's electorate overnight. The final act, in 1884, further increased the number of people who could vote to five million. The final act, introduced by Gladstone came at a time of political unrest and increasingly loud demands from radical groups for Parliament to extend the power of franchise.

➞ *Benjamin Disraeli, William IV*

GREENWICH MEAN TIME (1884)

Means of standardising global time. Having charted most of the globe by the late nineteenth century, it became apparent that the world needed to be divided into standardised longitudinal sectors to avoid navigational confusion. Britain was a leading power at that time so the prime meridian ended up running right through the political heart of England. The Greenwich meridian, as it is called, runs straight through the Royal Observatory at Greenwich, London. Adopted in 1884, it signifies zero degrees longitude. The Greenwich meridian also denotes average solar time in the time zone containing the British Isles. This is known worldwide as Greenwich Mean Time (GMT).

GRENVILLE, GEORGE (1712-1770)

British politician. Grenville was an MP for almost 30 years between 1741 and 1770. He was related to William Pitt the Elder but even after his brother-in-law's fall he remained in office. He was, at various times, Treasurer of the Navy, First Lord of the Treasury and First Lord of the Admiralty. His time at the Treasury was marked by an inflexible economic policy and he introduced the Stamp Act in 1765.

GREY, CHARLES, 2ND EARL (1764–1845)

British prime minister (1830–34). Grey entered Parliament in 1786 and was created lord of the admiralty 20 years later and then foreign secretary. In his time as prime minister he pushed through the Great Reform Bill and the Abolition Act.

GREY, LADY JANE (1537–54)

Eldest daughter of Henry Grey, Marquis of Dorset and cousin of Edward VI. Lady Jane was used as a pawn by John Dudley, Duke of Northumberland who wanted to perpetuate his own power by making her queen in place of the rightful heir, Edward's elder half-sister Princess Mary. In 1553, the duke married his son, Guildford Dudley, to an unwilling Lady Jane. After Edward's death on 6 July 1553, Northumberland proclaimed Jane queen, and Guildford Dudley proclaimed himself king. However, there was a public outcry and after nine days, he had to admit defeat. Lady Jane was imprisoned in the Tower of London, but the new Mary I was loath to have her executed. Mary was, however, forced to execute both Jane and Guildford Dudley on 12 February 1554, after the violent protests that arose over her own plans to marry Philip of Spain.

➠ ***Lord Guildford Dudley, Edward VI, Mary I, Tower of London***

GRUFFYD, DAVID AP (d. 1283)

Welsh prince. David opposed his brother, Llewellyn ap Gruffyd when he became sole Prince of Gwynned (1255) but like Llewellyn, fought against the encroachments of the English kings in Wales. David became Prince of Gwynned on Llewelyn's death (1282) but was captured and hung, drawn and quartered as a traitor in 1283.

➠ ***Edward I, Edward II, Llewellyn ap Gruffyd***

GRUFFYD, LLEWELLYN AP (d. 1282)

Welsh prince. The last native Welsh prince to be recognised by the English as Prince of Wales. In 1255, Llewellyn seized power in Gwynned. He attempted to make Gwynned all-powerful in Wales and received the homage of other Welsh princes in 1258. In 1276–77, Edward I of England conquered Wales and defeated Llewellyn. Llewellyn and his brother David raised a rebellion in 1282, but after Llewellyn was killed in a skirmish near Builth, the rebellion collapsed.

➠ ***Edward I, David ap Gruffyd***

GULF WAR (1990–91)

Conflict between Iraq and an international coalition (2 August 1990–3 March 1991). By 1990 Iraq owed $80 billion and demanded that Kuwait, its neighbour, cancelled their part of the debt and helped with repayments. Iraq also accused Kuwait of over-producing oil, thus contributing to the depression of the price of oil, Iraq's main export. Negotiations and mediation failed.

ABOVE The Royal Observatory, Greenwich

LEFT US M-1 Tank used in the Gulf War
BELOW The conspirators of the gunpowder plot

Just after midnight on 2 August 150,000 Iraqi troops crossed the border and overwhelmed Kuwait's 20,000-strong army. By dawn Kuwait's city was in their hands. Four days later the UN Security Council imposed an economic embargo on Iraq, the latter responded by annexing Kuwait on 8 August. A week later a large, international force gathered in Saudi Arabia; some 400,000 US troops backed by 200,000 from Great Britain, South Korea and New Zealand. On 29 November the UN issued an ultimatum that Iraq must leave Kuwait by 15 January 1991. They failed to do so and in the weeks after the deadline 100,000 sorties by coalition aircraft pounded Iraqi targets. On 24 February the coalition invaded south-west Iraq, moving north then east to encircle Iraqi forces in the south and Kuwait. By February 28 Iraqi resistance had collapsed and a ceasefire declared. On 3 March Iraq accepted the ceasefire conditions. However, Saddam Hussein, the Iraqi President, was still in power and still continues to undermine the peace of the region, despite the continued presence of coalition forces that continually over-fly Iraq. 100,000 Iraqis were killed; the coalition lost 240 dead 776 wounded.

GUNPOWDER PLOT (1605)

Catholic conspiracy to blow up the Houses of Parliament and James I in November 1605. The attempt proved unsuccessful after a letter warning a Catholic MP of the plot was intercepted. Robert Catesby led the group. The others included Robert Winter, John Wright and the most famous of them all, Guy Fawkes. They hid around 30 barrels of gunpowder in a cellar under the House of Lords. Guy Fawkes was arrested on 4 November when he was discovered next to the barrels. Catesby was a fanatical Roman Catholic and was shot once the plot was uncovered. All those involved were executed. The event is marked each year in Britain with Guy Fawkes (Bonfire) night when millions of people set-off fireworks in memory of the failed plot.

➠ ***Guy Fawkes, James I***

GWENT, KINGDOM OF

Kingdom in south-east Wales secured by the Normans. Just 20 years after the Battle of Hastings, the Normans had, under William Fitz Osbern established their rule as far west as Gwent. Several castles were built to protect the new administrative region.

GWYNN, NELL (1650–87)

Mistress of Charles II. Nell Gwynn, who was born into a poor family in Hereford, met Charles, 20 years her senior, when she was an orange-seller outside the Theatre Royal, Drury Lane. She later became a popular actress at the Theatre. She had two sons by the king. Nell was witty, loving, unassuming and undemanding and very popular with the public. Her humble birth, however, prevented the king creating her Countess of Greenwich.

➠ ***Charles II***

HADRIAN'S WALL

Roman defence against tribes from the north. Twenty years before the Antonine wall was built, Publius Aelius Hadrianus had Hadrian's Wall constructed to mark the northern boundary of the Roman Empire some eighty miles farther south, between Maryport and Wallsend. The fortified wall, built AD 122–26 was eventually abandoned by the crumbling Roman Empire in around AD 383. Although now only a fragmented ruin, the wall still runs approximately 185 km (115 miles) roughly east to west.

➠ ***Antonine Wall, Romans***

HAIG, GENERAL SIR DOUGLAS (1861–1928)

British Commander. Haig, having served on the general staff in India was made lieutenant-general and given command of the First Army Corps of the British Expeditionary Force when war broke out in 1914. Later he was made a full general and after huge British losses at Loos-en-Ghelle in 1915, replaced French as supreme commander. His handling of the major campaigns on the Western Front came under criticism, particularly from the prime minister, David Lloyd George. British casualties were severe in 1916 on the Somme and at Passchendale in 1917 Many blame Haig for the wasteless loss of life and poor tactical understanding.

➠ ***Battle of the Somme, World War I***

HALIDON HILL, BATTLE OF (1333)

Battle between Archibald Douglas's Scots and the English under Edward III and Edward Balliol (19 July 1333). Positioned defensively Edward's professional army slaughtered the Scottish warriors attempting to march up the hill through a swamp. Over 4,000 Scots were killed, including Douglas, after they were broken and pursued by English knights and bowmen.

Siege of Berwick, David II, Edward III

HAMPTON COURT PALACE (c. 1520s)

Tudor palace designed by Christopher Wren. The site, on the banks of the Thames, was owned by Cardinal Wolsey. In 1529, Henry VIII seized Wolsey's land and his newly built house. Subsequent monarchs, including Elizabeth I, lived at Hampton Court until the death of George II. George III turned it into 'grace and favour' apartments, a tradition that continues today. Hampton Court, which was opened to the public by Queen Victoria, is famous for its gardens – partially designed by Capability Brown – and large maze. The palace was damaged by fire in the 1980s, but quickly restored. It is reputed to be one of Britain's most haunted buildings.

Capability Brown, Elizabeth I, George II, Henry VIII, Thomas Wolsey, Christopher Wren

TOP LEFT General Sir Douglas Haig

HANDEL, GEORGE FREDERICK (1685–1759)

German composer and musician who moved to the London court of George I. Handel showed prodigious musical talent as a child, writing his first composition at the age of nine. While studying to become a lawyer, as his father had wished him to do, Handel supplemented his income by playing the organ. His love of music won out and he abandoned the law to move to Italy and study music. His great early works composed during this time include the opera *Agrippina* and the oratorio *Resurrection*. In 1710, Handel moved to England, where he was lauded. He remained in London for the rest of his life, making only occasional trips back to Germany. Two of his most famous works were composed while in England: *The Water Music* and *Messiah*. Handel wrote 50 operas and 23 oratorios. He is buried in Poets' Corner in Westminster Abbey.

George I, Westminster Abbey

HANOVERIAN DYNASTY

Royal dynasty of Electors of Hanover. The Hanoverians' right to the throne of England was based on their descent from Elizabeth, Queen of Bohemia, who was a daughter of the Stuart, James VI of Scotland and I of England. Elizabeth's daughter, Sophia, was Electress consort of Hanover, and the mother of George I. In 1701, after the death of the last child of the then Princess Anne, younger daughter of James II, Parliament passed the Act of Settlement: this named the Electress Sophia as Anne's heir. Anne, who was a Protestant, became queen after William's death in 1702. The reason behind the Act of Settlement was Parliament's determination to have a Protestant succession after Anne. Sophia and her son George were both Protestants, whereas their exiled Stuart rival, James Edward Stuart, son of James II, was a Catholic. It had been James Edward's birth in 1688 to the Catholic James, and his queen Mary of Modena, that led to the exile of both parents and child and their replacement by the Protestant William III and Mary II. Strictly speaking, as the direct descendant of the Stuart kings, James Edward had a superior right to the throne, but his Catholicism made him unacceptable. Despite two uprisings – the Jacobite Rebellions of 1715 and 1745 – led by James Edward and his son Charles Edward Stuart respectively, the Stuarts never regained the throne of England.

The accession of the Hanoverians to the English Crown posed certain difficulties. George I, who came to the throne in 1714, was very 'German', he disliked England and had no command of the language at all. Both he and his son and successor, George II, who became king in 1727, greatly preferred their Electorate of Hanover, where they were absolute monarchs. In England, they were constitutional monarchs, with powers limited by constitutional monarchy. The other monarchs of the Hanoverian dynasty were King George III, who succeeded to the throne in 1760, George IV (1820), William IV (1830) and Queen Victoria (1837). All these kings, like the first two Georges were Electors of Hanover as well as monarchs of England. Women and their royal descendants were not allowed to rule in Hanover, so that when Victoria became queen, the Electorate passed to her uncle, Ernest Augustus, Duke of Cumberland. The link between England and the Electorate was also maintained by a rule that the royal descendants of George II in Hanover had the right to British citizenship.

As a dynasty, the early Hanoverians were probably the most vulgar and outrageous monarchs ever to reign

in England. They indulged in vicious family quarrels. George I's spectacularly ugly German mistresses were hated in England for their greed. The profligacy of George IV, as both prince and king, made him the butt of lampoonists, pamphleteers and extremely insulting cartoons. Nevertheless, their place as monarchs was never seriously challenged and the Jacobite Rebellions were not supported by the English public.

➡ ***George I, George II, George III, George IV, William IV, Victoria***

ABOVE Queen Victoria
RIGHT George I
TOP RIGHT George II

FATHERS AND SONS

IT seems to have been a characteristic of the Hanoverian monarchs that they had quick tempers and rarely enjoyed good relationships with their son and heirs. George I was the first to prove this and during the king's final years, he and his son barely spoke. Despite his own mistreatment by his father, George II continued the trend with his own eldest son, Frederick, Prince of Wales. He showed no sign of sorrow when Frederick was killed after being hit by a cricket ball.

Perhaps the most unfortunate father–son relationship, though, was that of George III and the Prince Regent (later George IV). The king doted on his son in childhood, but as the prince grew up he showed signs of the decadence and ill-living that were to characterise his later years. George refused to support the prince's extravagences and the prince took his revenge later when the king began to suffer from mental illness: he spread rumours about his father's inability to run the country and had the old man incarcerated while he ruled as Regent.

TIMELINE

GEORGE I

Born: 28 May 1660
Ascends the throne: 1 August 1714
Crowned: 20 October 1714
Married: Sophia Dorothea of Celle
Died: 11 June 1727

GEORGE II

Born: 30 October 1683
Ascends the throne: 11 June 1727
Crowned: 11 October 1727
Married: Caroline of Brandenburg-Ansbach
Died: 25 October 1760

GEORGE III

Born: 4 June 1738
Ascends the throne: 25 October 1760
Crowned: 22 September 1761
Married: Charlotte of Mecklenburg-Strelitz
Died: 29 January 1820

GEORGE IV

Born: 12 August 1762
Ascends the throne: 29 January 1820
Crowned: 19 July 1821
Married: Caroline of Brunswick
Died : 26 June 1830

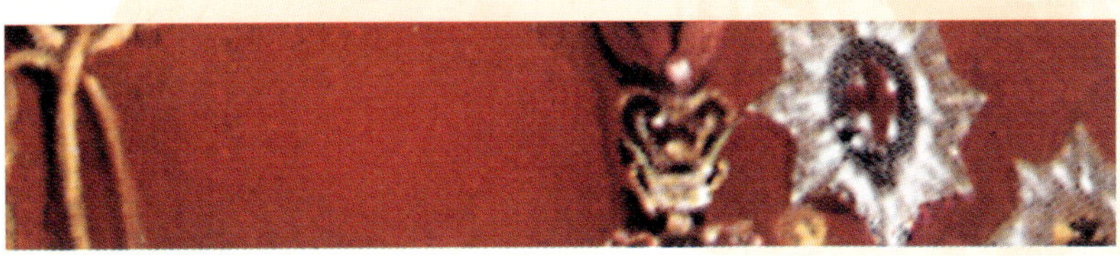

WILLIAM IV

Born: 21 August 1765
Ascends the throne: 26 June 1830
Crowned: 8 September 1831
Married: Adelaide of Saxe-Meinigen
Died: 20 June 1837

VICTORIA

Born: 24 May 1819
Ascends the throne: 20 June 1837
Crowned: 28 June 1838
Married: Albert of Saxe-Coburg-Gotha
Died: 22 January 1901

EDWARD VII (of Saxe-Coburg-Gotha)

Born: 9 November 1841
Ascends the throne: 22 January 1901
Crowned: 9 August 1902
Married: Alexandra of Denmark
Died: 6 May 1910

HARDIE, KEIR (1856–1915)

First Labour Politician. Working in a coal mine as a child, Scotsman, Keir James Hardie grew up developing socialist sympathies, having seen a need to improve the lot of his fellow miners at the pit face. At the age of 32, in 1886, he became the secretary for the Scottish Miners' Federation. He then became the first Labour candidate to run for Parliament in 1888, becoming a member of Parliament from 1892–95 and 1900–15.

HARDRADA, HARALD (1015–66)

King of Norway and Norse warrior. Half-brother to Olaf II, married to the daughter of Yarosalv, Grand Duke of Kiev, he became joint king of Norway (1046). After a war against Denmark he invaded England (1066) supporting Harold II's brother, Tostig. He was killed at the Battle of Stamford Bridge.

Harold II, Battle of Hastings, Battle of Stamford Bridge, William I

HARLEY, ROBERT (1661–1724)

British Tory politician. Harley served as chief minister to Queen Anne and negotiated the longed-for end to the War of the Spanish Succession in the Treaty of Utrecht (1713) His luck changed under George I, when he was imprisoned under charges of Jacobite sympathies.

Queen Anne, War of the Austrian Succession, Jacobites

HAROLD I (c. 1016–40)

King of the English (1035–40). Known as Harold Harefoot. Son of King Canute. Harold I was crowned in 1037, in the absence in Denmark of his younger half-brother Harthacanute. Harold's legitimacy was dubious. He died in 1040 and after Harthacanute returned from Denmark in 1042,he had the body exhumed and beheaded.

Canute, Harthacanute

RIGHT John Harrison's H1
ABOVE The burial of Harold II

HAROLD II (c. 1022–66)

King of the English (1066). Eldest surviving son of Godwine, Earl of Essex, Harold was ostensibly promised the throne when Edward the Confessor made him 'Duke of the English' in 1064. In 1065, however, King Edward also, apparently, named Duke William of Normandy as his successor. King Edward died in January 1066 and Harold was crowned. William of Normandy regarded this as treachery and prepared to invade England. Harold's estranged brother Tostig, Earl of Northumbria raided the south coast of England and then, with King Harold Hardraada, King of Norway, invaded Northumbria in September 1066. King Harold had to make a rapid march north to deal with them. Both Tostig and Hardraada were killed in battle at Stamford Bridge. William of Normandy invaded the south of England in October and Harold's army made another speedy forced-march southwards to fight him at the Battle of Hastings, where Harold was killed.

Edward the Confessor, Battle of Hastings, Norman Dynasty, Battle of Stamford Bridge, William I

HARRISON, JOHN

English clock-maker who solved the problem of longitude at sea. The great navigational problem with transoceanic voyages during the seventeenth century had been calculating longitude. Knowing how far west or east you were was vital to plotting co-ordinates, as ships could miss their intended landfall by 15 miles, wasting vital time. John Harrison was one of many who submitted designs for ships' chronometers to the British government from 1714, hoping to win a prize. His H4 design was eventually recognised the winner in 1772.

HARRODS

Department store in London's Knightsbridge. In 1849 Henry Charles Harrod set up his grocery business. By 1889 the business had grown to a point where the Harrods Store in Knightsbridge was established. Harrods has controlled various subsidiary companies over the years, but the flagship store remains its key symbol, representing goods of the highest quality.

HARTHACANUTE (c. 1018–42)

King of England (1035–42). Son of King Canute. Harthacanute was in Denmark, fighting to maintain his power there, when his father died in 1035. He returned to claim his English throne in 1040. Brutish, cruel, and vengeful, Harthacanute died suddenly while drinking at a wedding. He may have been poisoned.

➤ ***Canute, Harold I***

HASTINGS, BATTLE OF (1066)

Battle for the English Crown (14 October 1066). William of Normandy believed he had no option but to invade England following Harold's coronation. William had two reasons to claim the throne: Edward the Confessor had promised William succession; Harold had sworn allegiance to William. The invasion plan required building ships and as many as 3,000 were used to transport the 2,000 horses and 7,000 men on the 60-mile voyage from St Valery. Harold was heading south from York and his victory over Hardraada when hearing of the Norman landings. He arrived in London (6 October) and marched 58 miles to Battle, arriving on the night of 13 October. Harold drew his 7,500 men along a ridge, facing the Normans in three divisions. William's light troops attempted to break up the English formation with missiles but this had little effect until he launched a full-scale infantry and cavalry attack. In the confusion it appeared that William had been killed and the Normans retreated. Revealing himself by taking off his helmet, William rallied his cavalry and annihilated the English pursuers. For eight hours the English line withstood attacks until Harold and his brothers were killed and the remaining English army scattered.

➤ ***Harold II, William I***

HASTINGS, WARREN (1732–1818)

British colonial administrator who worked for the East India Company and who prepared the way for British rule in India. Hastings arrived in India aged just 18. By 1771 he had become governor of Bengal and the first governor general just three years later. His time there was turbulent. Although he was admired for his administrative reforms and his courting of some Indian leaders, he was also accused of high-handedness. He sentenced Maharaja Nandakumar to death by hanging after he had accused Hastings of corruption. On his return to England he was acquitted on charges of corruption following a seven-year trial in the House of Lords.

➤ ***East India Company***

HEATH, EDWARD (b.1916)

British prime minister (1970–74). An MP from 1950 until 2001, Heath has served British politics for over half a century. He was elected as prime minister in 1970 but his time in government was marked by deep industrial unrest that eventually saw him ousted by the electorate. A pro-European, his biggest achievement was to sign Britain up as a member of the European Economic Community. He was the last of the 'One Nation' Tory leaders before the more abrasive Margaret Thatcher took control. She was elected as leader of the Tories in 1975, ousting Heath. A noted musician and sailor, Heath retired from politics at the 2001 election.

➧ ***Margaret Thatcher***

HEIR TO THE THRONE

Next monarch to succeed to the throne. The heir *apparent*, eldest son of a reigning monarch, has a right to the throne senior to all others. Short of premature death, or being disinherited, he is certain to succeed. The heir *presumptive* – a daughter, brother, sister, cousin or other near relative of the reigning monarch is presumed to be the heir until a child is born to the monarch and supersedes them.

➧ ***Princes of Wales***

HENGIST

King of Kent. Hengist is said to have called for the assistance of two chieftains from Jutland around AD 449 in fighting the enemy Picts. The Jutish brothers Hengist and Horsa came to help as asked but, having defeated the Picts, took control of Kent for themselves, with Hengist as king.

➧ ***Danes, Vikings***

HENRY I (1068–1135)

King of England (1100–35). Youngest son of William I. In 1100, Henry succeeded his brother William II and was crowned within three days. Henry was challenged by his eldest brother, Robert, Duke of Normandy, whom he defeated in battle and imprisoned for life. Henry quarrelled with – and exiled – Anselm, his Archbishop of Canterbury, over papal authority in England but when threatened with excommunication, he gave in. After the tragic death of his only son, William, in 1020, Henry made his nobles swear alliegance to his daughter, Matilda, as their future queen, but after the king's death, they reneged.

➧ ***Saint Anselm, Matilda, William I, William II***

HENRY II (1133–89)

King of England (1154–89). First monarch of the Plantagenet (Angevin) dynasty. Henry was the son of Empress Matilda, who agreed with the usurper King Stephen in 1153 that he should succeed him. Henry's domains, later known as the Angevin Empire, were vast: in addition to England, they comprised Normandy, Anjou, Touraine and Maine and Aquitaine which came to him on his marriage to Eleanor of Aquitaine in 1152. Henry II established strong royal rule over his empire and reformed the operation of the law with the new jury system, among other important legal procedures. In an attempt to establish royal, as opposed to papal, control over the English church, Henry appointed his friend Thomas Becket as Archbishop of Canterbury in 1162. Becket, however, unexpectedly upheld papal rights in England and this led to his exile and, in 1170, his murder at Canterbury Cathedral. Afterwards, Henry was forced to do penance for the killing. Henry was also opposed by his own sons, who had been given important titles and positions, but were denied power. They rebelled against him, with the support of their mother Eleanor, and finally drove the king to his death in 1189.

➧ ***Thomas Becket, Eleanor of Aquitaine, King John, Matilda, Richard I, Stephen***

RIGHT Henry II in coronation robes

HENRY III (1207–72)

King of England (1216–72). Son of King John. Henry III came to the throne in 1216. He assumed his powers as king in 1227. Henry immediately quarrelled with his nobles over his refusal to accept their right to act as his advisers. Henry preferred to rely on favourites, but agreed to dismiss them when forcefully challenged.

However, the king changed neither his despotic ways, nor his reliance on favourites. In 1258 the nobles lost patience and, led by Simon de Montfort, Henry's brother-in-law, forced Henry to sign the Provisions of Oxford, which limited his powers. When Henry reneged, civil war followed in 1264–65. Henry was captured and imprisoned by Simon de Montfort, who directed his actions as king. In 1265, Simon was killed in battle by Prince Edward, Henry's son. Subsequently, Henry became senile and spent the rest of his life in artistic pursuits, including the rebuilding of Westminster Abbey.

Edward I, Simon de Montfort

HENRY IV (1367–1413)

King of England (1399–1413). Grandson of Edward III. Before becoming king, Henry – known as Henry Bolingbroke – was a much-admired chivalric figure. As one of the Lords Appellant in the 1380s, Henry had strongly opposed his cousin, King Richard, and his reliance on court favourites. In 1399, he usurped Richard's throne after the king had exiled him and illegally confiscated the lands of his dukedom of Lancaster. Despite the support Henry had received from Parliament, the usurpation and Richard's subsequent murder troubled his conscience and bedevilled his reign. First, he faced a rebellion by the earls of Kent, Salisbury and Huntingdon. The Welsh princes also rebelled against him, in 1400. In 1403, Henry Percy, son of the Earl of Northumberland, headed another revolt against the king. By 1405, Edmund Mortimer, Earl of March, who had a senior claim to the throne, was plotting with Northumberland to depose Henry and share his realm between them. On each occasion, Henry suppressed the revolts and plots with considerable force and cruelty. By 1408, Henry was reasonably safe from revolts, but by then he was a sick man, suffering from a disease thought to be leprosy. He died aged 45 in 1413.

Edward III, Henry V, Richard II

HENRY V (1387–1422)

King of England (1413–22). Henry V, who succeeded his father Henry IV, was one of England's great warrior-monarchs. When he was just 15, he fought for his father against the Welsh rebels and later against Henry Percy and Edmund Mortimer. Although he participated in his father's government, father and son did not always see eye to eye. For instance, in 1407, when the Burgundian and Armagnac factions were arguing over the succession to the French crown, Henry IV supported the Armagnacs and his son supported their opponents.

When he came to the throne, Henry V revived the claim of his great-grandfather, Edward III, to the throne of France. He invaded France in 1415, captured Harfleur after a punishing siege and, on 25 October, he confronted the French at the Battle of Agincourt. Henry's victory, where his army was outnumbered by the French, made him one of England's great hero-kings. Later, his victory was celebrated by William Shakespeare in his play *King Henry V* (1599). However, Agincourt did not give Henry the French throne. Despite support from the Burgundian faction, he got no further than recognition – at the Treaty of Troyes – as heir to the French king, Charles VI. To seal the bargain Henry married Catherine, Charles's daughter, in 1421. Henry was strongly opposed by the dauphin, Charles's son. War followed. In 1422, Henry was in France where he captured the dauphin's stronghold, Meaux. However, Henry fell ill with dysentery and died, aged 34, on 31 August.

Battle of Agincourt, Henry IV, Henry VI, Treaty of Troyes

ABOVE Henry V during the Battle of Agincourt

ABOVE TOP Henry VI invests John Talbot with sword of office

RIGHT A coin commemorating the marriage of Henry VII to Elizabeth of York

HENRY VI (1422–71)

King of England (1422–71). Son of Henry V. Henry VI was only nine months old when he became king. He was crowned in both London (1429) and Paris (1431), but never ruled in France. In England, his hold on power was very tenuous, not only because of his extreme youth but because of his mild, unwarlike, susceptible nature and his complete lack of interest in government. Henry VI was vulnerable to anyone who sought to manipulate him: his unscrupulous favourite, William de la Pole; his warlike uncle, Humphrey, Duke of Gloucester; or his strong-minded wife, Queen Margaret of France. Henry's gentle character, coupled with his bouts of madness after 1453, was a crucial factor in giving rise to rival claims to the English throne: these arose from the usurpation by his grandfather, Henry IV. There were several claimants, the most senior and most powerful being Richard, Duke of York. In 1455, the Wars of the Roses broke out between the duke's House of York and Henry's House of Lancaster. Henry was subsequently exiled, twice deposed and twice imprisoned in the Tower of London. He was eventually murdered there by Yorkist agents in 1471.

Battle of Bosworth, Henry IV, Henry V, Henry VII, Wars of the Roses

HENRY VII (1457–1509)

King of England (1485–1509). Henry's claim to the throne came through his descent from Edward III and the Beauforts, the children of Edward's son John of Gaunt by his third wife, Catherine Swynford. Henry was the only child of Lady Margaret Beaufort and her husband Edmund Tudor, Earl of Richmond. Henry's army defeated the last Plantagenet (Angevin) king, Richard III, at the Battle of Bosworth in 1485. Subsequently, Henry became the first king of the Tudor dynasty. During the Wars of the Roses (1455–85), the English nobility had so decimated themselves that Henry was able to create a new aristocracy which owed their positions solely to him. This was a great advantage and strength to him, considering the undue power the nobles had exerted over previous monarchs.

Henry was also determined to avoid another weakness of former reigns, the financial power exerted on the king by the English nobles and Parliament. Henry created a royal fortune which enabled him to do without Parliament for much of his reign. He avoided expensive wars, encouraged overseas trade and exploration and exploited Crown lands to the full. As a move to reconcile the opposing Houses of York and Lancaster, Henry, representative of Lancaster, had married Elizabeth, daughter of the Yorkist Edward IV in 1486. They had eight children. Henry used his children to cement alliances with other countries. His eldest daughter Margaret married James IV of Scotland, for example, and his eldest son and heir Prince Arthur married Catherine of Aragon, youngest daughter of Ferdinand and Isabella of Spain. When he died in 1509, Henry VII bequeathed a richer, more powerful throne than any England had known before to his successor, Henry VIII.

➡ ***Margaret Beaufort, Battle of Bosworth, Catherine of Aragon, Edward IV, Henry VIII, Lambert Simnel, Perkin Warbeck, Wars of the Roses***

HENRY VIII (1491–1547)

King of England (1509–47). Second son of Henry VII, Henry became heir to the throne on the premature death of his brother Prince Arthur in 1502, and succeeded in 1509. The same year, Henry VIII married Catherine of Aragon, Arthur's widow.

Henry was handsome, intellectually brilliant and the epitome of the multi-talented 'Renaissance' monarch. He was a skilled huntsman and dancer, a fine musician and – reputedly – a composer and he was able to discourse on theology, literature and other intellectual subjects with the greatest minds of the day. The court of Henry and Catherine was known for its glamour and lavish entertainments, and its hospitality towards the famous scholars and churchmen.

Henry relied heavily on his chief minister, Cardinal Thomas Wolsey who handled the day-to-day business of government on his behalf. It was once thought that Wolsey virtually ruled England, but Henry was not idle on this score: the policies Wolsey promoted were the king's own.

The one blight on Henry's brilliant reign was his lack of a son to succeed him. All his children by Catherine, except for a daughter, Mary, had been stillborn or died in infancy. In around 1526, Henry resolved to divorce Catherine and marry one of her ladies in waiting, Anne Boleyn, in hopes of having a son by her. Catherine strongly resisted Henry's attempts to get rid of her and in this, was backed by her nephew, King Charles of Spain. The pope, to whom Henry applied for a divorce, refused to give it. Ultimately, Henry removed the Church in England from the Pope's jurisdiction, pronounced his own divorce and married Anne Boleyn in 1533. This fundamental change involved the dissolution of England's monasteries by 1540 which provoked a protest, the so-called Pilgrimage of Grace, in 1536. The Pilgrimage was put down with considerable force.

The only surviving child of Henry and Anne Boleyn was a daughter, the future Queen Elizabeth I. Anne

Boleyn fell from favour and was executed for adultery and incest in 1536. Henry married four more times. His third wife, Jane Seymour, was one of Anne's ladies in waiting. She married Henry in 1536. Their son, the future Edward VI, was born in 1537, but Jane died as a result. Henry then married Anne of Cleves, whom he divorced, Catherine Howard, who was executed for adultery in 1542 and finally Catherine Parr, in 1543.

As his reign progressed, Henry grew more and more tyrannical and became the terror of his ministers and his family. His health declined and he was tortured for many years by an ulcerous leg. He grew extremely fat, which added to his health problems. Henry was fearful of a resurgence by the former Plantagenet (Angevin) dynasty and set about eliminating or exiling members of the family. He even had the 70-year old Countess of Salisbury beheaded in 1541. Henry, 55, died at Whitehall Palace, calling the name of his third wife, Jane Seymour. He was buried next to her at Windsor.

➡ ***Anne of Cleves, Anne Boleyn, Catherine of Aragon, Catherine Howard, Church of England, Dissolution of the Monasteries, Henry VII, Catherine Parr, Jane Seymour***

LEFT Songs and music at the court of Henry VIII

TOP RIGHT Henry VIII and his six wives

THE KING AND THE CARDINAL

DESPITE humble beginnings (he was the son of a Suffolk butcher), Thomas Wolsey (1475–1530) rose to become one of the most influential men of his age. Not only did he attain high office – Lord Chancellor of England and Archbishop of York – he also negotiated and concluded the Treaty of London in 1518 which promised peace between the Vatican and France, England and Spain. Prior to that he had helped plan the English campaign in France in 1512–13. As Lord Chancellor between 1515 and 1529, Henry VIII, desperate for a divorce from his first wife Catherine of Aragon in an attempt to produce a male heir, charged Wolsey with obtaining a divorce from Rome. Despite several long and arduous attempts, Wolsey was unable to procure this. Henry VIII took out his anger on Wolsey by accusing him of treason. Summoned from York to find out his fate, Wolsey died on the way on 29 November 1530. He was not universally popular. On hearing of his death members of the Royal Court held a banquet which depicted him descending to hell. He was also founder of Cardinal College, Oxford that later became known as Christ Church.

TIMELINE

1491 Henry born in Greenwich

1509 Henry ascends the throne and is crowned in Westminster Abbey; married his brother's widow Catherine of Aragon

1516 Birth of Henry's daughter Mary I

1520 Field of the Cloth of Gold between Henry and Francis I of France

1530 Thomas Wolsey dies while being transported to the Tower of London on charges of treason

1533 Henry marries Anne Boleyn; their daughter Elizabeth I is born in September

1535 Henry has his advisor Thomas More executed

1536 Anne Boleyn is executed on charges of treason; Henry marries Jane Seymour; Dissolution of the Monasteries begins, causing the Pilgrimage of Grace

1537 Birth of the longed-for son, Edward VI

1540 Henry's minister Thomas Cromwell is executed on charges of treason; the king marries Anne of Cleves but divorces her within six months and marries Catherine Howard

1542 Henry has Catherine Howard executed on charges of infidelity

1543 Marries Catherine Parr

1547 Dies at Whitehall on 28 January

HERALDRY

The study of coats of arms, armorial insignia and other methods by which descent can be traced. Although heraldry in Britain can only be traced formally back to the time of the Norman Conquest, there were probably heraldic systems in place well before that time. Coats of Arms were awarded by the monarch to a favoured subject. The insignia was then worn – on shields, armour, and flags – during tournaments as well as during battles.

➧ ***College of Arms, Tournaments***

HEREWARD THE WAKE

English rebel leader. William I did not have an entirely easy time ruling England after the Battle of Hastings. He certainly had his detractors, one of whom was Hereward the Wake, an English patriot leader. Hereward launched a revolt against William in 1070, from his stronghold on the Isle of Ely, Cambridgeshire. William's men managed to capture Hereward but he escaped their clutches and slipped into historic obscurity.

➧ ***William I***

HILDA, ST (AD 614–80)

Founder of Whitby Abbey and key player in the Synod of Whitby. Hilda was baptised *c.* AD 627. In AD 657 she founded her unisex abbey (Whitby or Streaneshalch Abbey) of which Caedmon was a significant member. Being now a prime Anglo-Saxon abbess, Hilda led the Celtic party in the Synod of Whitby, unfortunately unsuccessfully.

➧ ***Synod of Whitby***

HMS VICTORY (1759–1812)

Lord Nelson's flagship. Designed by Thomas Slade, construction began in Chatham on 23 July 1759. She was launched on 7 May 1765 and commissioned in 1778. She became the most successful 104-gun first-rate ship of the line. Prior to Nelson using her as his flagship at Trafalgar, she had been the flagship of Admirals Keppel, Kemperfelt, Howe and Jervis. She completed her active career on 7 November 1812. She is a major heritage attraction in Portsmouth dock.

➧ ***Napoleonic Wars, Admiral Nelson***

HOGARTH, WILLIAM (1697–1764)

English painter, caricaturist and engraver; also social reformer. Hogarth defined his age with story-telling series of engravings, such as *The Harlot's Progress* and *The Rake's Progress*. His engravings and caricatures, although humorous, show the grim side of London: gin palaces, violence and cruelty. His paintings include fine portraiture. After marrying the daughter of renowned artist Sir James Thornhill, Hogarth became influential in Thornhill's academy (forerunner to the Royal Academy). He gave strong support to British artists, in a world where foreign art was the vogue.

HOLBEIN, HANS (c. 1497–1543)

German artist who worked in Britain. Holbein first visited Britain in the 1520s. He also worked in Switzerland and Italy, as well as his native Germany. In 1533, he was employed as a court painter by Henry VIII, for whom he worked until his death. Holbein's most famous works include *The Ambassadors* and his pre-marriage portrait of *Anne of Cleves*: Henry later divorced Anne, reputedly because she proved to be less attractive than her portrait.

➧ ***Henry VIII***

HOLYROODHOUSE, PALACE OF (c. 1500)

The British monarch's official residence in Scotland, located in Edinburgh. The palace became a royal residence in the 1500s, after centuries of fighting over Edinburgh Castle between the Scots and English. The first monarch to live here was James IV of Scotland. Mary, Queen of Scots also lived here, for six years, after her arrival in Scotland (from France) in 1561. The palace stands at one end of Edinburgh's Royal Mile, with Edinburgh Castle at the opposite end.

➧ ***Edinburgh Castle; Mary, Queen of Scots***

HOME GUARD (1940–45)

Winston Churchill's local defence volunteers. On 14 May 1940 it was established for men that were too young, too old or in reserved occupations. Expecting 150,000 volunteers, within a month 750,000 had joined and one million by June. The Home Guard was to delay a German invasion force, giving the regular army time to reach the location.

➠ *World War II*

HOME RULE (19TH AND 20TH CENTURIES)

Attempt to give Ireland a domestic Parliament during the latter stages of the nineteenth century and the earlier twentieth century. Britain's political dominance of Ireland had been formalised through the Act of Union in 1801.

In the 1870s the Home Rule Association was formed and 59 Irish MPs who supported the movement were elected in the 1874 General Election. The big push for home rule came after the 1886 election. Led by the Irish nationalist Charles Parnell, the Home Rule Association held the balance of power after the election. The party supported the Liberals who, under Gladstone, had by then converted to the cause of Home Rule. The cause was eventually undermined by unionists within the Liberal Party defecting and failing to support the demands of its own leaders or those of the Home Rule Association. By the 1890s, Gladstone had returned to power and set about pushing another Home Rule bill through Parliament. This got through the House of Commons but was defeated in the Lords.

The scenario whereby the Irish party again held the balance of power was repeated in 1910. This time there was more success. The bill once again proceeded through the Commons, only to be delayed by the Lords. However parliamentary rules had changed by then and it means that the Lords could only delay bills for up to two years. Passed in 1912, the Home Rule Bill went onto the statute books in 1914 though it was suspended throughout the period of the World War II. By 1920 a modified bill was passed which provided for separate Parliaments for southern and Northern Ireland. Throughout the period, pressure to give autonomy/independence to Ireland grew through such events as the Easter Uprising of 1916. The leaders of this uprising wanted full independence for Ireland.

➠ *Easter Rising*

LEFT Hans Holbein, a self-portrait
BELOW Palace of Holyroodhouse

HOUSE OF COMMONS

Directly elected lower chamber of the British parliamentary system. The origins of the House of Commons can be traced to the thirteenth century when 'commoners', i.e. non-baronial representatives were summoned to Parliament. In the sixteenth century, the Commons acquired its permanent meeting place in Westminster. Its power increased enormously because of the Glorious Revolution that began in 1688 when control over taxation and free speech were won by the Commons. With the franchise being extended throughout the nineteenth century, its power and importance increased still further although the Lords often stymied many of its reforms. In the modern age, its importance has fluctuated. When there are small parliamentary majorities, it becomes very significant. There has been plenty of criticism though that its powers have waned over the last decade. Over 650 MPs are elected and debates have been televised since 1989.

➠ ***House of Lords***

HOUSE OF LORDS

The unelected upper chamber of the British parliamentary system and the highest court of appeal in the country. The term was first used in the sixteenth century. The House of Lords was abolished as a result of the Civil War but was later restored. Its membership increasingly grew as peerages were awarded for political service and no longer relied on family titles. During the 1800s, the house clashed with the Commons many times on the Reform Bills. In 1911 its powers were denuded with the Parliamentary Act which limited the Lords' actions, removing its veto on pecuniary bills giving it only a power to delay bills. The House of Lords has been subject to reform over the past few years with Tony Blair's Labour abolishing almost all of the hereditary peers. However there has been no announcement on further reform of the upper chamber.

➠ ***House of Commons***

HUGUENOTS

French Protestant minority in the sixteenth and seventeenth centuries. In 1523 the first French Protestant was burned at the stake and executions such as this soon escalated into nationwide massacres and mass imprisonment, such as the St Bartholomew's Day Massacre, 1572. With the Protestant King Henri IV's accession to the throne the Edict of Nantes, 1598, gave Huguenots religious freedom. This improved situation continued until Louis XIV's Revocation of the Edict of Nantes in 1685 when 250,000 French Protestants fled abroad. In England they became eminent craftsmen, such as silversmiths.

➠ ***Canterbury Cathedral***

HUNDRED YEARS' WAR (1337–1453)

Longest war in history. The Hundred Years' War raged through the reigns of five English and French kings. Henry I was the Duke of Guienne in south-west France and had allegiance to Philip VI, the French king. He was intent on destroying the power

TOP RIGHT The Hundred Years' War
RIGHT Hyde Park, London

of his Dukes. Edward III claimed the French Crown because his mother was the sister of the French king and Philip VI was only a cousin. The French declared the Crown could not be inherited through a woman. There were economic reasons for the war. In 1336 Philip V arrested all English merchants in Flanders. The Flemish towns revolted and allied with England. Edward III landed in Normandy with 10,000 men (July 1346) and defeated the French at Crecy, then at sea at Sluys and captured Calais (28 September 1347). The war was punctuated by the Black Death that wiped out a third of Europeans. In 1355 the English marched in Southern France and the Black Prince and his English longbowmen slaughtered the French at Poitiers (1356).

A treaty was signed in 1360 but when Charles V took the French crown in 1369 he broke the treaty and took the English possessions except Calais and Bordeaux. In 1415 Henry V defeated the French at Agincourt and the Treaty of Troyes (1420) decreed that after Charles VI's death Henry should be king of France and England. Henry died in 1422, followed by Charles. Two new monarchs, Henry VI and the future Charles VII disputed the treaty. Joan of Arc raised the English siege of Orleans and crowned Charles VII, was captured and executed by the English but French nationalism had been awoken. By 1453 only Calais was left. The war had lost the English their continental possessions despite numerous victories and France was free from foreign interference.

➠ ***Battle of Crecy, Edward III, Battle of Poitiers***

HYDE PARK (1536)

Largest royal park in London. In the Middle Ages Hyde Park was owned by monks and served as grazing land for wild deer and boar. In 1536, during the Dissolution of the Monasteries, Henry VIII seized the land for a hunting ground. In the seventeenth century, James I opened the park to the public.

➠ ***Buckingham Palace***

ICENI

Tribe of ancient Britain. During the Roman occupation of Britain there were native populations who attempted revolts against the Romans. One such population was the Iceni from eastern England. The Iceni had been ruled by King Prasutagus, a Roman tributary. Upon his death in AD 60, the Romans annexed the Iceni territory. Prasutagus's widow Boudicca (Boadicea) and her daughters were cruelly treated along with the other native Britons. In response Boudicca raised an army and launched a bloody, but short-lived revolt.

➧ *Boudicca*

INDIA, EMPRESS/EMPEROR OF

The title Empress of India was granted to Queen Victoria under the Royal Titles Act of 1876. Its main purpose was to emphasise British power as exemplified by its vast empire abroad. The title also put Victoria on a par with European royal families with imperial titles. Edward VII, George V, Edward VIII and George VI were called Emperors of India until the title was relinquished by George VI with the independence of India in 1947.

➧ *British Empire, George VI, Victoria*

INDUSTRIAL REVOLUTION (18TH CENTURY)

Period in the eighteenth century which saw great technological advance. The period of industrialisation in Britain, now known as the Industrial Revolution, lasted for some 100 years or so. As well as automating many tasks by use of machines, it saw a change in society. Millions of people migrated from rural areas to find work in urban environments, ultimately creating the urban working class.

Pinpointing the start of the Industrial Revolution precisely is not really possible. The Agricultural Revolution had already primed Britain for the change to begin by depriving many rural workers of their jobs. When industrial pioneers began inventing new industries there were plenty of people waiting to be employed. The cotton spinning factories of Richard Arkwright (1732–92), established over the latter third of the eighteenth century, are a good example of this. His machines saw the utilisation of water power, followed by steam power, the main driving force of the Industrial Revolution.

James Watt (1736–1819) had improved upon Thomas Newcomen's (1663–1729) steam engine in the 1760s. It was used initially for pumping flood water from mines which, in turn, provided the coal for fuelling the Industrial Revolution. By the early 1800s steam engines were also pulling the materials and products of industry along railway tracks and urban areas were black with their pollution. The iron and steel industry became the backbone of the Industrial Revolution, providing raw materials for the most impressive machines.

➧ *Agricultural Revolution*

INTERREGNUM (1649–60)

Meaning 'between the reigns', term used to describe the years of the English Republic created by Parliament, between the abolition of the monarchy in England in 1649 and the restoration to the throne of King Charles II in 1660. The Interregnum was divided into the Commonwealth (1649–53) and the Protectorate (1653–59). During the Commonwealth, power was exercised by the Rump Parliament, which angered the Puritans by failing to support their idea of a 'godly reformation' in the governance of England. Puritans regarded monarchy as tyranny, but to them the Rump, with its emphasis on materialism, was simply another form of tyranny. In 1652, the Rump was pressured by the army to introduce a bill calling for a new parliament. The army, however, did not trust the Rump Parliament and remained dissatisfied. So did Oliver Cromwell,

LEFT George Stephenson's 'Rocket' is admired
RIGHT A member of the IRA
FAR RIGHT Iron Age tools

who eventually expelled the Rump from Westminster. Subsequently, Cromwell became Lord Protector and head of state. His policy was to reconcile the opposing sides in the Civil War but divisions of opinion on policy within his Parliaments made this very difficult and it was never achieved. After Cromwell died in 1658, he was succeeded by his well-meaning but incompetent son Richard. England began sinking into chaos as law and order broke down and this led to the move to restore the Stuart monarchy in 1660.

➠ ***Charles I, Charles II, Oliver Cromwell, Rump Parliament***

IRA (1919)

Militant organisation campaigning for an independent Irish state. The Irish Republican Army was formed in 1919, helping to establish the Irish Free State in 1921. The movement split and was mostly unheard of between the 1920s and the advent of the Troubles in the late 1960s. The modern-day movement divided into the Officials and the Provisionals, the latter concerned with ejecting the British from Ireland. The Provisionals used terror to try and achieve their aims and were behind attacks such as the pub bombings in Guildford and Birmingham and the death of Earl Mountbatten. Following the limited success of the peace process, the organisation has split further with a faction known as the Real IRA continuing the violent struggle.

➠ ***Northern Ireland***

IRISH FREE STATE (1922)

The state created by the Irish Free State Agreement Act 1922. Ireland was divided as a consequence of the Act, with the north, a largely protestant area, ruled from Belfast and the south ruled from Dublin. The partition and other consequences of the act were extremely contentious. Michael Collins, one of the signatories of the Act, was murdered. It gave the new state limited autonomy and still meant the Irish had to accept the British monarchy. Republicans rejected the treaty and a civil war lasting until 1923 was launched. The Free State forces eventually overcame the Republicans. The first president of the republic was William Cosgrave. Eamonn De Valera replaced him in 1932. In 1937 the state changed its name to Eire, the Gaelic name for Ireland. It remained a member of the Commonwealth until 1949 when it changed its name to the Republic of Ireland. It became a member of the European Economic Community in 1973 and has enthusiastically embraced European government. It had the fastest growing European economy at the end of the 1990s and the beginning of the new century. Traditionally it has taken a neutral stance on matters of world affairs.

➠ ***Eamon De Valera***

IRON AGE

Period of prehistory. Metallurgy in Britain began with the Bronze Age. Bronze had been put to all kinds of technological uses and was a marked improvement on working stone because it could be melted and poured into shapes, and it could be reworked when cutting edges were blunted. Then came the arrival of iron. Iron was more difficult to work than bronze because it required far higher temperatures to soften it. Nevertheless, iron offered a material for tools and weapons that was far more hard wearing and tough than bronze. It eclipsed bronze and gave rise to the Iron Age culture in Europe.

JACOBITE REBELLION (1715–46)

Rebellion in support of the overthrown James II. When James became a Catholic in 1671 he suffered attempts to exclude him from the succession and in 1688 he was deposed and replaced by William of Orange. James came from the Stuart royal house, emanating from Scotland. His supporters were called Jacobites. In 1689, under the leadership of John Graham Claverhouse (1649–89) the Scottish Highlanders rose against the new king of England. Their rebellion was successful for a while, having defeated the loyalist forces at the pass of Killiecrankie. Further rebellions, under the leadership of James Edward Stuart – the Old Pretender – in 1715, and then his son Charles Edward Stuart – the Young Pretender – in 1745 were both effective at threatening the loyalist monarchy. Everything came to a head, though, in 1746 at the Battle of Culloden, where the loyalists finally defeated their enemy, bringing the Jacobite Rebellion to an end.

JAMES I OF SCOTLAND (1394–1437)

King of Scotland (1406–37). In 1424, James I inherited a poverty-stricken, lawless kingdom, controlled by the warlike Murdoch family, who were James's cousins. James imprisoned several of its members, then ruthlessly attempted to curb the power of the Scots clans and nobles. James made many enemies,and he was assassinated in 1437.

➡ ***Stuart Dynasty***

ABOVE The Battle of Culloden, 1746

FAR RIGHT The flight of James II after Battle of Boyne

JAMES I OF ENGLAND AND VI OF SCOTLAND (1567–1625)

King of Scotland (1567–1625) and England (1603–25). The only child of Mary, Queen of Scots. He had a claim to the throne of England based on his descent from Margaret, daughter of Henry VII, who married James IV of Scotland in 1503. James's father, Henry Stuart, Lord Darnley was also descended from Margaret. James became king of Scotland as an infant, on his mother's abdication in 1567, and was controlled for several years by the Stuart family and his nobles. He took power personally in 1586 and followed a policy of friendship with England (even after the execution of his mother in 1587), moderate government in Scotland and royal authority over the Presbyterians. James adhered to the Divine Right of Kings, the belief that monarchs were appointed by and responsible only to God, but encountered resistance to this idea in Parliament. The Anglican Church in England, however, welcomed James's Protestantism and his religious reforms, which included imposing moderation on the Puritans and introducing the Authorised Edition of the Bible, the King James Bible, in 1611.

James also worked to establish alliances with Protestant states in Europe, through the marriages of his children with Protestant rulers, but this threatened to involve him in European wars for which Parliament refused to vote the necessary funds. After 1614, the king came under the influence of the scheming George Villiers, later Duke of Buckingham. Villiers became his favourite, greatly angering Parliament and the nobles, who saw their own rights being curtailed. Puritans were enraged at the Catholic marriage James promoted, though failed to secure, for his son, the future Charles I. In 1624, the pressure forced James I to yield and agree, where previously he had refused, to take Parliament's advice on foreign affairs. He died the following year.

➠ *Charles I, Lord Darnley, Elizabeth I, Mary, Queen of Scots*

JAMES II OF ENGLAND AND VII OF SCOTLAND (1633–1701)

King of England and Scotland (1685–88). Second son of James I and VI. James's first wife, Anne Hyde, by whom he had two daughters, Mary and Anne, died in 1671. In 1673 James married the Catholic Mary of Modena, daughter of the Duke of Modena. By about 1668, James and Anne Hyde had converted to Roman Catholicism, but this was kept secret due to public and parliamentary antipathy to the faith. After the Restoration in 1660, James's brother, Charles II conferred many titles on him, including Duke of York and Lord High Admiral. He commanded the Royal Navy during the second (1665–67) and third (1672–74) Anglo-Dutch wars. Charles II had hoped to force toleration for Catholics through Parliament, but he failed and instead he was obliged to assent to the Test Act of 1673, which required all holders of public office to take the Anglican sacraments. Consequently, James had to resign as Lord High Admiral. Parliament attempted to exclude him from the royal succession, but Charles refused to allow it.

After Charles's death in 1685, James came to the throne as James II. From the first, he was determined to return his realm to Roman Catholicism and caused outrage as he promoted Catholics to high offices and positions of power. Due to residual guilt over the execution of his father, Parliament was willing to put up with James because his heir, Princess Mary, was a Protestant. This attitude changed in 1688, when a son was born to James and Mary of Modena, thus opening up the prospect of a line of Catholic monarchs. James was deposed and forced into exile with his wife and son. He attempted to retrieve his throne, but was defeated at the Battle of the Boyne in Ireland in 1690. James died in France in 1701.

➠ *Anglo-Dutch Wars, Battle of the Boyne, Charles II, Test Acts*

JAMES V OF SCOTLAND (1512–42)

King of Scotland (1513–42). James came to the throne of Scotland at the age of 17 months. In 1537, he married Madeleine, daughter of François I of France. James followed a policy of friendship with France and the pope and curbed the power of his nobles. They refused to support him against English invaders in 1542 as a result of which James was easily defeated. He went into a depression and died, leaving an infant daughter – Mary, Queen of Scots.

Mary, Queen of Scots

JENKINS' EAR, WAR OF (1739–41)

Struggle that grew out of the commercial rivalry between England and Spain. When Robert Jenkins, master of the ship Rebecca, had his ear cut off by Spanish coastguards in 1731, the ear was later shown to the House of Commons in 1738, forcing Sir Robert Walpole to declare war.

War of the Austrian Succession

JESUITS (1534)

Roman Catholic monastic order, also known as the Society of Jesus. Founded by St Ignatius of Loyola, who wrote *Spiritual Exercises*, the order's innovations included: lengthy probation, strict obedience, central authority and no female members. The Jesuits largely ignored Wales and their ministry in England was unwelcomed as it encouraged recusancy. English xenophobic fear of Jesuits was realised when the Catholic revival culminated in the Gunpowder Plot. A very significant English Jesuit, Edmund Campion, was hanged and other Jesuits during Elizabeth I's and James I's reigns resorted to hiding in priest holes.

Recusancy, Roman Catholicism

JEWS

Providers of commercial services and victims of persecution in an era of Christian dogmatism in Britain. Jews first traded in England in the sixth century, but it was at William the Conqueror's invitation that they first became significant in England's economy, being money-lenders at a time when Christianity forbade usury. The Norman and Angevin kings continued to use Jews, but public opinion often showed resentment. In 1189 the Third Crusade encouraged massacres back in England and in 1190 the Jews of York committed mass suicide rather than be murdered by their baronial debtors. Mistrust increased: the Statute of the Jewry, 1275, appointed Christians as wardens of their record chests and stigmatised them with compulsory yellow badges. Some Jews were even hung for coin-clipping. In 1290 Edward I expelled the Jews and in the following century Christian attitudes towards usury relaxed: Italian bankers arrived in England. By the Enlightenment the 20,000 Jews in London were tolerated, but largely poor.

Crusades, Edward I, Enlightenment, William I

JOHN OF GAUNT, DUKE OF LANCASTER (1340–99)

Third surviving son of Edward III. The name 'Gaunt' came from his birthplace, Ghent (Belgium). John of Gaunt was the richest and most powerful magnate in England. As a military commander, he took part in the Hundred Years' War with France after 1355 and his forces represented one quarter of the army raised for a campaign against Scotland in 1385. John of Gaunt called himself King of Castile (Spain) by right of his second wife, but renounced the title in 1387. During the senility of his father, John of Gaunt was virtual ruler of England. He used his power to advance his supporters, and was patron to the religious reformer John Wyclif. John Gaunt married three times. His first wife, Blanche, was the mother of the future Henry IV. By his third wife, Catherine Swynford, he fathered the Beaufort family, from which Henry VII was descended.

Margaret Beaufort, Edward III, Henry IV, Henry VII, Hundred Years' War, Richard II, John Wyclif

LEFT James V of Scotland
BELOW John of Gaunt

JOHN, KING (1167–1216)

King of England (1199–1216). Youngest and favourite son of Henry II. John was known as 'Lackland' because he was left without territory after his father distributed lands to his other, much older, sons. Henry II hoped that his heir, Richard, would transfer his own inheritance, the Duchy of Aquitaine, to John, but in this he was disappointed. In the quarrel between Henry and his sons, John supported his brothers against their father. This is said to have broken Henry's heart and hastened his death in 1189.

During the subsequent reign of his brother, Richard I, John tried to take advantage of Richard's frequent absence abroad to gain power in England. He was frustrated by the regents Richard left in charge, in particular his vigilant mother, Eleanor of Aquitaine. John became king after Richard's death in 1199, but he was not accepted as such in the territories of the Angevin Empire in France where his nephew, Prince Arthur of Brittany – the son of John's late elder brother Geoffrey – was preferred. Arthur disappeared in 1202 and John was accused of murdering him.

Contrary to popular belief, John was a responsible king, with a particular interest in justice for his subjects in the lawcourts. However, he made some serious errors. First, he angered the English Church by refusing the pope's choice for Archbishop of Canterbury. The pope then laid England under interdict (1208) and excommunicated the king (1209). These punishments were lifted after John's submission in 1213, by which time he had appropriated a great deal of Church wealth. Secondly, John infuriated his barons by refusing their rights as royal advisers. In addition, by losing Angevin possessions in France, John failed to display the military prowess expected of a medieval king. The result of these failings was that John's barons forced him to sign the famous Magna Carta in 1215, which set out their rights and privileges. Subsequently, John renounced the document. The barons again rebelled, but John died of a fever in 1216 during the consequent civil war.

➡ ***Eleanor of Aquitaine, Henry II, Magna Carta, Richard I***

ABOVE King John and his barons at the signing of the Magna Carta
TOP RIGHT Dr Samuel Johnson awaiting an audience

JOHNSON, SAMUEL (1709–84)

English lexicographer, poet and critic – the inventor of the *Dictionary*. Johnson's family was impoverished and lack of funds led him to abandon his degree at Oxford. His title of 'Dr' comes from two honorary doctorates awarded to him after the publication of his *Dictionary* in 1755. This brought him fame, but not financial security. His circumstances were only relieved in 1762 when George III awarded him an annual pension. In 1763 Johnson met James Boswell, who later became his biographer. In 1764 he founded 'The Club' with the painter Joshua Reynolds, frequented by the actor David Garrick and Charles James Fox. Johnson is buried in Westminster Abbey.

Oxford University

JONES, INIGO (1573–1652)

London-born architect, influential in bringing Italian-style architecture to England. Although he received no formal training in architecture, Jones travelled through Europe as a young man, where he studied the varied building styles of countries he visited. He was particularly impressed by the works of the Italian architect Palladio. The Britain in which Jones grew up was one of prominent Gothic edifices, so his contribution was vastly significant, leading as it did to the more fluid lines of Georgian architecture. Jones was favoured by the English kings James I and Charles I and, in around 1613, was appointed the king's surveyor of works. Shortly afterwards he designed the Queen's House at Greenwich, followed by the Banqueting House in Whitehall. He was also

instrumental in the re-design of Covent Garden and its splendid Palladian church, St Paul's (or 'The Actors' Church'). Jones also worked on properties outside London, including Wilton House, in Wiltshire.

Charles I, James I

JONSON, BEN (1572–1637)

English playwright, actor and poet, buried in Westminster Abbey. Jonson spent his life in and out of gaol for being too outspoken in his writings. In 1598 he killed another actor in a dual and was tried for murder – he defended himself, escaping execution by a legal loophole. Although best known for his comedies, Jonson also wrote tragedies. His works include the play *Every Man in his Honour* – in which one of the parts was acted originally by Shakespeare.

William Shakespeare

JULIAN OF NORWICH (1342– c. 1416)

Medieval mystic and writer. On 13 May 1373, now her remembrance day, Julian was healed after experiencing visions of Christ's suffering and of the Virgin Mary. She then wrote up her visions in *Revelations of Divine Love*, which also included discussions of predestination and evil. She ended her days as a recluse in Norwich.

KELLS, BOOK OF (8TH–9TH CENTURY)

Pre-eminent Celtic illuminated manuscripts. Produced on Iona, the highly coloured and detailed illustrations show Irish and Northumbrian influences. Their name probably originates from the migration of the Ionan community to Kells in Ireland in the face of Norse invasion. They are now kept in Trinity College, Dublin.

Columba, Vikings

KENT, KINGDOM OF

Province of ancient Britain. The Angles, Saxons and Jutes seized power in Britain with the departure of the Romans. They all emanated from the Germanic region of central Europe and shared out the new territory by dividing it into kingdoms. The south-eastern corner of England, Kent, had been ruled by a Briton who was having trouble with an enemy force called the Picts. He requested help from the Jutish chieftain brothers Hengist and Horsa. They obliged the Briton king by defeating the Picts but then overthrew him to seize control of Kent themselves. The Jute territory comprised the Kingdom of Kent and South Hampshire.

Anglo-Saxons

KEW GARDENS (c. 18TH CENTURY)

Royal Botanic Gardens. Kew Gardens encompass more than 300 acres of land. The first known botanic garden in the area was laid out in 1759. This small plot was extended and remodelled several times; in the 1770s it was restructured by Capability Brown. Today Kew Gardens boasts a scientific research centre for botany as well as the gardens that are open to the public. One of its most famous landmarks is the great conservatory.

Capability Brown

RIGHT A General Kitchener recruitment poster
FAR RIGHT John Knox admonishing Mary Queen of Scots

KEYNES, JOHN MAYNARD (1883–1946)

British economist. In the years between the two world wars the economy of Britain was not buoyant, and the British Empire was in decline. In 1936 the economist John Maynard Keynes published his *General Theory of Employment, Interest and Money*. In it he proposed a solution to the worsening unemployment problem. The idea was that government should counteract the causes – lack of demand for goods and decreased national income – by increasing expenditure from the national purse. This policy became dubbed 'Keynesian economics' and is opposed by 'moneterism' which proposes *cuts* in government spending by way of a solution.

KING JAMES BIBLE (1611)

Also known as the Authorised Version of the Bible. In 1604 James I called the Hampton Court Conference to decide religious issues between the Anglican party and the Puritan party. The only Puritan demand at the Hampton Court Conference that James I accepted was the request that the Bible be translated and used nationwide. James is credited with the idea for the eponymous Bible and it remained the official version for many centuries.

James I

KITCHENER'S ARMY (1914)

Name given to the volunteers for the army at the beginning of World War I. At the outbreak of war, Horatio Herbert Kitchener, one of Britain's foremost generals, was made secretary of state for war (the first serving British officer to hold the post). Reliant upon a volunteer army, Kitchener used extensive rallies and advertising to expand the British army from 20 divisions to 70 in a relatively short period of time. The campaign had overwhelming results and

over one million men had signed up by Christmas 1914. The momentum continued for some months but eventually conscription had to be introduced (1916).

Lord Kitchener, World War I

KITCHENER, LORD HORATIO HERBERT (1850–1916)

Military commander and statesman. Kitchener joined the Royal Engineers in 1871 and was promoted in 1883 to captain for his service in Palestine, Egypt and Cyprus. In 1884 he served in the abortive attempt to relieve Khartoum. He was Governor General of Eastern Sudan (1886–88) and became Commander-in-Chief of the Egyptian Army in 1892. He successfully invaded Sudan in 1895 and defeated the Khalifa at Omdurman in 1898. Kitchener was promoted to major general in 1896 and baron in 1898. He served in the Boer War and was made commander in India (1902–09), during which time he was promoted to field marshall. He became Consul General in Egypt in 1911 and was made Earl of Broome in 1914. From 1914–16 he held the position of Secretary of State for War and recruited the Volunteer British Army. Kitchener was lost at sea on 5 June 1916 when the cruiser Hampshire hit a mine and sank.

Boer War, Kitchener's Army, World War I

KNIGHTS

Medieval Britain was a place where warrior skills were highly prized. The most honourable military rank was knight. A knight was usually raised by the sovereign, having served as a page and squire. Knights were mounted soldiers in armour. This meant having to acquire riding skills and be robust enough to do battle dressed in metal. Only a select few were up to the job and so were accorded considerable respect, social status and wealth.

Order of the Garter

KNOX, JOHN (c. 1514–72)

Leader of the Reformation in Scotland. Details of Knox's early life are few, but it is known that by 1540 he had been ordained and in 1547 he unwillingly became leader of the Scottish Reformation. After a 19-month capture by the French in 1547–48, Knox helped Edward VI with his Protestant reforms. In 1559 Roman Catholicism ceased to be the official religion in Scotland and Knox returned from Geneva full of Calvinist ideas. Knox publicised his view that the body and blood were not literally present at Communion and his idea that ministers should be elected by the people was a key to the Presbyterianism of the future. His quote, in *Predestination* (1556–58) 'against the monstrous regiment of women', and his attitude regarding women and religion led to Elizabeth I banning him from England and continual confrontation with Mary, Queen of Scots. Despite his austere language Knox's ideas were moderate when compared with the extremism to come.

Church of Scotland, Elizabeth I, Mary, Queen of Scots, Protestantism, Reformation

LABOUR PARTY (1900)

British political party. The party was formed in 1900 and first held office in 1924. Its socialist principles were evident during its first government (1945–51), when it introduced the National Health Service and social security. The Labour Party won its most overwhelming victory in 1997, ousting 18 years of Conservative government, under the leadership of Tony Blair and the banner of New Labour. The roots of the Labour Party lie with Keir Hardie and John Burns, who entered Parliament as independent Labour members in 1892, but it took nearly a decade for an official party to be set up. By 1922, however, the party was established enough to be seen as the official opposition party to the Conservatives – a position it has maintained since.

➠ ***Tony Blair, Conservative Party***

LANCASTER, HOUSE OF (1399–1461)

Branch of the Plantagenet (Angevin) dynasty, descended from John of Gaunt, Duke of Lancaster, third surviving son of Edward III. The first Lancastrian king, Henry IV, usurped the throne from his cousin Richard II in 1399. Henry IV was succeeded by his son Henry V, one of the most popular romantic warrior-kings in history. His early death meant the throne passed to his son Henry, who was less than a year old at the time. Henry VI could not live up to his father's reputation and the Wars of the Roses ensued between the Lancastrian line and the House of York. Henry VI was to be the last Lancastrian king.

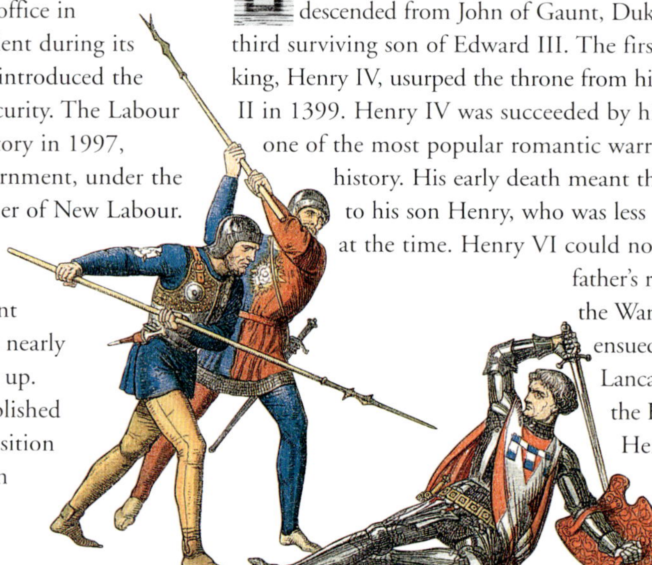

Usurpation has always been the most reprehensible of royal crimes and the Lancastrian hold on the throne was weakened because of it. Henry IV faced several rebellions during a troubled reign. However, the military prowess of his son, Henry V, who succeeded him in 1413, to a large extent diverted the unrest and divided loyalties that accrue to a monarch whose power was based on usurpation. Henry V's victory over the French at Agincourt in 1415 made him one of England's greatest hero-kings, an image perpetuated by William Shakespeare in his play *King Henry V* (1599). Tragically, Henry died young, in 1422, leaving his throne to his infant son, Henry VI.

Henry VI was as different from his father as it was possible to be: he was studious, pious, unworldly and subject to bouts of madness which he inherited from his maternal grandfather, Charles VI of France. Henry VI's weakness as well as his extreme youth on coming to the throne, were disastrous for the House of Lancaster. It permitted a strong challenge for the crown from Richard, Duke of York, who claimed descent from a son of Edward III who was senior to Henry's ancestor, John of Gaunt. The dispute between York and Lancaster led to the Wars of the Roses (1455–85) in which the two Houses fought for the Crown. In 1471, Henry was murdered and his son, Prince Edward, was killed at the battle of Tewkesbury. The Lancastrian line was now represented by Henry Tudor, descendant of John of Gaunt through his mother, Gaunt's great-granddaughter, Lady Margaret Beaufort. The Lancastrians ultimately triumphed in the Wars of the Roses in 1485 but Henry Tudor afterwards ascended the throne as Henry VII, first monarch of the new Tudor dynasty.

→ *Henry IV, Henry V, Henry VI, Richard II, Wars of the Roses*

LAND LEAGUE (19TH CENTURY)

Organisation, also known as the Irish Land League, that tried to achieve land reform in Ireland in the nineteenth century by boycotting unpopular landlords. It was established by Michael Davitt, an Irish nationalist, and proved successful in achieving its aims. In 1881, Gladstone introduced the Irish Land Act that gave in to the group on many of its demands for land reform. It was disbanded shortly after.

→ *Michael Davitt, William Gladstone, Charles Parnell*

LEFT The Battle of Barnet during the Wars of the Roses between the Houses of Lancaster and York
RIGHT William Laud

LANFRANC, ARCHBISHOP (c. 1005–89)

William the Conqueror's Archbishop of Canterbury (1070–79). The Italian Benedictine, Lanfranc, began his career teaching in Normandy. In 1070, however, Stigand was deposed and Lanfranc became the first Norman primate. He initiated reorganisation of the English Church and Norman bishops replaced Anglo-Saxons. He also secured the younger brother William II's succession, rather than Robert Curthose's.

→ *William I*

LAUD, WILLIAM (1573–1645)

Anti-Puritan bigot and Archbishop of Canterbury (1633–45). Charles I's religious adviser, Laud, regarded the Church and the State as inseparable and therefore hated Nonconformism. His imposition of Anglicanism, his *English Prayer Book* and his policy called 'throrough' were ultimately unsuccessful. In Scotland the Bishops' Wars and the covenants resulted. In Ireland his ally, Strafford, was executed. In England his trial of Prynne only emphasised the strength of Puritanism. In spring 1640 Parliament met and petitions against Laud were numerous. By December he was imprisoned in the Tower for treason. Ironically it was Prynne that tried him in 1644 and he was beheaded in January 1645.

→ *Bishops' Wars, Charles I, Nonconformism, Puritanism*

LAW, ANDREW BONAR (1858–1923)

British Conservative politician. Bonar law was elected leader of the Conservatives in 1911 and played a major role in the coalition government led by Herbert Asquith in the immediate post-war years, holding the positions of Chancellor of the Exchequer and Lord Privy seal.

→ *Herbert Henry Asquith*

LAWRENCE, T. E. (1888–1935)

English soldier. During World War I, English soldier Thomas Edward Lawrence was assigned to the military intelligence department in Cairo, Egypt, as a translator. In 1916 he became involved with negotiations

for an Arab revolt against the Ottoman Turks. He became a guerrilla leader with a genius for tactics, combining sabotage raids on Turkish communications with organising the Arab revolt. His success earned him such a reputation that he became known as Lawrence of Arabia.

World War I

LEICESTER HOUSE SET

Court set up by Prince George (later George II) in opposition to his father. Relations between George I and his son declined seriously after the first Hanoverian became king. Eventually the prince decided to set up a rival court at Leicester House, across the river. This became the centre of society and political opposition for a time. Robert Walpole was won over to it.

George I, George II

LEVELLERS (1647)

Democratic party during the English Civil War. Among the allies of Cromwell's Parliamentarians, or Roundheads, were the Levellers, led by John Lilburne, a democratic party campaigning for the Republic, male suffrage and religious toleration. The Levellers found widespread support in the New Model Army – Cromwell's fighting force – but Cromwell disagreed with their demands for radical reforms and executed their leaders in 1649. From then on the Levellers movement lost its political momentum, although it continued to exist until 1688.

John Lilburne

ABOVE Lawrence of Arabia
CENTER David Owen and David Steele
RIGHT David Livingstone

LIBERAL PARTY (19TH CENTURY)

British political party. The Liberals grew out of the former Whig party, whose emphasis had been on liberalism, in the nineteenth century. With the rise of the Labour Party to the far left of the Conservatives, the Liberals found themselves taking the middle road, and their momentum was lost. In 1988 they merged with the Social Democratic Party to become the Liberal Democrats.

Labour Party, Whigs

LILBURNE, JOHN (c. 1614–67)

Leader of the Levellers. The Levellers were a group of fundamentalist, democratic, republicans active during the English Civil War. They found considerable support in Oliver Cromwell's New Model Army but Cromwell himself found their views too radical. John Lilburne had served time in prison (1638–40) for distributing Puritan pamphlets. Having served in the parliamentary army he was elected to lead the Levellers in advocating ambitions for a democratic republic. He spent his time in and out of prison, his views considered dangerous and rebellion-inciting.

Levellers

LINDISFARNE GOSPELS, THE (7TH/8TH CENTURY)

Hiberno-Saxon illuminated manuscripts. They were illuminated in a style that amalgamated Irish, classical, Byzantine and Saxon influences and are renowned for their rich colour, detail and beauty. Probably produced for a bishop of Lindisfarne, Eadrith, they were made by the monastic community on Lindisfarne, established by Aidan in AD 635 and abandoned in AD 875 because of Danish attacks. The monks fled with St Cuthbert's body and presumably also the manuscripts, so explaining their remarkable survival. They are now kept in the British Museum.

➡ ***Saint Aidan, Book of Kells***

LIVERPOOL, ROBERT BANKS JENKINSON, 2ND EARL OF (1770–1825)

British prime minister (1812–27). Liverpool became a member of the Tory Party in 1790 and served a number of roles there, including home secretary and war minister, before becoming prime minister in 1812. His government saw the country through the Napoleonic Wars, but his policies were not always popular.

➡ ***Napoleonic Wars***

LIVINGSTONE, DAVID (1813–73)

Scottish missionary. Livingstone was a missionary who devoted his life to the exploration of Africa. He arrived on African shores in 1841 at the age of 28. In 1849 he reached Lake Ngami. He then travelled the upper Zambezi with his wife, Mary Moffat, and his children, but they fell ill and returned to England. He then explored Loanda and followed the Zambezi to its mouth in 1856, when he discovered the falls he named after Queen Victoria. From 1866 he set out on a mission to discover the source of the Nile, reaching Ujiji in 1871. It was here that Henry Morton Stanley (1841–1904) famously tracked Livingstone down. They went on to jointly explore the north end of Lake Tanganyika before Livingstone died of fever.

LLOYD GEORGE, DAVID (1863–1945)

British prime minister (1916–22). Lloyd George first entered Parliament in 1890 for the Caernarfon Boroughs. Although associated with the Welsh, Lloyd George was actually born in Manchester to Welsh parents. His surname was originally George. He added the Lloyd in honour of his mother's brother, Richard Lloyd, who helped raise him as a child after the death of his father. A Liberal, Lloyd-George was chancellor of the Exchequer between 1908 and 1915 under Herbert Asquith. There he made his mark as a social reformer unveiling a Budget in 1909 aimed to help those at the bottom of the social scale and imposed a high tax on those who earned over £3,000 a year. During World War I he became minister of munitions, a task he excelled in. By the end of the war he had taken over as prime minister. At the Paris Peace Conference he resisted calls to impose retributive terms on Germany. At home his government was destabilised by the situation in Ireland and the revelations about Lloyd George selling honours for contributions towards party campaign expenses. He was ousted as prime minister in 1922 after losing the support of Conservatives in his government.

➡ ***World War I***

LOCKERBIE BOMBING (1988)

On the night of 21 December 1988 tragedy struck the village of Lockerbie, Dumfries and Galloway, south-west Scotland. A Pan Am Boeing 747 airliner, en route to America, was sent plummeting to earth by a bomb which exploded in its cargo hold. The wreckage scattered over several miles, but the main portion of the fuselage came down on the village. Eleven villagers died along with all passengers and crew from the aircraft.

LOLLARDS (14TH CENTURY)

Fourteenth-century religious reformers. As Christianity began to develop in the Middle Ages people evolved different opinions on how it should be practised. The Roman Catholic division celebrated their faith with a flamboyant style which grated with the instincts of those who followed the Orthodox Church. In the fourteenth century a religious reformer, John Wycliffe, asserted that the Bible, and not the Church, was the supreme authority. His followers, the Lollards, believed the church should help people to live lives of evangelical poverty, thereby imitating Christ. They abhorred showy ritual, particularly the transubstantiation of the bread and wine of the Eucharist.

➡ *John Wycliffe*

LONDON UNDERGROUND (1863)

System of railways under London. By 1863 London was already such a densely packed city that there was only one solution for putting in new railway lines – to go underground. The first section of the London Underground system, known as the Tube, was between Farringdon and Paddington. The carriages were open topped and pulled by a steam locomotive, so the ride must have been extremely unpleasant with the choking, filthy fumes. That pioneering first section was built by the Metropolitan Railway Company, having been conceived by politician Charles Pearson. It had seven stations in all and the ride from one end to the other took thirty-three minutes.

LONDONDERRY, SIEGE OF (1689)

Battle of the War of the English Succession (19 April–30 July 1689). The forces of James II besieged 30,000 Ulster Protestants defended by 7,000 armed citizens under Major Henry Baker. Failing in successive assaults the besiegers withdrew, having lost 5,000 men against the garrison's 3,000. Major Baker was one of the casualties.

➡ ***Battle of the Boyne, Glorious Revolution, James II, William III***

LONG PARLIAMENT (1640–60)

Parliament assembled by Charles I. At a time of turbulence in British politics, Charles II tried to use the Parliament to push through reforms that ultimately led to the outbreak of the Civil War in 1642. During its existence competing factions held sway over the Long Parliament. By the mid-1640s, the New Model Army dominated the parliament. It was purged in 1648 and what became known as its Rump, those members who retained their position after the purge, helped to establish the Commonwealth. In the 1650s the Rump itself was expelled by Cromwell and Parliament was not recalled until 1659. In 1660 it reconvened only to dissolve itself to be succeeded by the Convention Parliament. This led in turn to the restoration of the monarchy.

➡ ***Charles II, Short Parliament***

LUDDITES (1811–16)

Members of a movement against the burgeoning revolution in industry. With the Industrial Revolution came the realisation that machines may take away valuable jobs from the people. Between 1811 and 1816 protesters, known as Luddites, organised sabotage attacks to destroy machinery that threatened their livelihoods. The cotton and wool mills of northern England, in particular, were targeted by the Luddites as machines became more and more automated. They claimed to be led by a mythical figure called General Ludd.

TOP RIGHT The Siege of Londonderry

LUTYENS, SIR EDWARD (1869–1944)

English architect. Lutyens began his tuition with the architect Ernest George. In later years he became strongly associated with the landscape gardener Gertrude Jekyll, with whom he often worked in partnership. His work was classical in style, greatly influenced by architecture of the Baroque era. He is famous for, among other achievements, the planning and creation of New Delhi in India (then part of the British Empire); for the Cenotaph in Whitehall, London; for the Monument to the Missing of the Battle of the Somme, at Thiepval, France; and for Queen Mary's Dolls' House, which is housed in Windsor Castle

➡ ***Windsor Castle***

MACDONALD, RAMSAY (1866–1937)

British prime minister (1924, 1929–31). MacDonald was elected to Parliament in 1906 and became leader of the new Labour Party. He lost this position when he took a stand against World War I, but was re-elected in 1922. He became prime minister in January 1924 but was forced to resign again in October the same year. After his second term in 1931 MacDonald left the Labout Party and formed a coalition government with the Conservatives and Liberals.

MACKINTOSH, CHARLES RENNIE (1868–1923)

Scottish artist, strongly associated with Glasgow. Mackintosh trained as an architect – one of his best-known buildings is the Glasgow School of Art – but was also fascinated by interior decor. His architectural projects (such as Hill House near Glasgow) were created homogenously, with Mackintosh designing the interiors as well. His catalogue of works includes watercolours of landscapes, sketches of nature and textile designs. Mackintosh was a member of the Glasgow Four, with J. Herbert MacNair and the artist sisters Frances and Margaret Macdonald. In 1900 Mackintosh married Margaret. The group exhibited in Britain and in Europe, alongside the Viennese Secessionists.

MACMILLAN, HAROLD (1894–1986)

British prime minister (1957–63). An MP from 1924, Macmillan was a critic of appeasement in the years before World War II. Under the Churchill government of the early 1950s he was minister of housing, defence and Chancellor of the Exchequer. Following Eden's resignation after the Suez Crisis, Macmillan became prime minister in 1957, winning an election in 1959 where he was closely associated with the famous phrase: 'You've never had it so good'. He encouraged the independence of many of Britain's overseas colonies with his 'Winds of Change' speech. Macmillan tried to get Britain into the European Economic Community but was vetoed by the French. He retired in October 1963 through ill health. His last year in office was marked by the turmoil of the Profumo affair.

MAGNA CARTA (1215)

The Great Charter sealed at Runnymede on 15 June 1215 by King John and barons that has become one of the most important constitutional documents in British political history. Angered by the king's foreign policy and his dictatorial approach, the barons tried to get codified constraints on Royal power. One of the provisions of the Magna Carta secured the right of justice for everyone. It failed, though, to prevent the first Barons' War, Copies of the original document can still be found in Salisbury and Lincoln Cathedrals and the British Library.

➡ *King John*

MAJOR, JOHN (b. 1943)

British prime minister (1990–97). Major took over as prime minister in 1990 when Margaret Thatcher resigned and led the Conservatives to a somewhat surprising victory at the 1992 General Election. He was first elected as an MP in 1979 and Thatcher made him chancellor of the Exchequer in

ABOVE Furniture by Mackintosh from Glasgow House
RIGHT King John signing the Magna Carta
FAR RIGHT John Major launches the citizens charter

October 1989. Wide divisions within his own party on the issue of Europe marked his time as prime minister. His party never recovered from the collapse of the British entry in the European Exchange Rate Mechanism in 1993 an event that became known as 'Black Wednesday'. His party was elected out of office in a stunning defeat by Tony Blair's Labour in May 1997.

➠ ***Conservative Party, Margaret Thatcher***

MALCOLM I (c. AD 886–954)

King of Scotland (AD 942–44). Malcolm's reign was troubled by recalcitrant Scots nobles and invasions and attacks on his Viking allies by King Edmund of Wessex. Edmund gave Malcolm Cumbria in exchange for his alliegance but his wars with his nobles continued. Malcolm died in battle against them in AD 954.

➠ ***Eric Bloodaxe, Edmund of Wessex***

MALCOLM III (c. 1031–93)

King of Scotland (1058–93). Known as Canmore, meaning 'Bighead'. Son of Duncan I. Malcolm established alliances with his father's old enemies, the Earls of Orkney and became an ally of Harold Haardrada of Norway, overlord of Orkney and the Western Isles. Malcolm supported the invasion of England in 1066 by Haardrada and Tostig, rebellious brother of King Harold II. Malcolm, however, was a Saxon sympathiser and his sister Margaret married Edgar the Atheling, Saxon claimant to the English throne. He aided Edgar in his unsuccessful bid to unseat the Norman William I. Subsequently, Malcolm raided the north of England, prompting William to invade Scotland and force Malcolm to recognise him as his overlord. After William's death in 1087, Malcolm prepared to invade England, but was defeated by William II in 1090. In 1093, Malcolm was ambushed and killed by Robert Mowbray, Earl of Northumberland.

➠ ***Donald III, Duncan I, William I, William II***

MALCOLM IV (1141–65)

King of Scotland (1153–65). Malcolm became king at the age of 11, but was treated as a vassal by Henry II of England. This roused fears of anglicisation among the Scots nobles. They rebelled in 1160 and 1164. With the aid of his Anglo-Norman barons, Malcolm suppressed both rebellions. He promised to become an impressive king, stronger than the nobles imagined, but had no chance to prove it. He died suddenly when he was just 23 years old.

➠ ***Henry II***

MARLOWE, CHRISTOPHER (c. 1564–93)

English playwright and poet, contemporary of Shakespeare. Marlowe took the dramatic world by storm with *Tamburlaine the Great*. His other plays include *The Jew of Malta* and *Dr Faustus*. Amongst his poems are 'The Passionate Shepherd' and 'Hero and Leander'. The details of his life are shady and it has been suggested he was a 'secret agent' for Elizabeth I. He died in a brawl in a pub in Deptford (reputedly over money), where he was living in an attempt to escape the plague.

➠ ***Elizabeth I, Plague, William Shakespeare***

MARSHAL, WILLIAM

British nobleman, advisor to the monarch in the thirteenth century. Marshal was a key advisor to King John at the time of the signing of the Magna Carta, where he counselled caution. He was the monarch's chief advisor from 1213. Prior to that he had been on the crusades with Richard I from 1183 to 1187. He also served under Henry III and expelled Louis of France from Britain.

➧ *King John*

MARSTON MOOR, BATTLE OF (1644)

Royalist defeat in the north (2 July 1644). 27,000 Parliamentarians and Scots under Thomas Fairfax and Oliver Cromwell attacked 18,000 Royalists under Prince Rupert. Rupert's cavalry were soundly beaten by Cromwell's Ironsides, although the Parliamentarian right was crushed. Under Cromwell's command the Royalists were driven from the field, losing 4,000 men. Parliament now had control of the north. Rupert's attempt to relieve York had failed; the Royalists were reduced to a handful of beleaguered garrisons in the north.

➧ ***Charles I, Oliver Cromwell, Battle of Edgehill, English Civil War***

MARY I (1516–58)

Queen of England (1553–58). Daughter of Henry VIII and Catherine of Aragon. Mary was their only surviving child. On becoming queen Mary set about re-establishing England as a Catholic country and the persecution of the Protestants during her reign has caused her to be dubbed 'Bloody Mary'. She was married to Philip II of Spain, whom she adored, and died believing she was about to produce the heir needed to maintain Catholicism in England.

Although Henry adored his daughter, he longed for a son to succeed him. After 1526, Henry's efforts to divorce Catherine inevitably involved Mary. Like her mother, she was kept in confinement and threatened with dishonour or death. Psychologically, the effect on Mary was devastating. However, she refused to abandoned her Roman Catholic faith or, for a long time, to declare herself illegitimate as Henry demanded. When she finally submitted and signed the necessary declaration, she never forgave herself. When she was re-admitted to her father's court, she was so terrified that she fainted at the sight of him.

Mary became the first Queen regnant of England in 1553 on the death of her brother Edward VI. John Dudley, Duke of Northumberland tried, but failed, to deny her the throne by substituting his own candidate, his daughter-in-law, Lady Jane Grey. As queen, Mary resolved to halt Protestant reforms, return England to the jurisdiction of the pope and restore Catholicism. She was fiercely resisted by her subjects. Mary's marriage to the Catholic Philip of Spain in 1554 was unpopular and caused violent public demonstrations. She twice imagined she was pregnant, but her hopes proved unfounded. Philip's interest in Mary, whom he found personally unattractive, revolved around the chance to use England's resources for Spain's wars in Europe. In an effort to impose Catholicism, Mary ordered the burning of some 300 Protestants, who became regarded as martyrs.Greeted with joy and celebration on her accession, Mary died in 1558, deserted by Philip, and vilified by her subjects. The day of her death, 17 November, was kept as a public celebration for many years.

➧ ***Catherine of Aragon, Edward VI, Elizabeth I, Henry VIII***

ABOVE The Battle of Marston Moor
FAR RIGHT TOP The Mary Rose

MARY II (1662–94)

Joint queen of England (1689–94) with her husband, William III. Mary was the direct heir of her deposed father, James II. She was content to leave the government of England to her husband but, to his great grief, died of smallpox in 1694. The couple had no children.

➧ ***Queen Anne, James II, William III***

MARY ROSE

Henry VIII's flagship. In 1982, after an 11-year project, the wreckage of the warship Mary Rose was raised from the seabed off Southsea, Hampshire. The vessel was Henry VIII's flagship but sank suddenly on 19 July 1545. Experiments have shown that modifications to the ship, and severe overloading, had made it capsize.

➜ ***Henry VIII***

MARY, QUEEN OF SCOTS (1542–87)

Queen of Scotland (1542–67). Mary became queen of Scotland aged six days. She was married three times: to the young king of France (1559–60); to Henry, Lord Darnley (1565–67); and to James Hepburn, Earl of Bothwell (1567–78). Although Mary permitted religious freedom in Scotland, her Catholic marriage to Lord Darnley angered the Scots nobles and alienated the Protestant English queen Elizabeth I. The nobles believed Mary was relying on favourites, like David Rizzio, her Italian secretary. He was murdered in 1566 with the co-operation of the jealous Lord Darnley. Mary was implicated in the killing of Darnley in 1567, which was believed to have been masterminded by James, Earl Bothwell. Bothwell was acquitted of the murder, but suspicions remained. Mary was totally discredited by these events, all the more so after she married Bothwell in May 1567. Mary and Bothwell fled but were soon captured. Bothwell afterwards escaped to Denmark, where he died mad in 1578. Mary was sent to Lochleven Castle, where she miscarried of twins in July 1567. The Scots nobles forced Mary to abdicate in favour of her son by Darnley, who became King James VI of Scotland and, after 1603, James I of England. Mary escaped and fled to England, to seek protection from Queen Elizabeth. Mary was kept under house arrest, but she was executed in 1587 for her involvement in several Catholic plots aimed at murdering Elizabeth and restoring England to Catholicism.

➜ ***Earl of Bothwell, Lord Darnley, Elizabeth I, James Hepburn, James VI***

MATILDA, EMPRESS (c. 1102–67)

Daughter of Henry I. The title 'Empress' came from her first marriage to Emperor Heinrich V of Germany. When the English barons renaged on their promise to Henry to support Matilda as Queen Regnant, she and her second husband Geoffrey of Anjou invaded England in 1139. This precipitated a civil war with the usurper King Stephen. The arrogant Matilda alienated the English and she abandoned her efforts to acquire the crown in 1148.

➜ ***Henry I, Henry II, Geoffrey Plantagenet, Stephen***

MELBOURNE, VISCOUNT (1779–1848)

British prime minister (1834, 1835–41). First elected as a Whig MP in 1806, Melbourne was viewed as a moderate though he supported suppression of radical and working-class anger. His first government was brief, falling through disunity of its members. But he was asked to form another government in 1835. It was a period of turbulence, economic depression and Chartist opposition as well as the accession of the new monarch, Queen Victoria. His wife Lady Caroline Ponsonby had a love affair with Lord Byron.

MERCIA, KINGDOM OF

Province of Ancient Britain. The Angles claimed three kingdoms: East Anglia, Northumbria and Mercia. Mercia lay in central England with its western perimeter bordered by Wales. It covered most of England between the Humber and the Thames, except East Anglia. In AD 633 the king of Mercia, Penda, defeated and killed Edwin, who had declared himself Overlord of Britain. Penda was assisted by the king of Wales, Cadwallon. He also defeated the Christian King Oswald of Northumbria in AD 642.

➡ *Anglo-Saxons*

METHODISTS

John Wesley's attempt to revive the Anglican Church. Wesley, an Anglican priest, began to preach, motivated by his personal salvation. His brother, Charles, wrote hymns and George Whitefield joined them. Methodists believe in the power of the Holy Spirit and value simplicity and spirituality. Although Wesley intended only to create a society within the Church of England, in 1795, four years after his death, Methodism and Anglicanism split. In the nineteenth century harsh economic conditions increased the appeal of Methodism's thriftiness and concern for social improvement.

➡ *Church of England, John and Charles Wesley*

METROPOLITAN POLICE (1829)

London's law-enforcement. The predecessors to the Metropolitan Police force were the Bow Street Runners, a body of men introduced in 1749 by Henry Fielding. London got its first effective police force however, in 1829, under Robert Peel as Home Secretary. Bobbies, or peelers, as they were known, proved so successful that they were introduced to other parts of the country from 1856. In 1878 the London Metropolitan Police force established its Criminal Investigations

Department (CID) at New Scotland Yard. Members of the CID are specialists at surveillance, detection and forensic science.

MILL, JOHN STUART (1806–73)

Philosopher and social reformer. His friend, Thomas Carlylye, encouraged Mill's idealism. Mill wrote extensively, including *A System of Logic*, *Principles of Political Economy* and *Subjection of Women*, which showed an interest in women's rights. Intellectual followers of Mills' utilitarian philosophy made moves towards the implementation of religious equality in the 1860s and 1870s. Consequently the Church of Ireland was disestablished and the Second Reform Bill opened universities to people of any religion.

➠ ***Church of Ireland***

MILLENARIANISM (1603)

Beliefs behind the Millenary Petition, 1603. The petition, signed by 1,000 Puritan ministers, was presented to James I requesting ceremonial changes to the Church of England; for example, the abolition of wedding rings and surplices. James, fancying himself a theologian, called the Hampton Court Conference to consider these demands.

➠ ***Hampton Court***

MILLENNIUM DOME (1999)

Exhibition centre in south-east London. The Millennium Dome was built to celebrate the year 2000. It opened on 31 December 1999 and closed exactly a year later. Despite the hype and spectacular exhibits, the Dome was unsuccessful. It did, however, regenerate the formerly downtrodden area in which it was built.

ABOVE John Milton

MILTON, JOHN (1608–74)

English poet and writer; famous for *Paradise Lost* and *Paradise Regained*. Amongst his works are *Samson Agonistes* and *Areopagitica* (calling for freedom of the press). He wrote many controversial pamphlets: attacking the monarchy; calling for relaxation of the divorce laws; and on matters of religion. He went blind in 1651 but continued to write, dictating his works. Milton was an outspoken follower of Oliver Cromwell, who gave him a job in his government. After the Restoration Milton's works were publicly burned.

➠ ***Oliver Cromwell, Restoration***

MODEL PARLIAMENT (1295)

Parliament summoned in November 1295 in order to allow Edward I to obtain money for wars. It got its name because of the make-up of the Parliament that was supposed to be the most representative ever assembled, at that stage. By today's standards it does not impress in those terms as it was made up only of earls, barons, bishops and knights. Around 150 men attended the Parliament in total.

➧ *Edward I*

MONMOUTH'S REBELLION (1685)

Short-lived rebellion against the rule of James II. The rebellion was so called because it was led by the Duke of Monmouth. The illegitimate son of Charles II, Monmouth believed the throne was rightfully his. After being forced into exile he returned with 150 supporters and landed at Lyme Regis to denounce the king as a usurper of the throne. Supporters from across the West Country joined him but his luck ran out at Bridgewater where he was cornered by the king's troops and captured. His troops were slaughtered and Monmouth was tried and executed. Survivors were punished severely at the trials that became known as the Bloody Assizes, presided over by the bloodthirsty Judge Jeffreys.

➧ *Bloody Assizes, James II*

MONMOUTH, JAMES SCOTT, 1ST DUKE OF (1649–85)

Illegitimate son of Charles II who tried to claim the English throne. Monmouth made his name as a military commander and was thought to be extremely popular as the Protestant candidate for the throne. However his claim was never legitimised and he in 1685 he led a rebellion to try and remove James II. It ended in disaster with his troops being slaughtered. He was captured, tried and executed.

➧ *James II*

MONTFORT, SIMON DE (1208–65)

English baron who opposed the power of the royals and led the opposition to Henry III. De Montfort was born in France but came to England in 1230 and claimed the title of Earl of Leicester through his English grandmother. He was married to the sister of Henry III, Eleanor. Initially he served the king but later emerged as leader of the reforming barons and helped draw up the Provisions of Oxford to allow constitutional reform. However this did not head off conflict and the barons went into armed revolt. In 1264 he captured Henry and his son Edward becoming the virtual ruler of England. He summoned a parliament, which included, for the first time, women. However Edward escaped and defeated and killed Simon.

➧ *Henry III*

MONTGOMERY, FIELD MARSHAL (1887–1976)

British military leader. Montgomery joined the army in 1908 and served as captain during World War I. He replaced Auchinleck in 1942 as commander of the British Eighth Army in Africa. He defeated Rommel in the second Battle of El Alamein, Cyrenaica and Tripolitania and Battle of the Mareth Line, 1943. He became field marshal and was involved in the D-Day invasion of June 1944. He also masterminded Operation Market Garden in September of the same year. Later Viscount and Chief of the Imperial General Staff and served as Deputy Supreme Commander of NATO (1951–58).

➧ *World War II, Battles of El Alamein*

MORE, THOMAS (1478–1535)

English author and politician. More came to prominence during the reign of Henry VIII, serving as lord chancellor. He fell out with the king, however, over the issue of religious policy, deeply disapproving of his marriage to Anne Boleyn. He was executed in 1535.

➜ *Henry VIII*

MORRIS, WILLIAM (1834–96)

English artist, founder of the Arts and Crafts Movement. Morris was a painter, designer and craftsman, as well as a political activist (Socialist), poet and novelist. In addition Morris was a businessman, setting up Morris & Co, which produced textiles, furniture, stained glass and ceramic tiles. Early in his career, he was strongly associated with the Pre-Raphaelite Movement, especially Dante Rossetti, and with the painter Edward Coley Burne-Jones. In his later career, Morris established the Merton Abbey workshops based on Utopian ideals of shared labour and shared finances. Morris was married to Jane Burden, who became famous as a Pre-Raphaelite model.

➜ *Arts and Crafts Movement, Pre-Raphaelites*

MORTIMER, ROGER, EARL OF MARCH (c. 1287–1330)

Roger Mortimer took part in a rebellion against Edward II in the Welsh marches, but escaped from the Tower of London to Paris in 1324. There, he became the lover of Queen Isabella, the king's estranged wife and later aided her in the overthrow of her husband in 1327. The subsequent rule of Mortimer and Isabella in England was corrupt and incompetent. Isabella's son, Edward III, had Mortimer seized in 1330 and executed.

➜ *Edward II, Edward III*

MOSLEY, OSWALD (1896–1980)

British fascist. Mosley was an MP from 1918 until 1931 serving, in turn, the Conservative Party, standing as an Independent and the Labour Party. Following the trend of right-wing policies in Europe, Mosley created the British Union of Fascists in 1932. The party was anti-Jewish, condemned free speech but was a supporter of the Commonwealth. An admirer of Mussolini's, Mosley's attempts to create disorder largely failed though there were clashes with left-wing extremists in East London in the 1930s. Mosley was imprisoned during World War II.

MOUNTBATTEN, LORD LOUIS (1900–79)

Earl Mountbatten of Burma. Son of Prince Louis of Battenberg. A man of remarkable drive and ability, Mountbatten joined the Royal Navy and distinguished himself during World War II as Supreme Allied Commander in South-East Asia (1943) and the last British Viceroy of India (1946-1947). Subsequently, he became First Lord of the Admiralty (1949), but clashed with the government over British actions at Suez in 1956. He was murdered by the IRA in 1979.

➜ *IRA, House of Windsor*

ABOVE Roger Mortimer is arrested and taken to the Tower
TOP LEFT Simon de Montfort

NAPOLEONIC WARS (1803–15)

Campaign waged by Europe against Napoleon's expansionist policies. Distrust between Britain and France sparked off a series of wars dragging most European states into conflict.

Napoleon's armies would fight from Portugal to Moscow. The Treaty of Amiens that aimed to restore lost territories after the French Revolutionary Wars required England to return Malta to France. England refused and war broke out. The English captured many French colonies but Napoleon aimed to cut off English trade with Europe and invade England. In 1804 Napoleon was crowned Emperor and proclaimed himself king of Italy annexing some Austrian territory, bringing Austria into the coalition against France, along with Britain and Russia. Spain allied itself with France. Threats of French invasions were halted by Nelson's victory at Trafalgar (21 October 1805) but Napoleon had defeated the Austrians and Russians at Ulm (20 October) and Austerlitz (3 December). In 1806 Napoleon created the Confederation of the Rhine, uniting the German states. From 1806–12 the Russo-Turkish War raged, the Turks siding with the French. Prussia joined Russia and declared war on France (6 October 1806) but they were defeated six days later at Jena-Auerstadt; the French captured Berlin. On 21 November the Berlin Decree blockaded British trade with Europe.

After defeats in 1807 Russia and Prussia allied with France and occupied Portugal. In 1808 the British invaded Portugal driving the French out of the country and Spain. In 1809 Austria allied with Britain, losing two battles, forcing them out again. In 1812 Napoleon invaded Russia and by 1813 most of Europe was against him. He won his last battle at Dresden (27 August 1813) but now Europe was poised to invade France. He abdicated on 11 April 1814 and was exiled to Elba. He returned for 100 days culminating in the Battle of Waterloo and his final defeat. The Treaty of Paris (20 November 1815), formally ended hostilities.

➤ ***Battle of Trafalgar, Battle of Waterloo, Duke of Wellington***

NASEBY, BATTLE OF (1645)

Battle of the English Civil War (14 June 1645). After sacking the city of Leicester, the Royalist army was chased and cornered near Market Harborough by 13,000 Parliamentarians under Fairfax. The 9,000 Royalists under Charles I and Prince Rupert broke the Parliamentarians but Cromwell meanwhile had overwhelmed their infantry. The Royalists lost 5,000 men and all their artillery.

➤ ***Oliver Cromwell, English Civil War***

NATIONAL COVENANT (1638)

Scottish anti-Laudian oath. The National Covenant of February 1638 aimed, via Presbyterian government, to assert the rights of Parliament rather than those of Charles I in the Scottish Church. As the agreement urged continued loyalty to Charles most of the nobles and a third of the clergy in Scotland signed it. Charles's disapproval of the abolition of Episcopalianism led to the first Bishops' War. By the Solemn League and Covenant, 1643, the English Parliament was allied with the now more extreme Presbyterian covenanters; more

LEFT French troops hail Napoleon

FAR RIGHT Nelson boarding a captured ship during the battle of St Vincent

moderate covenanters remained loyal to Charles and war resulted. With the restoration of Episcopalianism in 1662 the covenanters were persecuted. With the accession of William and Mary in 1689, the Covenanters' mission was complete and Presbyterianism in place.

Covenant Martyrs, Presbyterianism

NATIONAL DEBT (1693)

Debt incurred by the government of a country. In Britain the first national debt was owed in 1693 when the government issued stocks to raise £1 million. The Bank of England, under the Treasury, is the body which deals with national debt in Britain. There has been a direct historical relationship between national debt and warfare in Britain, simply because wars cost a lot of money. World Wars I and II pushed the British national debt up considerably. Since then other factors, such as keeping the economy buoyant by overseas borrowing, have increased national debt.

NATIONAL HEALTH SERVICE (1948)

Government-run public health service. In 1946, following World War II, the National Health Service (NHS) Act of Parliament was passed, under the Labour government, as a scheme to provide comprehensive free medicine to a beleaguered nation. The NHS was brought into operation in July 1948, with the Ministry of Health assuming direct responsibility for hospital services. Administration was entrusted to regional and local offices. Any British national has the right to free medical attention under the NHS without the need for insurance. The National Health Service is paid for primarily by the tax payer and has now become part of the British cultural tradition.

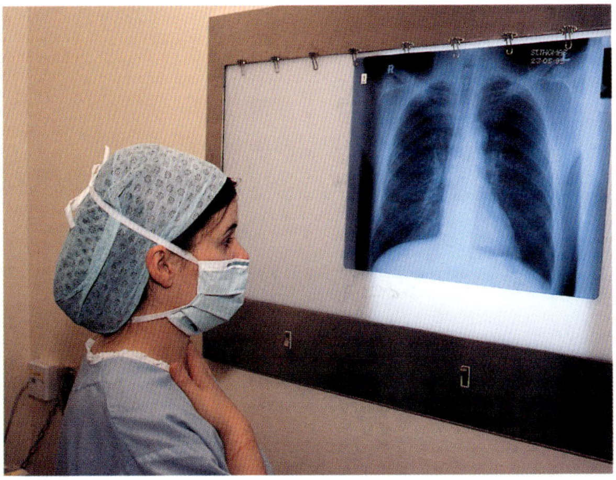

NELSON, ADMIRAL HORATIO (1758–1805)

British Admiral during the Napoleonic Wars. Nelson joined the Royal Navy at the age of 12 in 1770 and was a captain by 1778. When the French Revolutionary Wars broke out in 1793 he began his distinguished naval career by defeating the Spanish at Cape St Vincent (1797) and crushed the French fleet in Abukir Bay (1798). He crippled the Danish fleet at the Battle of Copenhagen (1801) and by this time he had lost the sight of one eye (1794) and his right arm (1797). Nelson was by now a baron and a viscount. In 1803 Nelson blockaded the French at Toulon but they escaped and united with the Spanish fleet. At the Battle of Trafalgar (21 October 1805) he cornered these navies but was killed, not before knowing of his victory, and uttering the immortal 'England expects that every man will do his duty'. Nelson had saved Britain once more.

Napoleonic Wars, Battle of Trafalgar

NEVILLE, RICHARD (1428–71)

English politician, known as the 'Kingmaker'. Originally he supported Richard, Duke of York, but after his defeat was forced to flee abroad. He then returned and helped Edward, Duke of York become king. He wielded enormous power in his post as lord chamberlain until he fell out of the king's favour. He was then instrumental in restoring the deposed Henry VI to the throne,

Edward IV, Henry VI, Wars of the Roses

NEW LANARK (1800)

Utopian industrial community. In 1800, at the age of 29, Robert Owen became the manager of a mill in a place called New Lanark, Scotland. Owen used his position to create a model community which fulfilled his socialist ideals. He achieved this by improving working and housing conditions for the employees in his charge and provided schools for their children. Others became inspired by his vision of 'villages of co-operation' and he stimulated the creation of the co-operative movement which was established in 1844.

Robert Owen

NEW TOWNS (1945)

Post-war style of town reconstruction. Following World War II Britain had a housing shortage problem on its hands which required the building of new towns. The hearts of many British cities were either destroyed by bombs or in a state of urban decay. This left millions of people refugees in their own homeland. The most immediate solution was to build entire towns from scratch, using the American model of regular street patterns and series of self-contained neighbourhoods. Classic examples of this are Milton Keynes and Stevenage. In 1976 the new town planning policy was dropped in favour of inner city rejuvenation projects.

ABOVE Robert Owen's New Lanark community
RIGHT Isaac Newton discovers the refraction of light
FAR RIGHT Florence Nightingale

NEWCASTLE, THOMAS PELHAM-HOLMES, DUKE OF (1693–1768)

British prime minister (1754–56 and 1757–62). As a Whig politiciam Newcastle was secretary of state for over 30 years before succeeding his brother Henry as prime minister. He resigned after his first term in office after criticism of his policies in the Seven Years' War, but later returned.

Henry Pelham, Seven Years' War

NEWTON, ISAAC (1642–1727)

English physicist and mathematician, most famous for developing his theory of gravity. Newton was born in Lincolnshire, on Christmas Day; a fragile, sickly child unexpected to live beyond infancy. His delicate health led to most of his childhood being spent in reading. In 1661 he entered Cambridge University where he studied a variety of scientific and mathematical subjects, including astronomy, as well as ancient languages. Among his discoveries, Newton demonstrated that white light is made up of several different colours of light, made headway in the study of differential calculus, created the basis for celestial mechanics and invented the world's first reflecting telescope. In 1687 his book *Mathematical Principles of Natural Philosophy* was published and secured his contemporary reputation as Britain's foremost physicist. The book contained his theories of the law of gravitation, famously discovered by Newton after watching an apple fall from a tree.

Enlightenment

NIGHTINGALE, FLORENCE (1820–1910)

English philanthropist and medical reformer. In 1854 Florence Nightingale arrived in the Crimea with a staff of nurses to set up a field hospital for the wounded British soldiers fighting in the war there. Conditions were so inefficient and unhygienic that 42 per cent of the injured were dying from infections to their wounds. Nightingale and her team improved the situation so considerably that the death rate fell to a mere two per cent. Florence Nightingale won great praise for her achievements in the Crimea and dedicated her life to raising the status of nursing, receiving the Order of Merit in 1907.

➡ *Crimean War*

NINE YEARS' WAR (1688–97)

War between England and France. This war is also known as either King William's War or the War of the Grand Alliance. William of Orange became William III of England in 1688. He hoped to make England an active ally in his struggle against France. The French Louis XIV supported James II, the Roman Catholic claimant to the throne. The war saw Louis XIV supporting James II in numerous attempts to regain the throne. The Grand Alliance was aimed at forcing France back to borders that had been agreed as early as 1648. While the Anglo-Dutch reigned supreme at sea, Louis won three battles in the Netherlands but could not make any progress in Germany. It soon became clear that neither side would achieve a victory and the Peace of Ryswick was signed in September 1697. The peace did not deal with the problems of North America where the French and the English had fought alongside their respective Native American allies and included an unsuccessful English attempt to take Quebec. This was the first of a series of wars fought between England and France to control the continent, otherwise known as the French and Indian Wars.

NORMAN CONQUEST (1066)

Struggle for the English throne. Harold was shipwrecked in Normandy in 1064 and secured his release by pledging his allegiance to William, Duke of Normandy. When Edward the Confessor died childless the English Royal Council elected Harold king. With the sanction of Pope Alexander II, William landed his army at Pevensey on 28 September 1066 and defeated Harold at Hastings. He then proceeded to London, brushing aside all resistance and was crowned King on Christmas Day. The Danes supported Saxon rebels in the north but in a series of campaigns the Norman Conquest was complete by 1070.

➡ ***Battle of Hastings, Norman Dynasty, William I***

NORMAN DYNASTY

French royal dynasty that conquered England under William of Normandy. The Norman dynasty originated in the Duchy of Normandy in northern France where a Viking i.e. 'Northman' chieftain called Rollo was granted lands in the early tenth century.

In 1035, the eight-year old William, illegitimate son of Robert the Magnificent, became Duke of Normandy. In 1051, the duke was apparently promised the English throne by Edward the Confessor, who, it seems, made the same promise to his kinsman, Harold Godwinson. On Edward's death, in January 1066, Harold proclaimed himself king. In October, William invaded England, killed Harold at the Battle of Hastings and was crowned King as William I, first monarch of the new Norman dynasty.

Although the dynasty lasted less than 90 years, the Normans transformed England. They introduced the feudal system and eliminated the existing Anglo-Saxon aristocracy, replacing them with Normans in all the richest and most powerful offices of state. William I died in 1087 and was succeeded by his son William II, also known as William Rufus. Rufus was killed in a hunting accident in 1100, and though his elder brother Robert, Duke of Normandy, had a claim to the English throne, his youngest brother, Henry, pre-empted Robert and was crowned as Henry I. The death of his only son in 1120, obliged Henry to elicit a vow from his barons that they would support his daughter, Matilda, as Queen Regnant after him. However, after Henry's death in 1135, Matilda was pre-empted by her cousin, Stephen of Blois, who usurped the throne. Civil war followed but, in 1153, King Stephen accepted Matilda's son, Henry, as his heir. Henry came to the throne as King Henry II in 1154, not as a Norman monarch but as the first of the new Plantagenet (Angevin) dynasty.

➡ ***Domesday Book, Harold II, Henry I, Henry II, William I, Empress Matilda, William II***

NORTH ATLANTIC TREATY ORGANISATION (NATO) (1949)

Military alliance. Formed in 1949 and originally composed of 12 countries from Europe and North America including Britain, France, Canada and the United States. Greece, Turkey and Germany later became members. Originally it was a Cold War organisation and thus was composed of countries from the west. However, since the collapse of the Soviet Union, it has remodelled itself as a 'peacekeeping' body. NATO sanctioned and led the air raids over Kosovo in 1999.

➡ ***World War II***

NORTH, LORD FREDERICK (1732–92)

British prime minister (1770–82). Most notably this was the time of the American Revolution. His rule was marked by loyalty to the king, George III, even though he had reservations about the policy the king was taking. He introduced the Intolerable Acts in 1774 that led to the closure of Boston Harbour as retaliation for the Boston Tea Party in 1773.

➜ ***American Revolution, George III***

NORTHERN IRELAND

Country formed by six counties in the north east of Ireland. The counties are Antrim, Armagh, Down, Fermanagh, Londonderry (Derry) and Tyrone. The Government of Ireland Act 1920 established the country. Following the peace progress in the 1990s and the Good Friday Agreement, Northern Ireland has once again become an autonomous region within the United Kingdom with its own Assembly and limited powers to make law. This followed almost 30 years of direct rule from Westminster initiated during the height of the troubles. Prior to that, from 1921 to 1972, there was a Parliament at Stormont. The government was always composed of a majority of Ulster Unionists, a party that reflected the wishes of the majority Protestant community. The history of Northern Ireland has been shaped by British rule there over the centuries. During the 1960s a civil rights movement was vociferous in trying to eradicate the discrimination among the Catholic minority. This discrimination was felt most keenly in jobs and housing. Protestant reaction to the movement led to the intervention of the British Army and Stormont was suspended in 1972 pre-signalling a rise in sectarian attacks.

➜ ***Good Friday Agreement***

NORTHUMBRIA, KINGDOM OF

Province of ancient Britain. Northumbria was a kingdom which comprised the north-east of England and south-east Scotland and was governed by t he Angles. In the sixth century Northumbria comprised the two lesser kingdoms of Bernicia and Deira, but by the seventh century they had been united. In AD 664 King Oswy of Northumbria asserted the supremacy of the Roman Church in Britain by calling the Synod of Whitby. In AD 827 Northumbria fell under the Overlordship of Wessex and by AD 886 was subject to Danelaw following invasion by the Danes.

➜ ***Anglo-Saxons***

ABOVE John Hume and Seamus Mallon following the announcement of the verdict in the Referendum on the Good Friday Stormont peace agreement

O'CONNELL, DANIEL (1775–1847)

Irish nationalist and barrister. A central figure in Catholic Ireland's struggle for liberation from the British. O'Connell sought to improve the rights of the Catholics by non-violent means. He is revered in Irish history as the 'Liberator'. O'Connell established the Catholic Association in 1823 that sought to gain Irish emancipation from Britain. It survived on duties paid by members from of the Catholic community. This became known as the Catholic tax. O'Connell also successfully achieved his goal of getting Catholics the right to sit in Parliament. He was one of the first to benefit from this. In 1830, a year after the right was granted, O'Connell was elected as MP for County Clare. His popularity waned due to his commitment to a peaceful solution, Many at the time thought the only way to secure a political solution was through violent means if necessary.

➠ *George IV*

ODO, BISHOP OF BAYEUX (11TH CENTURY)

French bishop and half-brother of William the Conqueror. Odo was also thought to be the man to commission the Bayeux Tapestry. After the Norman Conquest of England in 1066, Odo was made Earl of Kent. When William was out of England, Odo acted as the King's regent. His relationship with William was not always good. He was imprisoned in 1082 until William's death in 1087. He returned to France in 1088 and died on a crusade with Robert, Duke of Normandy.

➠ *Norman Conquest, William I*

OFFA'S DYKE (AD 757)

Defensive network running frm the mouth of the River Dee to that of the River Severn. Built by King Offa, the Anglo-Saxon ruler of Mercia.

OIL CRISIS (1970s)

Worldwide recession due to inflated oil prices. In 1960 a body was established called the Organisation of Petroleum-Exporting Countries (OPEC). Its members included most of the Arab nations in the Middle East. Through OPEC these countries were able to co-ordinate the price and supply policies of oil to consumer countries. In 1967 the Arab/Israeli war began and Western involvement prompted Arab nations to react. By the early 1970s they had triggered a worldwide recession by demanding inflated prices for oil. This became known as the 'oil crisis' as it threatened the infrastructure of consumer countries. By the 1980s demand for their oil had lessened and the crisis ended.

OWEN, ROBERT (1771–1858)

Welsh social reformer. Robert Owen was one of the first people to promote the ideas of socialism. Socialism is essentially a movement aiming to remove any class structure from society by giving communities private ownership of the means of production, distribution and exchange of goods. The members of the community should therefore enjoy social equality. Robert Owen set out to show that socialism could be put into practice by establishing a model community in New Lanark, Scotland. The success of this project led to the establishment of the co-operative movement, but socialism has never secured a true foothold in Britain.

New Lanark

OWEN, WILFRED (1893–1918)

English poet, famous for his war poetry. Owen, who worked as a tutor before the war, was invalided out in 1917 with shell shock. He was returned to the fighting in 1918 and killed seven days before the Armistice. He was awarded the Military Cross. Most of Owen's poetry was not published until after his death, when his works were tirelessly lauded by his great friend and fellow poet, Siegfried Sassoon. His poems include 'Anthem for Doomed Youth' and 'Dulce et Decorum Est'.

World War I

OXFORD MOVEMENT (1833)

Catholic revival. In 1833 Anglican divine and poet John Keble (1792–1866) gave a sermon at Oxford, attempting to revive Catholic religion in the Church of England – the Anglican communion. From that point on the Catholic Revival or Tractarian Movement became popularly known as the Oxford Movement. The Oxford Movement had a transforming effect on Anglican communion, and emerged as Anglo-Catholicism, as opposed to Roman Catholicism which is far more conservative in its doctrines, rituals and traditions.

OXFORD UNIVERSITY (1100s)

English university. The most ancient seat of learning in Britain is Oxford University, which was established through the 1100s. The founding of the oldest existing college is dated to 1249. Oxford University comprises some 39 colleges which are run by the Hebdomadal Council and Curators. Matters that fall under the common university banner are managed by the Houses of Congregation and Convocation. The university owns a number of academic buildings of note. They include the Bodleian Libraries, the Sheldonian Theatre and Divinity School. The university suffered land confiscation during the Reformation, 1534, but Henry VIII's daughter Elizabeth I reorganised the situation in 1571.

BELOW Oxford University
LEFT Daniel O'Connell

PAINE, THOMAS (1737–1809)

American republican supporter. Thomas Paine was a left-wing political writer and activist. In 1774 he arrived in America and published a pamphlet entitled 'Common Sense' in 1776, an influential piece of republican propaganda. Paine fought on the side of the colonists during the American Revolution, or War of Independence, won in 1783. He returned to England in 1787 to write *The Rights of Man*, published 1791. Indicted for treason in 1792, he escaped to France.

PALE, THE

English enclave in Ireland. During the fourteenth and fifteenth centuries Irish chieftains recovered much of the territory invaded by Anglo-Normans in 1167. The enclave of land still under English control, which ran 50 miles inland from Dublin, was known as the Pale. The Pale remained under English rule and subsequently proved the foothold needed for the Tudors to impose the Reformation and English law on Ireland. They adopted a policy of conquest, confiscation of land and settlement by Englishmen.

➡ ***Elizabeth I***

PALMERSTON, HENRY JOHN TEMPLE, 3RD VISCOUNT (1784–1865)

British prime minister (1855–58, 1859–65). Originally a Tory, Palmerston broke with the party in 1830 and became foreign secretary for the Whigs. In his time he saw through a number of conflicts, including the Indian Mutiny and the Second Opium War.

PANKHURST, EMMELINE (1858–1928)

English suffragette. At the start of the twentieth century women were not allowed to vote in political elections. In 1903 Emmeline Pankhurst founded the Women's Social and Political Union to address the situation. Pankhurst launched the militant suffragette campaign in 1906, involving the organisation of protests, which included hunger strikes by imprisoned campaigners, herself among them. Her daughters, Christabel and Sylvia, were keen supporters of her activities. Women finally received the right to vote in the year of her death.

➡ ***Suffragettes***

PARIS, TREATY OF (1259)

Treaty between the French and English monarchies which formalised the loss of large parts of the Angevin empire under King John. The two kings signing the treaty were Louis IX of France and Henry III of England. Henry, by signing the treaty renounced his claims to large parts of France.

➡ ***Henry III, King John***

PARLIAMENT (13TH CENTURY)

Legislature of the British political system. In all Parliament consists of the Monarchy, the House of Lords and the House of Commons. Its base is in Westminster, London. It emerged from the Curia Regis in the thirteenth century. Parliament has taken many forms during the hundreds of years since. There has been the Barebones Parliament, the Long Parliament, the Short Parliament and the Model Parliament.

Throughout this time its meetings were irregular, nothing like today's Parliament and it met for special occasions such as to raise taxes for wars. Even after the events of the Glorious Revolution, Parliament's powers were still limited. Because of the power of the monarch, and the fact that the vote was extended only to landowners, Parliament's powers were limited up until the nineteenth century. But as the franchise extended, through the Reform Acts in the nineteenth centuries, the Lower House, the House of Commons, became more representative of the country as a whole and Parliament's power increased. The single most important act as far as the House of Commons was concerned was the

1911 Parliamentary Act which assured its supremacy over the House of Lords. Its prominence was helped in the latter half of the century by the beginning of radio broadcasts in 1978 and live television broadcasts from the House of Lords in 1986 and the House of Commons in 1989. In the past decade there has been speculation that its powers have been waning as the country's most important law-making body and has instead just become a rubber-stamping body whose importance has been bypassed by the desire of politicians to make announcements to the media before Parliament.

PARNELL, CHARLES (1846–91)

Irish nationalist. Parnell seemed an unlikely nationalist. He was a Protestant Anglo-Irish landowner but he proved a strong supporter of Irish rights. He was elected as an MP in 1875 and used the tactic of filibustering to try and draw awareness to the plight of the Irish. He was the first president of the Irish Land League and was arrested for inciting agrarian violence in 1881. He was a member of the Irish Home Rule Association and sided with Gladstone's Liberals when the Irish held the balance of power in parliament.

➜ ***Michael Davitt, Land League***

PARR, CATHERINE (1512–48)

Sixth and last wife of Henry VIII. Twice married before she wed the king in 1543, Catherine Parr was a kindly, tactful woman who created a calm, domestic atmosphere for Henry and his three children in the last four years of his life. After his death in 1547, Catherine married Thomas, Lord Seymour, who had been her suitor before she wed Henry. She died after giving birth to a daughter in 1548.

➜ ***Edward VI, Elizabeth I, Henry VIII, Mary I***

PASSCHENDAELE (1917)

Third battle of Ypres (31 July–10 November 1917). After the British took the village of Messines overlooking the German lines on June 7 a major offensive was planned. Persistent rain and artillery barrages made the battlefield a swamp. As the attacks went in the Germans slaughtered thousands with their machine guns and mustard gas. After months the Canadians captured Passchendaele. At a cost of 250,000 men the allies had gained just eight kilometres.

➜ ***World War I***

LEFT Emmeline Pankhurst is arrested
ABOVE A shell bursting, Passchendale

PATRICK, ST (5TH CENTURY)

Patron saint of Ireland. Patrick, a Romanized Briton, lived near the Severn until the Irish enslaved him. During these six years as a herdsman Patrick was converted, escaped back to England, then felt compelled to return to Ireland. He was at least partly responsible for the conversion of the Picts and Anglo-Saxons, but his English ecclesiastical superiors disliked him. By the seventh century the legends, that Patrick drove the snakes out of Ireland and used the shamrock (consequently the national flower of Ireland) to explain the Trinity, were prevalent. His humble diary, *Confessio*, contributed to his long-lasting popularity. His feast day is 17 March.

➡ Anglo-Saxons

PEASANTS' REVOLT (1381)

Uprising against the new poll tax. In June 1381 Richard II introduced a new poll tax in an attempt to sort out the economy following the Black Death (1348–49) which had seen between a third and half of the British population die from bubonic plague. Two previous poll taxes, in 1377 and 1379, had already been introduced but the new one was a threefold increase. The peasants of Britain, who still laboured under the system of serfdom and feudalism, were prompted to revolt in protest. Riots broke out all over England.

Two men – Wat Tyler and John Ball – emerged as rebel leaders and marched on London where they plundered and ransacked parts of the city. Richard, still only a teenager, attempted to appease the mob by announcing concessions but order was not restored until Tyler had been murdered. The king's concessions were then revoked and the revolt suppressed.

➡ ***Richard II, Wat Tyler***

ABOVE John Ball preaches to the Peasants
RIGHT The Peterloo Massacre

PEEL, SIR ROBERT (1788–1850)

British Prime Minister. Peel first entered parliament in 1809 and was a minister a year later. He served as Chief Secretary for Ireland from 1812 to 1818 and became Home Secretary in 1822. In this position, he became famous for a number of administrative and judicial reforms. He instituted the Metropolitan Police (or 'Peelers') in 1829. His career became steeped in controversy from 1829 when, against both his previous reputation as a hard-line Protestant and also the strong views of a majority in the Tory party, he persuaded Wellington to grant Roman Catholic Emancipation. He became leader of the party in 1834 and thereafter briefly Prime Minister in 1834-5. During this period he issued the Tamworth Manifesto which committed his party to a policy of judicious reform of 'proved abuses'. Some have seen this as marking the transition from the Tory to the Conservative parties. As prime minister from 1841-6, he instituted radical changes to the financial structure of the state, introducing income tax for the first time in peacetime, reducing or removing many protective tariffs and helping to pave the way for the long period of prosperity known as the 'mid-Victorian boom'. Repealing the Corn Laws in 1846, however, split his party and led to the end of his government. The Conservatives would not win another election for almost thirty years and Peel's career ended in controversy. He died as the result of a riding accident in 1850.

➡ ***Metropolitan Police***

PELHAM, HENRY (1696–1754)

British prime minister (1743–54). Pelham was from a well-to-do family and was first elected as an MP from 1717. He gained his reputation for his expert management of Parliament although he was considered to be a dull character. He led the 'Broad-Bottom Administration', so-called because of the broad political factions within it. His brother, the Duke of Newcastle was also a leading figure in this administration.

PEPYS, SAMUEL (1633–1703)

English diarist. Pepys is famous for his extensive diaries, covering the years 1660–69, which show life in London during the time of the Plague of 1665 and the Great Fire of London in 1666. His diary was not intended for publication. He worked as a secretary in the household of Sir Edward Montagu; he also worked as a clerk for the Navy and the Admiralty. His diary ends in 1669, the year his eyesight failed.

➠ ***Great Fire of London, Plague***

PERCEVAL, SPENCER (1762–1812)

British prime minister (1809–12). Initially Chancellor of the Exchequer, Perceval rose to become prime minister in 1809. He was assassinated three years later.

PERCY, HENRY (1364–1403)

Known as 'Hotspur'. A member of a very powerful north of England family, son of Sir Henry Percy, 1st Earl of Northumberland. An active military commander, he fought against the Scots in 1388. He supported Henry IV in his usurpation of the English throne in 1399, and joined his father to defeat a Scots invasion in 1402. Henry ordered the ransom of the Percys' prisoners, at which they rebelled against him. Hotspur marched to Wales to join the rebel Welsh prince Owain Glendower, but was intercepted and killed in battle by Henry's forces at Shrewsbury.

➠ ***Owen Glendower, Henry IV***

PETERLOO MASSACRE (1819)

Name given to the killing of protestors at a rally (16 August 1819). During an open-air meeting on parliamentary reform at St. Peter's Fields, Manchester, on 16 August 1819, the gathering was suddenly charged by infantry and cavalry. The British government had seen the meeting as a threat and over reacted. Eleven people died and many more were injured in what would become known as the 'Peterloo Massacre' an allusion to the Battle of Waterloo, such was the horror of the British public. The massacre would lead to an attempt to overthrow the government by the Cato Street Conspirators (1820), who planned to murder Viscount Castlereagh and his ministers on 20 February.

➠ ***Cato Street Conspiracy***

PHILBY, KIM (1912–88)

British spy. Kim Philby, Anthony Blunt, Guy Burgess and Donald Maclean all became communists whilst studying at Cambridge University. They ultimately formed an espionage ring as double agents between Britain and USSR during the early part of the Cold War, between East and West. Philby joined the KGB in 1963.

PHILIP OF SPAIN (1527–98)

King of Spain. Philip was first involved with England in 1554, when he married Mary I. He was less interested in her than in an alliance with England and the use of her resources for Spain's wars in Europe. After Mary's death in 1558, he proposed marriage to her half-sister and successor Elizabeth I, but was refused. Philip actively encouraged the Catholic plots to destroy Elizabeth and place Mary, Queen of Scots on the English throne. In 1588, the year after Mary's execution, Philip sent the Spanish Armada to England as part of a plan of invasion. It failed.

➠ ***Elizabeth I, Mary I, Mary, Queen of Scots, Spanish Armada***

PILGRIM FATHERS (1620)

Name given to the Puritans who left England and established the first English settlement in the New World. In 1620 the Mayflower set sail from Plymouth bound for the New World. Onboard were 102 people of whom fewer than 25 were Puritan refugees. The journey became known as the voyage of the Pilgrim Fathers. They landed in North America three months later and founded New Plymouth, Massachusetts.

➨ *James II, Mayflower*

PILGRIMAGE OF GRACE (1536)

Anti-Reformation uprising in northern England. Henry VIII and Thomas Cromwell's policies of increased central government and taxes and the Dissolution of the Monasteries led to uprisings. In October 1536 Aske took York and soon had 30,000 supporters. Thomas Howard delayed the rebels by false negotiations. On 2 December the rebels named their demands at Pontefract, namely that the papacy be restored and royal influence be limited. Howard vaguely agreed and the rebels consequently dispersed. In January and February 1537 the riots re-emerged, this time under government control: 220-250 rioters were executed, including Aske.

➨ *Robert Aske, Henry VIII*

PIRACY

Piracy was first practised by buccaneers in the Caribbean. Walter Raleigh (1552–1618) and Francis Drake (1540–96) were two famous British pirates who went on to achieve fame as ocean-going explorers. The heyday of piracy in the Atlantic fell between the 1650s and 1720s. There may have been as many as 2,000 pirates at any given moment during this period. The British Navy hanged more than 400 pirates between 1716–26.

➨ *Sir Francis Drake, Sir Walter Raleigh*

PITT, WILLIAM THE ELDER (1708–78)

British prime minister (1766–68). Known as a great orator, Pitt was first elected to Parliament in 1735. He was a strong proponent of going to war with France during this time to secure British trade routes.

ABOVE The departure of the Pilgrim Fathers
FAR RIGHT Samuel Pepys helps during the Great Plague

He was denied the chance of top office until the 1750s. As secretary of state he directed the war effort in North American and India with great success. When he achieved the office of prime minister he was dogged by ill health. Pitt suffered from depression and gout and for a year between 1767 and 1768 he was incapacitated by the former. He resigned in October 1768. In his last speech in the House of Lords he collapsed before he had finished and died within a month.

PITT, WILLIAM THE YOUNGER (1759–1806)

British prime minister (1783–1801, 1804–06). Pitt, son of William Pitt the Elder, became the youngest ever prime minister of Britain in 1781 at the age of just 24. Initially he embarked upon a programme of parliamentary reform but the French revolution of 1792 made him halt this for fear of civil unrest in Britain. He paved the way for British control of India by placing the East India Company under governmental control and oversaw the division of Canada into different spheres of influence between France and England. He also introduced income tax in 1799. The first rate was two shillings in the pound. Like his father he suffered from poor health and died in his 40s.

PLAGUE (1665)

Disease that ravaged England in the seventeenth century. Bubonic plague decimated European populations in the 1300s. As many as half of the people had been killed in some areas. It only abated when all of those vulnerable to infection had died. The epidemic earned the name Black Death. In 1665 a new strain of the disease – The Great Plague – hit the shores of Britain. It was not so virulent as the last, but still claimed the lives of a fifth of the population of London. The outbreak met its end in 1666 with the Great Fire of London, which probably cleansed the city of its rat problem.

PLANTAGENET, GEOFFREY (1113–51)

Husband of Empress Matilda. Father of Henry II. Geoffrey was Count of Anjou and Duke of Normandy. Though he supported her, Geoffrey did not personally participate in Empress Matilda's civil war against the usurper Stephen. Geoffrey's own ambitions centred around the conquest of the dukedom of Normandy which he began to attack in 1135. Geoffrey achieved his objective in 1144, so laying one of the most important foundations for the Angevin Empire in France later created by his son, King Henry II.

➠ ***Henry I, Henry III, Empress Matilda, Plantagenet Dynasty***

PLANTAGENET DYNASTY

Alternative name for the Angevin Dynasty. The Angevin kings of England did not use 'Plantagenet' as their surname, but they are most commonly called by this name. The Plantagenets were the longest-lasting dynasty to rule in England, over a period of 331 years. There were 14 Plantagenet kings in all. The first was Henry II, followed by Richard I the Lionheart, King John, Henry III, Edward I, Edward II, Edward III, Richard II, Henry IV, Henry V, Henry VI, Edward IV, Edward V and Richard III. None of these kings were nonentities except perhaps for the tragic child-king, Edward V. Henry II was a great administrator and the father of the 'common law'. Richard I the Lionheart, Edward I and Henry V and Edward IV were renowned warriors. Edward III, the longest reigning of the Plantagenets,was an inspirational king who promoted Arthurian ideals of chivalry at his court. He also precipitated the Hundred Years' War with France by laying claim to the French throne. The disastrous Plantagenet reigns were those of King Edward II, Richard II and Henry VI, all of whom were murdered. So was King Edward V. King Henry III was another weak Plantagenet king, who was imprisoned by his discontented nobles, but survived. King John, though popularly labelled a villain, was an able king but not a wise one: he made many powerful enemies who, ultimately, destroyed him. Henry IV precipitated the Wars of the Roses between the Houses of York and Lancaster by usurping the throne in 1399. Richard III also usurped the throne and was killed in battle in 1485 by the first of the successors to the Plantagenets, the future King Henry VII, first monarch of the Tudor dynasty. The first English Prince of Wales, who became King Edward II, was a Plantagenet.

[222] Geoffrey Plantagenet, father of Henry II
RIGHT Edward I seated with Monks and Bishops
FAR RIGHT Edward III

TIMELINE

HENRY II
Born: 5 March 1133
Ascends the throne: 25 October 1154
Crowned: 19 December 1154
Married: Eleanor of Aquitaine
Died: 6 July 1189

RICHARD I
Born : 8 September 1157
Ascends the throne: 6 July 1189
Crowned: 2 September 1189
Married: Berengaria of Navarre
Died: 6 April 1199

JOHN
Born: 24 December 1166
Ascends the throne: 6 April 1199
Crowned: 27 May 1199
Married: Isabella of Gloucester, Isabella of Angouleme
Died: 18 October 1216

HENRY III
Born: 1 October 1207
Ascends the throne: 18 October 1216
Crowned: 28 October 1216
Married: Eleanor of Provence
Died: 16 November 1272

EDWARD I
Born: 17 June 1239
Ascends the throne: 20 November 1272
Crowned: 19 August 1274
Married : Eleanor of Castile, Margaret of France
Died : 7 July 1307

EDWARD II
Born : 25 April 1284
Ascends the throne: 8 July 1307
Crowned : 25 February 1308
Married: Isabella of France
Died: 21 September 1327

EDWARD III
Born: 13 November 1312
Ascends the throne: 25 January 1327
Crowned: 29 January 1327
Married: Philippa of Hainault
Died: 21 June 1377

RICHARD II
Born : 6 January 1367
Ascends the throne: 22 June 1377
Crowned : 16 July 1377
Married : Anne of Bohemia, Isabella of France
Died: 14 February 1400

PLASSEY, BATTLE OF (1757)

Battle for control of Bengal (23 June 1757). Following the recapture of Calcutta in January 1757, Robert Clive, the British commander, allied himself with disaffected local leaders. He attacked a huge Bengali army under Siraj-ud-Dawlah with little more than 3,000 men and routed them, securing control of Bengal and ultimately India.

Robert Clive, East India Company

POET LAUREATE (1668)

Originally an honorary name given to many poets, the first Poet Laureate in its modern meaning was John Dryden (1668). For the first time a Poet Laureate became a salaried member of the Royal Household. Formal duties originally included writing poems on specific occasions, such as a royal birth or death, or an occasion of national importance. Today the role is less defined. Poet Laureates have included Wordsworth; Alfred, Lord Tennyson; Cecil Day-Lewis; John Betjeman; Ted Hughes and Andrew Motion.

John Betjeman, John Dryden, William Wordsworth

POITIERS, BATTLE OF (1356)

Battle (19 September 1356) of the Hundred Years' War. A 6,000-strong English army under Edward, the Black Prince had positioned themselves in vineyards and were attacked by an army of 20,500 French, under King John. The French cavalry charged into heavy fire from the English bowmen. The English charged and routed the French army. The French lost 4,500 men and King John was captured. English losses were small; they were able to safely retreat towards Bordeaux.

Edward III, Edward the Black Prince Hundred Years' War

POLE, EDWARD DE LA (1472–1513)

Nobleman. De La Pole, a Yorkist and Earl of Suffolk,had designs on becoming king. He fled the country after his ambition was thwarted. Although he returned to Britain, he quickly returned to the Continent in 1501. The Archduke of Burgundy handed him to the English. Imprisoned in the Tower, he was executed by Henry VIII.

POLE, REGINALD (1500–58)

Cardinal of Mary Tudor. After Henry's Break with Rome, Pole sided with the pope and left for Padua. Returning to England in 1554, as the papal legate, he encouraged a return to Catholicism. In 1556 he became Archbishop of Canterbury, but died demoralised in 1558 after papal accusations of heresy due to Anglo-Spanish alliances.

Break with Rome, Counter-Reformation, Henry VIII, Mary Tudor

POOR LAWS (1601)

Series of Acts of Parliament designed to alleviate the suffering of the poor in England. The Poor Law Act was passed in 1601 and was designed to address the problem of dealing with the poor among the British population. Parish overseers were empowered in various ways. They were charged with providing facilities and materials with which to set the unemployed to work. Profits were then used to provide relief for the aged, to apprentice pauper children and to build poorhouses. By 1834 when another Poor Law Act was passed, workhouses had become an established part of British society. The act forbade the granting of poor relief to all able-bodied persons, except those in workhouses.

However, conditions in workhouses were kept unpleasant enough to deter all those who actually had any alternative but starvation. Thus the poor were trapped in a vicious cycle.

➠ ***Elizabeth I***

PORTLAND, WILLIAM BENTINCK, 3RD DUKE OF (1738–1809)

British prime minister (1807–09). Portland took on the nominal role of prime minister during the coalition government of Frederick, Lord North, but assumed the role in full in 1807.

➠ ***Lord Frederick North***

PRE-RAPHAELITE MOVEMENT (1848)

English artistic movement of the nineteenth century. The Pre-Raphaelite Brotherhood was founded by Dante Gabriel Rossetti, William Rossetti, Frederick George Stephens, William Holman Hunt, Thomas Woolner, James Collinson and John Everett Millais. William Rossetti, brother of Dante (and of the poet Christina) was the only non-artist member of the group. He was a writer who came up with the movement's short-lived magazine, *Germ*. The brotherhood strove for an artistic ideal they felt had disappeared at the time of Raphael. Although trained at the Royal Academy, they were opposed to the methods taught by the Academy. They were especially concerned with techniques of lighting and developed a new style of painting – covering the canvas with a white background before painting the picture on the top, giving their works a spectacular luminosity. The prominent critic John Ruskin was an influential supporter of the group, helping to bring them to the notice of the conservative art world who, at first, were furiously opposed to them. Other artists associated with the movement include Edward Burne-Jones, William Morris, Arthur Hughes, Henry Wallis and Elizabeth Siddal (wife of Dante Rossetti). Key pictures of the movement include Rossetti's *The Girlhood of Mary Virgin*, Holman Hunt's *The Light of the World* and Millais' *Lorenzo and Isabella*.

LEFT A manuscript showing the Battle of Poitiers
ABOVE King Rene's Honeymoon by Rosetti

➠ ***William Morris, Royal Academy***

PRESBYTERIANISM

Doctrine supporting Church government by presbytery. Presbyterianism sees Christ as the head of the Church and the members as equals, from which the ministers are elected for a term of office, although ordination is for life. Several presbyteries combined made a synod and the central authority is the General Assembly. Presbyterianism developed out of the Protestant Reformation and became very popular in Scotland, where it was propagated by Calvin. However, the Calvinism of James I was less extreme: when he declared, 'no bishop, no king', at the Hampton Court Conference he was denying the implementation of Presbyterianism. Religious intolerance led to some Presbyterians fleeing to America. Presbyterianism's only era of significant power in England was during the English Civil War and its conflict with Episcopalianism led to the National Covenant and the Bishops' Wars in Scotland. In 1972 Presbyterianism in England and Wales took the form of the United Reformed Church.

➠ ***Covenant Martyrs, English Civil War, Episcopacy National Covenant, Protestantism***

PRIDE'S PURGE (1648)

Purge of the Long Parliament in 1648 named after Thomas Pride, a colonel during the Civil War. The purge left just the Rump Parliament. It expelled around 140 MPs from the parliament, there were only just over 150 in total, and paved the way for the vote that led to Charles I being brought to trial. Pride also happened to be a judge at the subsequent trial and also signed the King's death warrant. Some of those purged from the Parliament were arrested.

➠ ***Charles I, Rump Parliament***

PRINCES IN THE TOWER (1483)

The princes were the child-king Edward V and his brother Richard, Duke of York, sons of King Edward IV. They disappeared while in the Tower of London awaiting Edward's coronation in 1483. In 1502, Sir James Tyrell confessed to the crime, saying he acted on Richard's orders. The Tudors, however, had a vested interest in vilifying Richard III and it is possible that the culprits may have been agents of the future Henry VII. In 1674, the remains of two young children, believed to be the two princes, were discovered at the Tower. They were reburied in Westminster Abbey.

→ *Edward IV, Edward V, Henry VII, Richard III, Tower of London.*

PRIVY COUNCIL (16TH CENTURY)

Governing body of the realm. Now largely ceremonial and membership is granted to those who have obtained high office. It first emerged in the sixteenth century. Members in that time were drawn from those holding high state office. It used to meet wherever the Sovereign happened to be located. From the 1700s the Cabinet took over control and functions of the council. Although largely ceremonial it still holds powers used to administer legal disputes from Britain's overseas dependencies, including capital punishment cases.

PROMS (1895)

Season of classical concerts held in the Royal Albert Hall, London. The Promenade Concerts, or 'Proms' for short, were founded by conductor Henry Wood and Robert Newman. Their purpose was to bring classical music to everyone – of all social backgrounds – in an enjoyable atmosphere. When Wood died in 1944, he bequeathed the rights of the concerts to the BBC. The Proms consist of around 70 concerts which take place annually from mid-July to mid-September.

→ *British Broadcasting Corporation, Royal Albert Hall*

PROTESTANTISM

Christian belief that emerged out of the Protestant Reformation. Protestantism was marked by the belief in justification by faith alone and the authority of the Bible. It emerged in England, then the rest of Britain, with Henry VIII's rejection of papal authority and it was furthered by the religious reforms that simultaneously came over from the Continent.

Under Edward VI Protestantism was applied more fanatically, namely via the Prayer Book and the Act of Uniformity, both 1549. The next monarch, Mary Tudor, nicknamed Bloody Mary, burnt several hundred Protestants at the stake, including the bishops, Latimer and Ridley, at Oxford in 1555, and the archbishop, Cranmer, 1556. When faced with the flames Latimer presciently declared: 'We shall this day light such a candle, by God's grace, in England, as I trust shall never be put out.' Elizabeth's accession and the Acts of Uniformity and Supremacy, 1559, re-established Protestantism as the religion of England, although her self-professed intent was 'not to make windows into men's souls'.

During the English Civil War and the Commonwealth mainstream Anglicanism was usurped by minority Puritan

sects. With the Restoration Charles II's reign supported Protestantism, but in the form of Anglicanism. Nevertheless wider Protestant dominance and political power led to the Glorious Revolution. From then on Protestantism, manifest in all its denominations and break-aways, remained the main religion of England, Scotland and Wales. The Catholic-Protestant conflict in Ireland continues to this day.

➠ ***Break with Rome, Dissolution of the Monasteries, Edward VI, Elizabeth I, Glorious Revolution, Henry VIII, Mary I, Reformation***

PROVISIONS OF OXFORD (1258)

Constitutional reform in the thirteenth century. It granted executive power to the king who was to be supported by a council of 15. It made provision for Parliament to meet three times a year and local government became a responsibility of the council.

➠ ***Henry III, Simon de Montfort***

PURCELL, HENRY (1659–95)

English composer. As the son of a musician in the court of Charles II, Purcell began his own musical career as a choirboy at the Chapel Royal. In 1677, he was appointed composer to the king and, in 1679, he succeeded his music teacher and became the organist at Westminster Abbey. Although he began composing at a young age, little of Purcell's work prior to 1680 has survived. In his position as royal composer, Purcell wrote a great deal of state and ceremonial music; he is also known for his songs (including 'Nymphs and Shepherds'), anthems, church music and operas, especially *Dido* and *Aeneas*. He also wrote the music for many plays – a significant and popular form of entertainment in the Restoration years, as theatricals had been banned during the time of Cromwell. Amongst the playwrights with whom Purcell worked were William Congreve and John Dryden.

➠ ***Charles II, Oliver Cromwell, John Dryden, Mary II, Restoration, Westminster Abbey, William III***

TOP LEFT The Princes in the Tower

LEFT The last night of the Proms at the Albert Hall

PURITANISM (LATE 16TH AND 17TH CENTURIES)

Doctrine aimed at purifying the Church of England. Puritans developed Calvinism: combining strict Bible reading and his theory of Predestination they concluded that they alone were the 'elect'. Dissatisfaction emerged with Elizabeth I's religious settlement of 1559 as some regarded it as having too many remants of Roman Catholicism. Also separatist Puritans emerged who wanted the Church and State to be separate. Under Charles I and Laud intolerance towards Puritans increased. In contrast the Commonwealth was tolerant to Puritan sects such as Levellers, Diggers, Fifth Monarchy Men and Quakers. In Wales and Scotland Puritanism continually had proportionally more dominance than in England. Although a disparate group, Puritans were recognisable by their black and white dress and rigid morality.

➠ ***Calvinism, William Laud***

QUAKERS

Also known as the Society of Friends. The Quakers were founded by George Fox in England in the middle of the seventeenth century. He renounced church buildings, liturgy and clergy and valued the inner voice and spirituality. At the monthly meetings the group would wait for God to choose a member to receive his word and 'quake'. Despite persecution (450 died in prison because of the Quaker Act, 1662) Quakerism spread rapidly from the north of England. Quakers earned respect for their dignified calm. They also advocated the abolition of slavery and supported women's rights and pacifism.

➠ ***Abolitionists***

RALEIGH, WALTER (1552–1618)

English navigator and pirate. Like Francis Drake, his contemporary, Walter Raleigh (1552–1618) too fell into favour with the Virgin Queen, Elizabeth I. Raleigh made several unsuccessful attempts to establish a British colony in Virginia, North America, between 1584 and 1587. He then made an exploration to the north coast of South America in 1595. He is accredited with bringing both the potato and tobacco from the Americas to Europe. He was beheaded for conspiracy by James I.

➡ ***Elizabeth I, Piracy***

RATIONING (1939)

Process of limiting food supplies to the public during World War II by the Ministry of Food. The Ministry controlled the procurement, distribution and prices of most foodstuffs, so that people were treated as fairly as possible, regardless of wealth or status. Post-war derationing didn't end fully until 3 July 1954.

➡ ***World War II***

RECUSANTS

Those who refused to attend Church of England services. Persecution for recusancy began under Edward VI, came to a head under Elizabeth, due to the activity of the Counter-Reformation, and continued under James I. Punishments included fines, confiscation of property, imprisonment and even death. Covert priest-holes were used to secret Jesuits and other Roman Catholic priests to prevent their capture and persecution.

➡ ***Counter-Reformation, Elizabeth, James I, Roman Catholics***

REFORMATION (16TH CENTURY)

Sixteenth-century reform movement in the western Christian Church. Wyclif and Erasmus wrote attacks on the corruption within the Church, namely absenteesim and the sale of indulgences and relics. Then Luther acted, famously pinning his 95 theses on the door of Wittenberg Cathedral in October 1517. Luther was not actually anti-pope, just anti-corruption, nevertheless Calvin, Zwingli and Knox developed the original Reformation ideas and an independent Protestant church emerged in northern Europe. Henry VIII took advantage of the era of religious change, appointing himself Supreme Head of the Church of England. Religious reform continued to be a key political, and religious, issue in Britain for the nest 150 years.

➡ ***John Calvin, Henry VIII, John Knox, Protestantism, John Wyclif***

RENAISSANCE (15TH CENTURY)

Period of great change in every sphere of society, considered by scholars to be the beginning of modern history. The term Renaissance comes from the French and literally means rebirth. It was a movement that began in the north of Italy in the fifteenth century and spread throughout Europe, it continued to expand for the next two centuries. The cultural changes affected every area of life, including the arts, architecture, sciences and philosophy. In art and architecture, the movement saw a return to the classical influence of ancient Greece and Rome, and a move away from the rigidity of the austerely religious medieval world – a central figure of the Italian Renaissance was Leonardo da Vinci. In Britain the movement was particularly prominent during the reign of Elizabeth I – a world in which William Shakespeare was a key Renaissance figure – and into the Stuart dynasty. Charles I, a committed patron of the arts, was a key part of the continuing movement, which at his death was crushed into submission under Cromwell's puritanical government. The Restoration of Charles II to the throne in 1660 led to a new period of rebirth, in which the arts once again flourished.

➜ ***Charles I, Charles II, Oliver Cromwell, Restoration, William Shakespeare***

RESTORATION (1660)

Reinstatement of the English monarchy in 1660. Charles II was made king after the collapse of the Protectorate. Following the downfall of Richard Cromwell, there was much confusion over the immediate political future of England. With the Rump Parliament discredited, the Convention Parliament sought ways of returning Charles II from nine years of exile. He eventually returned to the country in May 1660 after receiving assurances about his constitutional position and safety.
The new political order was cemented by the work of the Cavalier Parliament. Charles II, in 1662, married Catherine of Braganza, a Portuguese princess. Although there were no offspring, he fathered several illegitimate children sparking a battle for the Crown upon his death in 1685. The same period was marked by a rebirth in English culture especially in the writing of plays and poetry.

➜ ***Charles II, English Civil Wars***

RETAINERSHIP

medieval system by which all land ultimately belonged to the Crown, but effective ownership of land was retained by the payment of feudal dues. A hierarchy meant that land rent was paid upwards until it reached the monarch's purse.

➜ ***Feudalism***

BOTTOM FAR LEFT Ration books for both first and second world war
BELOW Leaders of the Reformation in Europe including Luther (centre)

RICHARD I (THE LIONHEART) (1157–99)

King of England (1189–99). Third son of Henry II. Richard, who succeeded his father in 1189, has a glorious reputation as a warrior-king, and as the crusader saviour of Christendom. Richard was certainly a valiant soldier. Fighting wars was his prime passion. He cared little for England, where he spent only around six months of his 10-year reign. He preferred his duchy of Aquitaine and the task of guarding it against French incursions. Richard financed his crusade by selling offices, lands, estates or rights. He even contemplated selling London, but could not find anyone rich enough to buy it. In 1192, on his way home from the Third Crusade, he was imprisoned by a rival. In 1194, after an enormous ransom had been paid, he was back in England, but soon left for France and never returned. He died during a siege in 1199 when an arrow wound turned poisonous.

➠ ***Eleanor of Aquitaine, Crusades, Henry II, King John***

RICHARD II (1367–1400)

King of England (1377–99). Son of Edward, the Black Prince. Richard succeeded his grandfather, Edward III. He acquired a hero's reputation in 1381 when he confronted Wat Tyler, leader of the Peasants' Revolt. Heroics, however, were not typical of Richard. He was despotic and relied on favourites, ignoring the rights of his nobles and his Parliament. In 1386, five disgruntled nobles, the Lords Appellant, imposed their own advisers on the king. One of the Lords Appellant was Richard's cousin, Henry Bolingbroke, son of John of Gaunt, whom the king exiled in 1398. Richard afterwards appropriated Henry's duchy of Lancaster. Henry proved to be the most dangerous of all the king's many enemies.

In 1399, he returned to retrieve his duchy, forced Richard to abdicate and afterwards took his throne as King Henry IV. Richard was imprisoned in Pontefract Castle where he died, probably from starvation, in February 1400.

➠ ***Edward III, Edward, the Black Prince, Henry IV, Peasants' Revolt, Wars of the Roses***

RICHARD III (1452–85)

King of England (1483–85). Youngest son of Richard, Duke of York. Richard fought bravely and loyally for the Yorkist cause in the Wars of the Roses.

His brother, the first Yorkist monarch, Edward IV, put Richard in charge of government in the traditionally unruly north of England. Despite his youth, Richard proved a just and much-admired administrator. The problem with understanding Richard III is the vast difference between the admirable reputation he earned in the North and his actions in 1483 when he usurped the crown from his young nephew, Edward V, and afterwards, reputedly, murdered both him and his brother. Other suggested victims of Richard's ambition were Henry VI, murdered in 1471, and Richard's brother George, Duke of Clarence, killed in 1478, both of them

FAR RIGHT Red deer in Richmond Park
TOP RIGHT The burial of Richard II

in the Tower of London. Richard's involvement has never been definitely proved. However, the fifteenth century was a very violent period in British history and achieving ambitions by force was not uncommon. It is therefore likely that Richard was no more violent than his contemporaries. His life story was, however, worked over by Tudor propaganda to create the popular picture of Richard as an evil monster. This derives mainly from Richard's biography (1513–18) as written by Sir Thomas More and William Shakespeare's play *King Richard III* (1592). There is, however, no evidence that Richard was a hunchback, or that he was born in sinister fashion, complete with teeth, as depicted by Shakespeare. These were metaphors for evil, designed to inspire fear and loathing among a superstitious public. There is no doubt, though, that by usurping the throne from his nephew, Richard made many powerful enemies. They combined with Henry Tudor to defeat and kill the usurper at the Battle of Bosworth in 1485.

Edward IV, Henry VII, Thomas More, William Shakespeare, Wars of the Roses

RICHMOND PALACE (14TH CENTURY)

Ruined historic building, in which many British monarchs lived. Richmond Palace was destroyed in the late 1300s, but rebuilt during the reign of Henry V (1413–22). It was the favourite residence of Henry VII and his son, Henry VIII, was born here. The palace was ruined again after Charles I's execution.

Charles I, Henry V, Henry VII, Henry VIII

RICHMOND PARK (1637)

Park in Surrey, bordering south-west London. This area was one of Henry VIII's favourite hunting grounds. Charles I made it an enclosed park, in 1637. Today it is home to colonies of red and fallow deer. There are several buildings within the park, including the home of the Royal Ballet School.

Charles I, Henry VIII

RIZZIO, DAVID (1533–66)

Italian adviser to Mary, Queen of Scots. He entered the court of the Queen initially as a musician. His relationship with the Queen provoked jealousy in her husband Lord Darnley. In 1566, just a year after the marriage of Mary to Darnley, Scottish noblemen stabbed Rizzio to death. Darnley who had Rizzio dragged from the Queen's presence to his death arranged the murder.

Lord Darnley, Mary Queen of Scots

ROCKINGHAM, 2ND MARQUESS OF (1730–82)

British prime minister (1755–66 and 1782). Rockingham is remembered mainly for his stand in support of American independence during the Revolution and as initiator of peace negotiations at the end of the war. He died in office.

American Revolution

ROCKINGHAM, COUNCIL OF (1095)

Synod to resolve William II's and Anselm's conflict over investiture. The bishops agreed with William that he should choose his own pope. Anselm, however, supported the pope and wanted his own religious appointment to be out of the king's jurisdiction. After his defeat at Rockingham Anselm left for Rome until Henry I's reign.

Saint Anselm, William II

ROMAN CATHOLICISM

Major branch of Christianity, headed by the pope. Roman Catholics particularly believe in Transubstantiation. Rome was established as headquarters of the western Church in the third century and during the Dark Ages papal authority developed. In 1054 the Church split and so the distinct Roman Catholic branch emerged. By the sixteenth century the demand for reform of this long-established faith covered most of northern Europe.

After the Dissolution of the Monasteries the Roman Catholic Church in England not only lost much of its influence, but also its wealth and even Bloody Mary could not turn the tide. Initially tolerant regarding religion, even Elizabeth executed some recusants. Roman Catholicism attempted to regain pre-eminence firstly by the persecutions of the Inquisition, then by the reforms of the Council of Trent. Foxes' *Book of Martyrs*, the Armada and the Gunpowder Plot, 1605, contributed to Roman Catholicism being associated with treason and xenophobia (particularly fear of Spain), thus anti-Catholic restrictions were implemented. Catholics fared little better in Britain during the High Anglican era of Laud and the Puritan extremism of the Commonwealth. Then fear of Catholics re-emerged, this time due to the Treaty of Dover and Charles II's alleged promise to re-establish Catholicism in England. This resulted in the anti-Catholic Test Act, 1673.

The accession of a Roman Catholic king, James II, and the birth of his Catholic heir, were the catalysts for Protestant reaction, namely the Glorious Revolution: Roman Catholicism was consigned to the sidelines of power in England. Today the principal Roman Catholic place of worship in England is Westminster Cathedral.

➡ ***Counter-Reformation, Reformation, Test Acts***

ROMAN CHRISTIANITY

In Britain, the branch of Christianity founded by missionaries from Rome. Whilst Britain was still part of the Roman Empire Constantine legalised Christianity by the Edict of Milan, AD 314. St Augustine was sent by Pope Gregory to revive the conversions in the sixth century. From Kent, Roman Christianity spread, coming into conflict with Celtic Christianity at the Synod of Whitby. Here Bishop Wilfrid, on the Roman side, secured a victory for Roman practice in Britain. The Viking raids initiated the demise of the Celtic Church in the north of England, so from then on the Roman Church, with its papal infrastructure, became the pre-eminent Church in Britain until the Reformation.

➡ ***Saint Augustine, Constantine, Celtic Christianity, Synod of Whitby***

ROMAN EMPIRE

In AD 43 Emperor Claudius I added England, Wales and lowland Scotland to the Roman Empire. He called the new territory Brittania. Brittania was the northernmost outpost of the Roman Empire. The Romans had seized territory reaching as far south as Egypt (Aegyptus), as far east as Iraq (Mesopotamia) and as far West as the Iberian peninsula (Hispania) by the height of expansion in AD 117 under Emperor Trajan.

Hadrian who was emperor AD 117–38 is famed for having a defensive wall built at the boundary between Britannia and Scotland to fend off attacks from clansmen, such were hostilities between the Romans and the natives. Nevertheless, the Romans occupied Britannia until AD 410, when Rome fell to the Visgoths and the Roman legions were withdrawn.

During the 367 years of Roman occupation, the Britons did not make life entirely easy for the Romans. There were several uprisings against the Romans from native populations within Britannia, although the Romans were quite capable of dealing with them effectively and efficiently whenever the need arose, primarily because they were so well organised. In fact the key to the Romans' success was its organisational strength and ability to embrace new technologies that made life and warfare easier to conduct.

This is demonstrated most clearly by its eventual downfall. In AD 180 Emperor Marcus Aurelius died. It sent the empire into a century of internal warring and the outcome was a divided empire. This meant the empire's infrastructure was flawed and its death knell sounded.

➡ ***Roman Invasion***

ROMAN INVASION (AD 43)

Julius Caesar had proved (55 BC) that the Romans could carry out a successful campaign across the Channel. Nearly 100 years later, four legions began to assemble at Boulogne supported by 20,000 auxiliary troops. They landed at Richborough in Kent, but the Belgae tribe gathered 80,000 men to contest the Roman crossing of the Medway. Using diversionary tactics the Romans outmanoeuvred the British forcing them to retreat into Essex. Emperor Claudius arrived shortly after Medway and stayed in Britain for 16 days, entering Colchester, with elephants, to accept the surrender of many British tribes. Over the next few years the Romans advanced and subjugated the southwest, the north as far as Lincoln and the northwest to the midlands. Caratacus, leading a guerrilla war, was finally cornered to the west of the Severn, near Caersws and taken captive. Boudicca (AD 61) rebelled but 10,000 Romans slaughtered her 230,000 strong force. Following the Battle of Mons Grauprus (AD 84) to the northwest of Aberdeen, where 13,000 Romans defeated 30,000 Caledonians, Roman expansion in Britain was nearly complete. By AD 50 England and Wales, up to Carlisle, had been conquered and much of the Lowlands of Scotland by AD 90.

➠ ***Boudicca, Julius Caesar, Emperor Claudius***

ROMANS

When the Romans arrived in ancient Britain they found a land full of heathen, warlike, Celtic tribes. The Celts were an Iron Age people who lacked the organisational skills of the Romans. Although they put up some resistance, the Celts were quickly conquered by the Roman army who were considerably better armed and skilled in the field of battle. Having arrived, in AD 43 the Romans set about building settlements for themselves, using the technologies they had mastered during the expansion of the empire since 753 BC. They also built a communications infrastructure across Britain, so that soldiers and materials could be moved from one place to another as efficiently as possible.

Roman houses were masterfully constructed using blocks of stone and clay bricks held together with mortar. Roofs were made from tiles on wooden frames and floors were made from tiles. In essence they were the template for most building design ever since. Some Roman houses had the luxury of under-floor heating and were elaborately embellished with floor and wall mosaics.

Public buildings were even more impressively constructed. They featured pillars and arches which enabled the Romans to build very large structures without using enormous amounts of material. The same technology was used in building bridges, viaducts, aquaducts and defensive walls.

Roman roads were remarkable feats of engineering. They comprised various layers of building material and included cambers and gullies for drainage. Their roads are well known for being extremely straight. This is because they were designed to take the shortest route possible between locations.

Roman towns often included sewerage systems carefully planned and built before the streets and buildings, so that they ran beneath. The towns were paved to keep the streets clean and carefully laid out so that public facilities could be utilised to optimum effect.

LEFT Minerva as seen on copper dupondius of Claudius
ABOVE LEFT Julius Caesar in Kent
ABOVE Roman Excavations

ROME, TREATY OF (1952)

International agreement that saw the formation of the EEC. On 25 March 1952 six European countries signed two international agreements. Belgium, France, West Germany, Italy, Luxembourg and the Netherlands established themselves as the European Economic Community (EEC) and became members of the Atomic Energy Commission (Euratom). Both of these agreements were signed in the capital of Italy and were seen as a bond of friendship between nations, so they became known as the Treaties of Rome. The EEC has since become the European Union (EU) in 1993. The EU membership now comprises many more of the European nations. The collapse of communism has resulted in further applications being submitted.

➡ *European Union*

RORKE'S DRIFT, BATTLE OF (1879)

Battle (22 January 1879) of the Zulu War. Zulu troops, flushed with their success at Isandhlwana, where they had wiped out over 1,000 British soldiers, descended on the outpost held by one company of the 24th Regiment. Under the command of Lieutenants Chard and Bromhead, the 139 men beat off the 4,000 Zulus who were compelled to withdraw back into Zululand, leaving 400 dead. British casualties were 25 killed and wounded and eight Victoria Crosses were awarded.

➡ *Zulu War*

ROSEBERY, ARCHIBALD, EARL OF (1847–1929)

British prime minister (1894). Rosebery's term lasted less than a year. His leanings were Liberal, but he was forced to stand down after his imperialist views caused dissention in the Liberal ranks.

ROUEN, BATTLE OF (1419)

Henry V's last major battle (19 January 1419). Henry V besieged the city in 1418 but Rouen held out until January of the following year before the garrison was forced to surrender. The city paid Henry a massive 300,000-crown ransom. In completing this campaign Henry had gained all the provinces he desired in France and after difficult negotiations, married Catherine in May 1420. The peace was short-lived however and he returned to France to extend English power.

➡ *Hundred Years' War*

ROUNDHEAD (17TH CENTURY)

Parliamentarian soldier during the English Civil War. As Puritans, Roundheads wore their hair closely cropped in stark contrast to the longer-haired Royalist Cavaliers. It is possible that the Parliamentarian leader, John Pym, began the fashion but it was often used as a sarcastic description or term.

➡ ***Cavalier, Charles I, Oliver Cromwell, English Civil War***

ROYAL ACADEMY (1768)

Oldest fine-art academy in England. The Royal Academy of Arts was founded by George III. Its first president was Sir Joshua Reynolds. The Academy served as an art school and an exhibition venue – today, its Summer Exhibition remains one of the art year's most prestigious events. The first Royal Academy building was in Pall Mall; today it is housed in Burlington House on Piccadilly. It houses some of the finest artworks in Britain.

➡ ***George III***

ROYAL ALBERT HALL (1871)

Concert venue in Kensington, London. Prince Albert proposed the building of a Hall of Arts and Sciences, to be paid for out of the profit made by

the Great Exhibition. As he died before the building was finished, Queen Victoria renamed it the Royal Albert Hall, in memory of him. The highly ornate Albert Memorial stands opposite it. The Hall is used for a host of musical events, despite its well-documented echo, including the annual Proms concerts.

➡ ***Prince Albert, Great Exhibition, Proms, Queen Victoria***

ROYAL MARRIAGES ACT (1772)

Act of Parliament designed to prevent princes from marrying unsuitable wives. It was prompted by the marriage of George III's brother Henry to a commoner. The Act made it illegal for princes under age 25 to marry without the king's permission. The Act is still in force today.

➡ ***George III, George IV***

RUMP GOVERNMENT (1648)

Government that retained only a handful of members from the Long Parliament after it was purged by Thomas Pride in December 1648. The Rump increasingly became ineffective and corrupt. It was eventually replaced by the Barebones Parliament. It was recalled by the army in 1659 but suffered from the same problems it had encountered before. It was dissolved in 1660 just prior to the return of Charles II.

➡ ***Oliver Cromwell, Interregnum***

RUSSELL, JOHN, 1ST EARL (1792–1878)

British prime minister (1846–52, 1865–66). Russell came to Parliament in 1813 and became a cabinet minister. He was a supporter of Catholic emancipation and was instrumental in drawing up the Reform Bill.

➡ ***Catholic Emancipation***

RYE HOUSE PLOT (1683)

Plot hatched against Charles II and his brother James, Duke of York. The conspirators, who appeared to oppose Charles' resolve that the Catholic James succeed to his throne, planned to intercept them at Rye House, in Hertfordshire, while they were on their way home from the races at Newmarket. Charles and James returned from Newmarket earlier than expected due to a fire at the race course and the plot was forestalled.

➡ ***Charles II, Exclusion Bills, James II***

LEFT Defence of Rorke's drift, in the Zulu War
ABOVE Cromwell dissolving the Rump Parliament

SALISBURY CATHEDRAL (1220)

Highest spire in Britain at 123 m (404 ft). Its location at New Sarum was allegedly determined by an arrow being shot from Old Sarum. Purbeck marble was used for the slender columns and the architecture is unique, being almost completely Early English.

SALISBURY, ROBERT GASCOYNE CECIL, 3RD MARQUESS OF (1830–1903)

British prime minister (1885–86, 1886–92, 1895–1902). Salisbury entered Parliament in 1853 and soon became foreign minister. His interest in foreign affairs extended into his office as prime minister, where he concentrated on British expansionist policies in South Africa.

SCONE, STONE OF

A little farther north than Perth, Scotland, is a village called Scone in Tayside. Scone is the location where most of the kings of Scotland were crowned. The coronations occurred on the Stone of Destiny or Stone of Scone which is now incorporated into the Coronation Chair at Westminster, London.

SCOTTISH ASSEMBLY (1998)

Autonomous government for Scotland created in 1998 with 129 members. The First Minister was Donald Dewar but following his death, Henry McLeish replaced him. It has minor tax-raising powers but has already shown that it can pursue an independent path from Westminster particularly over issues such as health provision and education

➠ ***Devolution, Welsh Assembly***

SEVASTOPOL, SIEGE OF (1854–55)

Siege that took place during the Crimean War. The Anglo-French army, under Canrobert and Raglan besieged a large force of Russians commanded by Prince Mentschikov. The city was under continual bombardment for nearly a year until the French stormed the southern defences. Over 54,000 Russians died.

➠ ***Crimean War***

SEVEN YEARS' WAR (1756–63)

European world rivalry. When Frederick the Great seized the Austrian province of Silesia in 1740 he triggered off the War of the Austrian Succession. In 1756 Maria Theresa attempted to recapture Silesia for the third time, thus began the Seven Years' War. England sided with Prussia and France supported Austria but the real struggle between France and England, the old enemies, would rage further and take place on three continents. The French-Indian Wars secured North America for the British and in India the French were defeated at Plassey (3 June 1757). In Europe after some initial French victories the British and their allies won at Rossbach (5 November 1757), Leuthen (5 December), Crefeld (June 1758), Minden (1 August 1759) and a planned French invasion of England was headed off at the Battle of Lagos off Portugal (August 1759). After further French defeats at Quebec (September 13), Wandiwash (22 January 1760) and Pondicherry (January 1761) the French had lost both India and North America.

RIGHT The Seven Years' War

The Treaty of St Petersburg, (5 May 1762), ended the war between Prussia and Russia and the Treaty of Fontainebleau (3 November 1762) and later the Treaty of Paris (10 February 1763) assured Britain's ascendancy over France.

George II

SEYMOUR, JANE

Third queen of Henry VIII. Jane Seymour came from a family of Wiltshire gentry and attracted the king's attention when she was lady-in-waiting to his second wife, Anne Boleyn. Jane married the king 11 days after Anne's execution in 1536. She gave birth to his longed-for son in 1537, but died shortly afterwards from childbed fever. Henry's grief was intense. In his will, Henry ordered that he be buried next to Jane at Windsor.

Anne Boleyn, Edward VI, Henry VIII

SHAKESPEARE, WILLIAM (1564–1616)

England's foremost playwright, also a poet. William Shakespeare lived during the reign of Elizabeth I, of whom he was a favourite, and achieved great fame and popularity in his lifetime. He was married to Anne Hathaway, with whom he had three children. They lived in Stratford-upon-Avon, the town in which he was born, but he moved to London in c. 1591, leaving his family behind in Stratford. The town is now a popular tourist attraction, based on its Shakespearean associations. He returned to Stratford in later years, as a rich man. He remained there for the rest of his life, and is buried in the town's Holy Trinity Church – the same place in which he was baptised. As well as being a writer, Shakespeare became an actor after moving to London. In 1597, he also became a shareholder in the Globe Theatre (which was being built on the south bank of the Thames) and subsequently acted on its stage. Many of his own plays were also performed at the Globe. Among his works are the comedies, *The Two Gentlemen of Verona*, *The Merry Wives of Windsor*, *Much Ado about Nothing* and *A Midsummer Night's Dream*; the tragedies, *Romeo and Juliet*, *Hamlet*, *Othello* and *Macbeth* and the history plays, *Henry V* and *King John*. In total, he wrote 35 plays (although some scholars contest they were all his own work). His works also include 154 sonnets, the majority of which were written to a young man and the others to a 'dark lady'. His poems include 'Venus and Adonis' and 'The Rape of Lucrece' (both of which were dedicated to the Earl of Southampton). His plays have been performed all over the world and have not lost their popularity.

Elizabeth I, Christopher Marlowe

RIGHT Shakespeare, at the height of his career, looks out on the life of London

SHELBURNE, WILLIAM FITZMAURICE, 2ND EARL OF (1737–1805)

British prime minister (1783). Shelburne was an outspoken oppponent of George III's policies regarding the American colonies and he was instrumental in concluding peace with the new United States during his time as prime minister.

American Revolution, George III

SHIP MONEY

Tax imposed from 1634 on maritime towns by Charles I to meet naval expenses. The tax was extended in 1635 to take in inland towns also. The tax was widely unpopular and came at a time when Parliament was not convened for 11 years. This became known as the 'Eleven Years' Tyranny'. Several refused to pay the tax including an ardent Parliamentarian John Hampden but in court, judges backed the Crown. However, it was eventually abolished and made illegal by the Long Parliament, whose members included Hampden.

Charles I, Long Parliament

SHORT PARLIAMENT (1640)

Parliament convened by Charles I between April and May 1640. The king wanted to raise funds for the Bishops' Wars that were prompted by his attempts to impose Anglicanism on Scotland. Because a Parliament had not been convened for so long, its members were apt to discuss other measures before they would concede to granting money for the king. An angry Charles I then quickly dissolved the parliament.

Charles II, Long Parliament

SIMNEL, LAMBERT

Joiner's son from Oxford, pretender to the throne. Lambert Simnel first impersonated Richard, Duke of York, who had been murdered in 1483. In 1487, Simnel's sponsor, the Earl of Lincoln, used him as a pawn aimed at seizing the throne for himself. Later, Simnel was made to impersonate Edward, Earl of Warwick, a nephew of Edward IV and Richard III. This was a big mistake. Henry VII had already imprisoned Warwick in 1485. When Henry paraded the real, live Warwick, Simnel's impersonation was revealed. Subsequently, he was allowed to work in the royal kitchens and was later appointed king's falconer.

Henry VII, Tudor Dynasty, Perkin Warbeck

SIMPSON, WALLIS

Duchess of Windsor (1937), wife of former King Edward VIII. Edward's relationship with the American divorcée Mrs Simpson provoked the Abdication Crisis of 1936. Opposition to the King's plans to marry Wallis forced him to choose between her and the crown. Edward chose Wallis and abdicated in 1936.

Abdication Crisis, Edward VIII, George V, George VI

SINN FEIN (1905)

Irish nationalist political party founded in 1905. In Gaelic, the term means 'We Ourselves'. The founder was Arthur Griffith a journalist from Dublin. The party's popularity grew through the failure of the Irish Home Rule Association to get any substantial reforms from London. Under Eamonn De Valera's leadership it won, in 1918, a majority of votes in southern Ireland. Its victorious MPs decided not to go to Westminster seeking to set up an alternative government in Ireland. The party split after the Easter Uprising, as some members wanted a full republic. Towards the end of the century, its fortunes were revived, as it became the political wing of the republican movement. It currently holds 18 seats in the Northern Ireland Assembly and is headed by Gerry Adams.

Irish Free State

SIX ACTS (1819)

Series of six repressive parliamentary statutes passed in an attempt to halt the spread of radicalism following the Peterloo Massacre of August 1819. A peaceful rally of up to 80,000 people in Manchester, campaigning for more rights for industrial workers, ended with 11 people dead killed by troopers' sabres. This became a symbol of repression. The Six Acts stopped any future meetings of more than 50 people.

Peterloo Massacre

SLAVERY

When European traders first visited the coast of West Africa, there was already a flourishing slave trade going on. Rich Africans were capturing tribesmen from villages in the interior and selling them into slavery

in the Middle East. It was easy therefore for the Europeans to establish their own slave trade. Ships would come from Europe to trade goods for slaves. The slaves were then shipped to the colonies in the Americas where they were sold at a profit. The money then went to buy cargoes of goods to bring back to Europe, setting up a trade triangle. In the eighteenth century philanthropists began campaigning for the abolition of slavery and it was eventually abandoned early in the nineteenth century.

➧ ***Abolitionists***

SLUYS, BATTLE OF (1340)

Naval battle (24 June 1340) during the Hundred Years' War. Under the command of Sir Robert Morley and Richard Fitzalan, the 200-strong English fleet attacked 70 French ships commanded by Hugues Quieret in Sluys Harbour. Quieret was killed and his whole fleet captured or destroyed. England was now safe from French invasion.

➧ ***Hundred Years' War***

SOLWAY MOSS, BATTLE OF (1542)

Invasion of England by James V of Scotland. James V was Henry VIII's nephew and when the Scots had defeated the English at Haddon Rig he sent an army to face him. James marched with nearly 20,000 men into Cumbria and encountered an English border force of about 800. Caught in the swamp and without clear direction, the Scots were routed and 1,200 prisoners were taken. James died a fortnight later after the Battle of Linlithgow.

➧ ***Henry VIII, James V***

SOMME, BATTLES OF THE (1916 1918)

Two major battles in North-East France during World War I. Seeking to relieve German pressure on Verdun, General Haig and French General Joffre launched a series of attacks against the German defences commanded by Von Hindenburg and Von Ludendorff. Little ground was made despite 500,000 allied casualties and 450,000 German killed and wounded. The allied advance amounted to seven miles along a 20-mile front. In the last year of the war the Germans successfully broke through the allied lines in the Somme, driving them back 40 miles. Again, Von Ludendorff commanded the Germans but when General Foch took over command of allied troops in the area, he managed to halt the offensive. By then 180,000 Germans and 200,000 allied soldiers had been killed. At one stage in the last battle the Germans were within two miles of the Paris railway. This was the first battle of the last German offensive.

➧ ***World War I***

LEFT Gerry Adams at a Sinn Fein press conference
ABOVE Machine gunners during the Battle of the Somme

SOUTH SEA BUBBLE

Financial crash. In 1711 the South Sea Company was founded. It had a monopoly on trade with South America at the time and proved to be extremely profitable. So profitable in fact that in 1719 it offered to take the British national debt into its own hands in exchange for further trade concessions. The 100 shares it started with quickly grew to 1,000, prompting a frenzy of speculation from investors. However, the South Sea Company grew too quickly and its 'bubble' of success eventually burst in 1720. The effect was like that of a stock market crash, and thousands of investors were financially ruined over night. Even worse, it exposed corruption in the British Cabinet. Robert Walpole (1676–1745) became the first prime minister as a result, and restored financial confidence.

George I, Robert Walpole

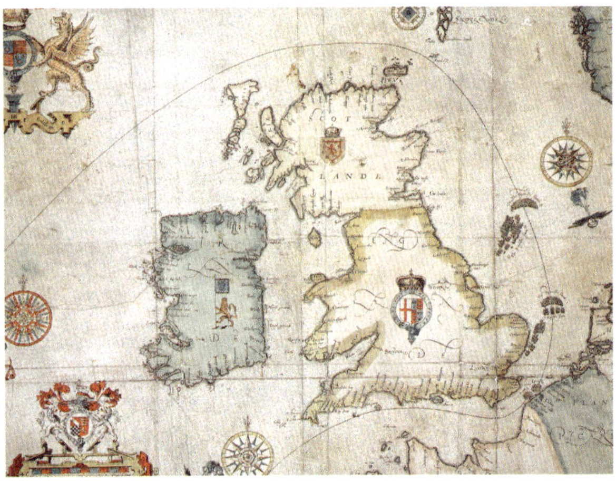

SPANISH ARMADA (1588)

Attempted Spanish invasion of England by the Spanish. Under the Roman Catholic Spanish King Philip II, a massive armada of 130 ships carrying 30,000 men was ordered to the Netherlands. Philip's intention was, at a stroke, to suppress the Protestant revolt in the Netherlands, that had been simmering since 1566, and was supported by Protestant England. He proposed that the fleet should invade England, seize Elizabeth I's throne and convert the English to Catholicism. The fleet was sighted off the English coast on July 29, and in a series of running battles off Plymouth and the Isle of Wight, the English attempted to break up the armada. When the armada anchored at Calais, awaiting the arrival of the invasion force to embark, Lord Charles Howard attacked, on August 8, and scattered the Spanish. Many were forced to sail around Scotland and Ireland to return to Spain and only 67 arrived home.

Elizabeth I, Philip II of Spain

SPANISH SUCCESSION, WAR OF (1701–14)

King Louis XIV's attempts to extend French power. On behalf of his son by a second marriage, Archduke Charles (who would later become Charles VI) Louis XIV claimed succession to the throne of the Holy Roman Empire. Although the French and imperial forces began fighting in Italy, the general war began in 1702 with France, Spain, Bavaria, Portugal and Savoy against the English, Dutch and the German states. The Duke of Marlborough enjoyed considerable success (1702–03) but the French missed their chance to take Vienna in 1703, finding themselves defeated at Blenheim by the Duke of Marlborough in 1704. The English also captured Gibraltar. In 1706 the French evacuated Italy and Marlborough beat them again at Ramillies to force them out of the Low Countries. In 1708, in partnership with Eugene of Savoy, Marlborough drove the French back into France and took Lille after the Battle of Oudenarde. Peace negotiations failed but the French were defeated again at Malplaquet in 1709. Meanwhile in North

ABOVE Map of the British Isles showing the route of the Armada
RIGHT The English capture Gibralter during the war of Spanish succession

America the conflict known as Queen Anne's War saw the English and French, both with Native American allies, fight many bloody battles. With the death of Joseph I, the Holy Roman Emperor, Charles VI took the throne in 1711. The Peace of Utrecht (1713) concluded the war as far as France, England and Holland were concerned. Charles VI continued the war, defeating Eugene in 1712 but finally he consented to peace in 1714, signing the Treaties of Rastatt and Baden.

Queen Anne, Treaty of Utrecht

ST JAMES'S PARK (1531)

London's oldest royal park – appropriated by Henry VIII in 1531. It was landscaped in 1603 for James I (James VI of Scotland). Charles I was walked through the park on the way to his execution. During the reign of Charles II its duckponds were filled with exotic birds, including the pelicans which remain today.

Charles I, Charles II, Henry VIII, James I (VI of Scotland)

ST PAUL'S CATHEDRAL (1675)

London's premier Protestant cathedral. In Roman times, a temple stood here; since c. 604 the site has been home to a cathedral dedicated to St Paul. The present building, designed by Sir Christopher Wren, was begun in 1675, although it wasn't completed until 1710. It was built to replace the third cathedral, which had been destroyed in the Great Fire. One of St Paul's most outstanding features is its huge dome, inside which is the famous Whispering Gallery – if you whisper against the wall at one side of the gallery, it can be heard all the way round on the opposite side. In the 1950s, a chapel in the cathedral was renamed the American Chapel, in honour of those Americans who died in World War II. Christopher Wren is buried in the cathedral, as are Admiral Nelson and the Duke of Wellington. In 1981, the wedding of Prince Charles and Princess Diana was conducted here.

Great Fire of London, Christopher Wren

STAMFORD BRIDGE, BATTLE OF (1066)

Battle of the Norman Conquest (25 September 1066). Nominally supporting William, Duke of Normandy's claim to the English throne, King Harold Hardrada and Tostig, his ally, invaded Yorkshire with 300 ships and 12,000 men. They enjoyed several successes against local Saxon Lords but were surprised at Stamford Bridge, near York, by Harold II. They were both killed and their army destroyed. Hardrada's son, Olaf, was allowed to sail away with just 24 ships carrying the survivors. Three days later, on the south coast, William the Conqueror landed and Harold had to force-march his troops south to meet him at Hastings.

Harold II, Norman Conquest

STAMP ACT (1765)

Imposition of tax by the British on the American colonies. In 1765 the British Parliament reacted to the threat of revolt in North America with the Stamp Act, a form of taxation designed to raise funds from its American colonies to pay for their defence. The colonies refused to use the tax stamps issued to them and a blockade of British merchant shipping forced the British government to repeal the act in 1766. Ironically the Stamp Act only served to precipitate the American Revolution (1775–83).

American Revolution

STAR CHAMBER (15TH–16TH CENTURIES)

Court of law in the fifteenth and sixteenth centuries. It was used first by Henry VII as a way of settling disputes arising from the Wars of the Roses. It was also used by Wolsey and Cromwell who tried to get those in dispute to use it in the first case rather than as a last resort. However it proved itself to be an unpopular institution. This arose from use as a way of maintaining

Royal influence. This was particularly marked during the time of Charles I especially in the time when he did not convene a Parliament. The chamber was eventually abolished by the Long Parliament.

Henry VII

STEPHEN, KING

King of England (1135–54). Originally Stephen of Blois, son of Adela, daughter of William I. In 1135, when the succession of Henry I's daughter the Empress Matilda as Queen Regnant of England was in dispute, Stephen made a pre-emptive strike and usurped the throne for himself. He was supported by English and Angevin nobles opposed to Matilda. In 1139, Matilda and her supporters invaded England and civil war ensued. During the hostilities, King Stephen was defeated in the only major battle, at Lincoln in 1141. Subsequently, he was imprisoned at Bristol. Stephen nevertheless clung on to his throne and, in 1147, Matilda gave up the struggle and returned to France. Stephen planned that his son Eustace should succeed him, but Eustace died in 1153. His heartbroken father agreed to accept Matilda's son Henry as his heir. When Stephen died in 1154, Henry succeeded him as King Henry II.

Henry I, Henry II, Empress Matilda, Geoffrey Plantagenet

STEPHENSON, GEORGE (1781–1848)

British engineer, inventor of the steam train. Although James Watt had improved the steam engine in the 1760s it was 50 years before it became efficient and reliable as a source of power for vehicles. Vehicles need to be able to pull their own weight effectively before they can be considered a viable means for transporting passengers or goods. George Stephenson set about the problem of building a steam powered locomotive in the early 1800s. By 1814 he had completed his first locomotive, *Blucher*. In 1829 he had perfected his experiments and designed *Rocket*, capable of 47 kph (29 mph).

James Watt

STIRLING CASTLE

Scottish stronghold. In 1297 Scottish nationalist William Wallace led a revolt against the English rule of Scotland. He won a battle at Stirling where there is a castle at a crossing point over the river Forth. He then declared himself 'governor of Scotland' but was defeated by Edward I in 1298, eventually being hung, drawn and quartered. Edward II invaded Scotland in 1314. He raised a siege at Stirling Castle. It led to the Battle of Bannockburn on 24 June when Edward was defeated by the army of Robert Bruce.

Robert Bruce, Edward I, Edward II

ABOVE George Stephenson with his Steam Locomotive The Rocket

STONEHENGE (c. 3000 BC)

Remains of a stone circle in Wiltshire, England. The exact origins of Stonehenge are a mystery. Archeological evidence has proved that the site has been used for religious and sacred rituals, including sacrifice, but no definitive initial purpose for the site can be given with certainty. There is also no rigid evidence as to how, and by whom, the monument was erected, but it was constructed in alignment with the orbit of the sun: at the summer solstice the sun rises directly overhead. Stonehenge is also strongly associated with Druidism, a religion that was prevalent in Britain in pre-Christian times.

➠ ***Avebury***

STUART DYNASTY

Originally a Scots dynasty that provided seven monarchs of England between 1603 and 1714.

The first Stuart king of Scotland was David II who came to the throne in 1371. The first of the Stuart kings of England, James I, was already James VI of Scotland when he succeeded the last Tudor monarch, Queen Elizabeth I in 1603. The royal Stuarts were an extremely unlucky family. Their history in Scotland was full of sudden deaths, deaths in battle, assassinations, depositions and rebellions against their rule. In England, the Stuarts' history was very troubled, due mainly to their adherence to the Divine Right of Kings: this was the principle that monarchs were appointed by God and answerable only to him. Both King James I and his son and successor King Charles I were devoted to the Divine Right. This ran counter to English principles of government, developed over centuries, in which kings were required to consult and rule in partnership with Parliament. The clash over these principles was worsened by the increasing predominance of Puritans in Parliament. Puritans tended to equate the rule of kings with tyranny and they clashed violently with the Stuarts over the question of religion. The plain, ascetic Puritan faith was at odds with the English form of Protestantism which still retained an aura of Catholicism.

Parliament successfully whipped James I into line during his reign, which lasted until 1625, but a head-on clash occurred with his son and successor, King Charles I. The result was the English Civil War of 1642–49 fought between the Royalists who supported the king and the roundheads who sided with Parliament. The war ended in 1649 with the execution of King Charles. When his son was restored to the throne in 1660 as Charles II, bringing an end to 11 years of Parliamentary rule,

ABOVE James I of England and VI of Scotland

ABOVE RIGHT Mary II

FAR RIGHT Coin commemorating marriage of Charles II to Catherine

the new king trod very warily in case he was forced into exile once again. Charles II was also very devious. He provided himself with an income by secret agreement with King Louis XIV of France, so rendering him less liable to financial control by Parliament. Charles was also a clandestine Catholic, but this was not revealed until he was dying in 1685. Where Charles II stood immovably firm was over Parliament's attempts to deny his Catholic brother, James, Duke of York, the right to succeed to the throne. James succeeded Charles as King James II and proceeded to ruin himself by attempting to restore Catholicism in his realm. He was ousted and exiled in 1688, and his Protestant son-in-law and daughter replaced him as King William III and Queen Mary II. By this time, Parliament had lost all patience with the use and abuse of their powers by the Stuart monarchs and instituted constitutional monarchy, under which kings reigned but did not rule. William and Mary accepted constitutional monarchy with reluctance, but observed its terms. So did their successor, Mary's sister Queen Anne, the last of the Stuart monarchs who died in 1714.

Church of England, Constitutional Monarchy, Parliament

AN UNFORTUNATE DYNASTY

THE kingdom that the first Stuart king, James I, inherited from his Tudor predecessor was secure and thriving. By the time the sun set on the Stuart dynasty the throne would have been lost twice, the country plunged into Civil War and a republic established for 11 years. Unlucky the Stuarts may have been, but most of them were guilty of serious errors of judgement as well. The firm belief in the Divine Right of Kings proved firstly to make James I very unpopular, then to result in the regicide of his successor Charles I. It was not only in dealings with Parliament that there were problems, though. Religious conflict dominated the dynasty. The fervent Protestantism of James I (after whom the Authorised Version of the Bible is named) was lost under Charles I, whose Catholic sympathies proved another bone of contention between the king and those in power. The problem continued with Charles II, so much so, that desperate attempts were made to prevent his brother James II – also a Catholic – from succeeding the throne. Eventually James was driven from the country and a new period of prosperity began with the reign of William and Mary (subject to constitutional monarchy). The reign that began with the unification of England and Scotland under one monarchy ended with political unity under Queen Anne.

TIMELINE

JAMES I
Born: 19 June 1566
Ascends the throne: 24 March 1603
Crowned: 25 July 1603
Married: Anne of Denmark and Norway
Died: 27 March 1625

CHARLES I
Born: 19 November 1600
Ascends the throne: 27 March 1625
Crowned: 2 February 1626
Married: Henrietta Maria of France
Died: 30 January 1649

CHARLES II
Born: 29 May 1630
Ascends the throne: 30 January 1649/29 May 1660
Crowned: 23 April 1661
Married: Catherine of Braganza
Died: 6 February 1685

JAMES II
Born : 14 October 1633
Ascends the throne: 6 February 1685
Crowned : 23 April 1685
Married : Anne Hyde, Mary of Modena
Died : 6 September 1701

MARY II
Born : 30 April 1662
Ascends the throne: 13 February 1689
Crowned : 11 April 1689
Married : William of Orange
Died : 28 December 1694

ANNE
Born : 6 February 1665
Ascends the throne: 8 March 1702
Crowned : 23 April 1702
Married : George of Denmark
Died : 1 August 1714

STUART, JAMES EDWARD 'YOUNG PRETENDER' (1688–1766)

Known as the 'Old Pretender'. Son of James II whose birth to his Catholic parents prompted the deposition of his father and lifelong exile. In 1708, James Edward attempted to invade Scotland and in 1715, he joined the Jacobite Rebellion which was aimed, unsuccessfully, at restoring him to his throne. Subsequently, James left the restoration of the Stuart throne to his son, Charles Edward Stuart (Bonnie Prince Charlie) who also failed to retrieve it.

➠ *Bonnie Prince Charlie, Jacobite Rebellions, James II*

SUEZ CRISIS (1956)

Attack by British and French forces on Egypt after it had decided to nationalise the Suez Canal Company in which Britain had a controlling stake. Stung by enormous international condemnation of the attack, British forces were forced to withdraw and it eventually led to the resignation of prime minister Anthony Eden. The British had controlled the canal, which connects the Red Sea with the Mediterranean, since 1875. In 1888, Britain became the guarantor of the canal's neutral status.

➠ *Anthony Eden*

ABOVE British troops search local people during the Suez crisis

SUFFRAGETTES

Movement to campaign for votes for women. Between 1886 and 1911 women's suffrage bills were repeatedly introduced and defeated in the British

Parliament. They were bills asking for women to be given the right to vote in political elections, for only men were able to vote; such was the air of male chauvinism in post-Victorian society. In 1903 a self-styled suffragette named Emmeline Pankhurst founded the Women's Social and Political Union. By 1906 she had launched a militant suffragette campaign designed to pursue women's right to vote by protest. Suffragettes, who were predominantly middle class, educated women, made all manner of protests

in the name of their just cause. Many suffragettes were arrested and imprisoned for their actions. Their tactic was to go on hunger-strike and gain public sympathy to secure release. Eventually the suffragette movement achieved its goal. Women over 30 were given the vote in 1918 and all women over 21 in 1928.

Emmeline Pankhurst, World War I

SUNDERLAND, ROBERT SPENCER, 2ND EARL OF (1640–1702)

English politician. Sunderland played an astute political game during the turbulent period of the Glorious Revolution. He converted to Catholicism under James II, but when it looked like the throne was under threat, he switched his own religious and political allegiances and served under William III.

Glorious Revolution

SUTTON HOO

Viking burial site. The British Museum, London, holds a collection of jewellery, armour and weapons unearthed at a site in Suffolk, England, 1939. Saxon ship burial and maybe the funeral monument to Raedwald, king of the East Angles, who died *c.* AD 624.

Vikings

SWING RIOTS (1830–31)

Riots against the use of machinery. The Swing Riots occurred in the south and east of England. The Luddites targeted machinery in cotton and wool mills, but the Swing Rioters turned their attentions to wrecking farming machines and attacking the landowners for introducing them. In both cases the riots were protests over rising levels of unemployment due to displacement by technology.

Industrial Revolution

ABOVE Replica Sutton Hoo Helmet

TALLIS, THOMAS (c. 1505–85)

English musician. Tallis was a gentleman of the royal chapel and began his career under Mary I. He retained his post when her half-sister Elizabeth succeeded and, with William Byrd, became the foremost music printer of the time.

➠ *William Byrd*

TEST ACTS (1673)

Three acts of the seventeenth century which tried to exclude nonconformists from high office in the civil and military arenas. From the date of the first act, 1673, all office holders had to swear allegiance to the monarch, affirm the monarch's supremacy as head of the Church of England, repudiate tenets of Roman Catholicism and receive the Anglican Communion. From 1678 all Roman Catholics were excluded from Parliament, except James II. The third act, in 1681, demanded that all government officials in Scotland had to be Protestants.

➠ *Roman Catholicism*

THAMES, RIVER

The artery of London. London began as a Roman settlement around the river. The river is 338 km (210 miles) long, making it the longest English river. It rises near Cirencester in the Cotswold Hills in the west of England and flows in a roughly easterly direction until it meets the North Sea at Southend. The Thames is tidal as far as Teddington just west of London. The Thames Barrier, completed 1982, was built downstream of London to prevent flooding.

THATCHER, MARGARET (b. 1925)

First female British prime minister who won three General Elections and ruled from 1979 to 1990. Her rule caused deep splits in the country between those who supported her and those who opposed her. It was marked by the Falklands Conflict of 1982, the Miners' Strike in 1985 and a programme of privatisation. She first served in government in the 1960s. She was elected as Tory leader in 1975 and took it to the right of the political spectrum. Elected in 1979, her government's policies were deeply unpopular at first, provoking many inner-city riots. However the success of the Falklands resurrected her fortunes and she was returned in 1983 and 1987 continuing policies of low taxation, inflation and public spending. Her economic policies transformed Britain but at a high social cost. Her image abroad was of a tough leader, the 'Iron Lady'. She was eventually relinquished of her leadership in 1990 when Tory MPs saw her as an electoral liability. She described this as a 'betrayal of the highest order'. She was succeeded by John Major.

➠ *Conservative Party, John Major*

THIRTY YEARS' WAR (1618–48)

Series of wars in the seventeenth century. Although the wars originally began as a conflict between Catholics and Protestants, this was really a major struggle

for political power in Europe. In 1618 the Bohemians refused to recognise Ferdinand II as their King and chose Frederick V instead. As a part of the Holy Roman Empire this brought them into conflict with the other members of the empire. After defeating the Bohemians in 1620 Ferdinand became King anyway, but resolved to wipe out Protestantism in Europe. This brought Protestant England, Denmark and Norway into the war. Tilly and Wallenstein defeated their invading armies. Protestant Sweden invaded Germany in 1630 and defeated the Catholics at Breitenfeld (1631). In 1632 the Swedes were defeated at Lutzen. In 1634 the French, seeing an opportunity to defeat the Spanish and the Austrians, joined the Protestants. For the next 14 years war raged in Italy, Flanders and Germany. In 1648 Ferdinand III, succeeding his father, signed the Peace of Westphalia (October 24). Holland was now independent, Sweden had gained territory on the Baltic and France had considerably improved her position in Europe. Half the population of Germany had been killed as a result of the wars.

➠ *James I*

TITHES

Taxes levied in the Middle Ages. Tax was paid by members of a parish community for the upkeep of the church and its incumbent priest. This tax was known as the tithe and typically amounted to 10 per cent of each parishioner's income. It was often produce, stored in the tithe barn.

TOLPUDDLE MARTYRS (1834)

Group of six trade unionist from the village of Tolpuddle in Dorset who were deported to Australia for forming a trade union in 1834. The six were farm labourers. Trade Unions had been ruled legal since 1824 but they still provoked panic in government circles largely because of perceived secret rituals. This is what the six were convicted for. The six – James Brine, James Hammett, George and James Loveless and John and Thomas Stanfield – were sentenced to seven years' transportation. They were pardoned in 1836 following a long public campaign to clear their name.

TOURNAMENTS (c.1066)

Medieval contests fought by jousting knights, sporting their distinct coats of arms. Knights on horseback armed with a lance (a long, blunt-edged weapon) attempted to unseat their opponent, without being thrown from their own horse. Tournaments were often held as entertainment, but could also be used to settle quarrels – in which case they resembled a battle proper. Tournaments were also important for providing training in combat skills. They were often fought by rival families or rival towns. The earliest tournaments were very rough and deaths often occurred. In later centuries they became more spectacular and theatrical. Jousting's popularity waned in the 1500s.

➠ *College of Arms, Heraldry*

ABOVE Meeting of the Tolpuddle martyrs

TOWER OF LONDON (c. 1066)

Most complete medieval fortress in Britain. The Tower of London was begun by William I, as a symbol to the people of Britain that he was not to be challenged. The first, temporary, fort was augmented by a stone tower, from which the building takes its name. King Stephen was the first monarch to live in the Tower, but successive monarchs also made it their residence and added to the building, as well as excavating a large ditch, or moat, all around the fort. At one time a royal menagerie of exotic animals was kept at the Tower, including elephants and big cats – in 1835 they were moved to London's new zoo. From the 1100s, the Tower was used as a prison. After 1285, prisoners were transported to the dungeons through Traitors' Gate. The most famous prisoner to have been taken through the gate was Princess Elizabeth, later Elizabeth I. Others to have been imprisoned here include Edward III, Henry VI and Guy Fawkes. Those to have been executed at the Tower include Lady Jane Grey and Anne Boleyn. The Tower is no longer used as a royal residence. The Tower, and its Yeoman Warders (better known as 'Beefeaters'), is now one of London's premier tourist attractions.

➡ ***Anne Boleyn, Edward III, Elizabeth I, Henry VIII, Princes in the Tower, William I***

TRAFALGAR, BATTLE OF (1805)

Naval battle (21 October 1805) of the Napoleonic Wars. The French Admiral Villeneuve, commanding 40 ships, was ordered to slip out of Cadiz to land troops in Southern Italy on the night of 19 October. Admiral Nelson, commanding 31 vessels, intercepted the Franco-Spanish fleet on the morning of 21 October, leading the attack himself aboard HMS Victory. The battle took place off Cape Trafalgar, on the southern coast of Spain. By the afternoon 20 Franco-Spanish vessels had been destroyed or captured and Villeneuve had been taken prisoner. This action ended Napoleon's plans of an invasion of England and claimed 14,000 Franco-Spanish lives. Nelson was mortally wounded and 1,500 British were killed. Most of the captured ships were lost in a storm but the British had gained naval supremacy that they would keep for over a century. On the same day Napoleon was winning the battle of Ulm against the Austrians under General Mack.

➡ ***Admiral Nelson, Napoleonic Wars***

TRENT, COUNCIL OF (1545–63)

Nineteenth ecumenical council of the Roman Catholic Church. The council opened under Pope Paul III. An interval occurred, 1555–59, due to Pope IV's opposition, then it continued under Pius IV. It implemented some self-reform and so helped the Catholic revitalisation, namely the Counter-Reformation. For example, a revised Bible appeared and corruption was tackled. On the other hand the council also reconfirmed some traditional viewpoints: Latin usage was to be continued, original sin was defined and Luther's beliefs in God's grace were rejected. By 1563 it had solved many of the Protestants' original disagreements and the Jesuits continued their mission to return Catholics to the fold.

➡ ***Counter-Reformation, Jesuits, Martin Luther, Recusants***

TRIPLE ENTENTE (19TH–20TH CENTURIES)

Diplomatic and military alliance between Britain, France and Russia. Originally designed as a counter-measure against the Triple Alliance of Germany, Austria-Hungary and Italy. A Franco-Russian military pact, signed in January 1894; in the following year a more comprehensive alliance was agreed. The French, smarting from defeat by the Germans in 1870–1871, opened negotiations with Britain. It was not until 1904 that traditional rivalries were put aside. Britain and Russia concluded an agreement in 1907, completing the Triple Entente. The tension between the Triple Entente and the Triple Alliance culminated in the outbreak of World War I.

➡ ***Allies, World War I***

TROYES, TREATY OF (1420)

Agreement between the French and British monarchies to establish claims and succession to the thrones of each country. The treaty was signed on 21 May 1420 during the Hundred Years' War. The terms of the treaty allowed for the French king, Charles VI to betroth his daughter Catherine to Henry V. It also made Henry regent of France. Henry died two years later of dysentery, leaving his son Henry VI, who was only a year old, to take advantage of the terms set out in the Treaty of Troyes. Henry VI was also the son of Catherine despite the brief marriage. Henry VI turned out to be a weak and ineffective leader who eventually ended up in the Tower before being murdered in 1471.

➡ ***Hundred Years' War***

TUDOR DYNASTY

The Tudor dynasty which reigned between 1485 and 1603, was descended from John of Gaunt, Duke of Lancaster, third surviving son of Edward III. Lady Margaret Beaufort, the mother of the first Tudor king, Henry VII, was the great-great granddaughter of Edward III. The name of the dynasty derived from Lady Margaret's husband, Edmund Tudor, Earl of Richmond.

The Tudor claim to the crown was very distant and was complicated by the fact that the Beaufort family, the product of John of Gaunt's third marriage, was not considered legitimate: the Beauforts had to be legitimised in 1397. Nevertheless, Henry VII's right to the crown was susceptible to challenge on the grounds that he was the descendant of a 'bastard' royal line. The uncertainty about his ancestry was not the end of Henry VII's problems as king. He had personally won his crown in battle, at Bosworth where the last of the Plantagenet (Angevin) kings, Richard III had been killed. Although this means of inheriting a crown was considered valid, it left a large number of Plantagenets who had a better claim to it than the victor. Plantagenet backing for the impostors Lambert Simnel (1487) and Perkin Warbeck (1494) as long-lost Plantagenet princes were, in fact, attempts to retrieve the throne.

CENTER LEFT Council of Trent inaugural session
TOP RIGHT Edward VI

The second Tudor king, Henry VIII created his own problems for his dynasty. His second marriage, to Anne Boleyn, was considered illegal in Catholic Europe because the Pope had not sanctioned his divorce from his first wife, Catherine of Aragon. This meant that the king's daughter by Anne Boleyn, Elizabeth I, was regarded as illegitimate. Henry's successor as king, his nine-year old son Edward VI was a sickly youth and died aged 15 in 1553. Edward's half-sister Mary I, who succeeded him, caused a serious upheaval in the life of her realm by her attempts to discard the Protestant faith and return England to the jurisdiction of the pope. She died in 1558 detested and reviled by her subjects. Because of her illegitimacy and the fact that the pope had excommunicated her, Mary's successor, her half-sister Elizabeth I was in a dangerous position. Elizabeth's reign was plagued by Catholic plots to kill her and replace her with her Catholic cousin, Mary, Queen of Scots. Elizabeth, however, cleverly concealed the weakness of her position and that of her realm by presenting herself as a glamorous, romantic and glorious figure, and the inspiration behind the achievements of her time in poetry, drama and overseas exploration. The great English triumph over the much-vaunted Spanish Armada in 1588 strengthened her position as queen and the last years of her reign, to 1603, were much more secure. Elizabeth had no heir of her own and her throne passed to the Stuart King James of Scotland, a direct descendant of King Henry VII through his daughter Margaret.

➡ ***Battle of Bosworth, James VI, Spanish Armada, Stuart Dynasty,***

TURPIN, DICK (1705–39)

Highwayman. Richard Turpin was an innkeeper's son from Hampstead Heath, Essex. He turned to highway robbery, gaining notoriety as Dick Turpin. England was not policed at that time in its history, so earning one's keep as a robber was an attractive idea to someone who was not born into privilege. Turpin was also involved with cattle rustling and smuggling contraband. He was eventually caught however, and hanged by the neck at York. It is likely that his legendary ride from London to York, on Black Bess, was actually completed by another highwayman John Nevison (1639–84) in 1676.

TYLER, WAT (d. 1382)

Leader of the Peasants' Revolt. Wat Tyler emanated from the east of England and probably learned his battle and leadership skills in the French wars. The Peasants' Revolt was catalysed by a rise in poll tax under Richard II. The peasantry took up arms and began ransacking towns by way of protest. Having invaded London, the king promised to address their grievances, but Tyler was murdered at a conference.

➠ ***Peasants' Revolt, Richard II***

UTRECHT, TREATY OF (1713–14)

Series of international treaties ending the War of the Spanish Succession. These treaties aimed to prevent France and Austria from dominating the Spanish empire. Philip V, grandson of Louis XIV of France, became King of Spain but renounced his claim to the French throne. Austria received Milan, Naples, Sardinia and the Spanish Netherlands. Britain acquired Gibraltar, Minorca, Nova Scotia, Hudson Bay, Newfoundland and St Kitts. France agreed not to support Jacobite claims to the English throne. Prussia was given three provinces and the Duke of Savoy was given Sicily. Britain emerged as a great colonial commercial and naval power.

➠ ***Queen Anne, War of the Spanish Succession***

VALOIS, CATHERINE DE (1401–37)

Queen Consort of Henry V. Catherine, daughter of Charles VI of France, married Henry in 1420 coinciding with the signing of the Treaty of Troyes making him her father's heir. The only child of Henry and Catherine de Valois became Henry VI on his father's death in 1422. In 1428, Catherine secretly married her Welsh servant, Owen Tudor. Their grandson became Henry VII, the first king of the Tudor dynasty in 1485.

➠ ***Henry V, Henry VI, Tudor Dynasty***

VANBRUGH, JOHN (1664–1726)

English architect and playwright. Vanbrugh began his career in the army, under the command of the Duke of Marlborough (for whom he later designed Blenheim Palace). He was captured by the French and, for two years, was imprisoned in the Bastille, during this time he started writing his play *The Provok'd Wife*. As well as Blenheim Palace, Vanbrugh designed Castle Howard, in Yorkshire.

➠ ***Blenheim Palace***

VERSAILLES, TREATY OF (3 SEPTEMBER 1783)

British recognition of American independence (3 September 1783). Following the end of the war between American Revolutionaries and Great Britain (1775–83), American independence was recognised and boundaries fixed. The treaty went further in dealing with possible problems by giving Florida to Spain and Minorca and Senegal and Tobago to France. The American negotiators included Benjamin Franklin and John Jay. The treaty, also known as The Treaty of Paris, was followed by British evacuation of New York (5 November 1783).

➠ ***American Revolution, George III***

ABOVE The signing of the Treaty of Versailles

VICTORIA, QUEEN (1819–1901)

Queen of England (1837–1901). Victoria succeeded her uncle, William IV, in 1837. In 1840, she married Prince Albert of Saxe-Coburg-Gotha and they had nine children. Victoria adored Albert and after an initial period, when she refused to allow him any royal powers, he became her adviser, mentor, tutor and devoted supporter. Albert was not particularly popular in England, so that when Victoria wanted to create him Prince Consort in 1857, she did so as a personal gift, by Letters Patent. She did not trust Parliament to pass the necessary legislation. When Albert died in 1861, Victoria was distraught and she mourned him extravagantly for the next forty years until her own death in 1901. Even posthumously, she was guided by Albert, so that 'what Albert would have wanted' became her criterion. Victoria was a woman of strong, Hanoverian-style passions, and she was subject to obsessive likes and hatreds. She became greatly attached to Lord Melbourne, her first prime minister, and to Benjamin Disraeli, another, later prime minister who flattered her shamelessly. On the other hand, Victoria detested her stentorian prime minister, William Ewart Gladstone and complained that he used to address her as if she were a public meeting. Victoria was a talented artist and painted many beautiful scenes at Balmoral House, the home built for the Royal Family in Scotland in 1853–56. None of Victoria's children married English spouses, which explains her nickname 'Grandmother of Europe'.

Eventually, the royal houses of Germany, Spain, Russia, Romania, Norway and Sweden were descended from Victoria and Albert. Tragically, Victoria inherited, probably from her father, Edward, Duke of Kent, the gene for the incurable 'bleeding' disease, haemophilia, in which the blood fails to clot normally. Through her, haemophilia struck the royal houses of Russia and Spain, and contributed to their eventual violent downfall. Victoria was very much in advance of her time in her social opinions. She valued the loyalty of the working classes above that of the aristocracy and had no racial prejudice whatever. During Victoria's 63-year reign, the longest yet in British history, Britain made substantial social progress, with acts of Parliament designed to control working hours and conditions in factories and mines, establish education for all children, improve the position of women and emancipate Catholics and Jews. There were also many important scientific, medical and technological developments in which Prince Albert took a particularly strong interest. While Victoria was queen, Britain became the dominant world power, with a vast, far-flung empire on which 'the sun never set'. This was quite literally true: there were so many British colonies scattered across the world that at any one time, the sun was always shining on one or other of them. India was considered the 'jewel in the crown' of the British Empire and in 1876, Victoria was granted the title Empress of India by Parliament. Throughout her reign, Victoria's popularity waned on occasion, especially after she shut herself away in her mourning for Prince Albert. Nevertheless, she died in 1901 respected and revered.

➡ ***Prince Albert, Boer War, British Empire, Crimean War, Edward VII***

VIKINGS

Scandinavian inavders. Following the Anglo-Saxon invasion of Britain, there came raids by Norsemen from Scandinavia, otherwise known as the Danes or Vikings.

Initially the Vikings seem to have only been interested in making short-term sorties onto Anglo-Saxon territory for the purposes of plunder and pillage. They would sail or row their long-boats across the North Sea and make surprise attacks along the east coast of England, scaring the living daylights out of the Britons by their aggressive, warlike behaviour.

Although heathens, the Vikings were not the unsophisticated barbarians that history has portrayed them. In fact they were very skilled at metallurgy, ship building and navigation, making them formidable Medieval explorers. They are known to have reached North America several hundred years before Columbus.

Eventually, the Vikings did harbour ambitions to conquer Britain however, and they achieved it in the ninth century. By AD 886 the Vikings had secured about half of England and the territory was divided by a line which became known as the Danelaw boundary, which ran roughly north-west from London to Liverpool. Lands north of the boundary were under Danelaw, which meant that Viking laws, customs and languages predominated. The Anglo-Saxons even paid tribute tax – Danegeld – to the Vikings.

➡ ***Anglo-Saxons, Canute, Sweyn Forkbeard***

WALES, (ENGLISH) PRINCES OF

Title held since 1301 by the heir apparent to the throne of England. The first Prince of Wales was the future King Edward II, who was said to have been presented to the Welsh after the last of their own, native, princes was killed. Since 1301, there have been twenty further Princes of Wales. The Princes' estate, the Duchy of Cornwall, was created in 1337 for Edward, the Black Prince, heir to King Edward III.

➡ ***Edward I, Edward II, Edward, the Black Prince, Heir to the Throne***

WALLACE, WILLIAM (1272–1329)

Scottish nationalist. Wallace led an uprising against English rule in Scotland in 1297. He shared the uprising with Robert Bruce but declared himself 'governor of Scotland' following the success of his campaign at Stirling. He was defeated however, in 1298, by Edward I, and put to death in 1305. Robert the Bruce was eventually recognised as king of Scotland in 1328 at the Treaty of Northampton.

➡ ***Robert Bruce, Edward I***

WALPOLE, ROBERT (1676–1745)

British Prime Minister. He first became an MP in 1701 and held numerous offices under Queen Anne. He was imprisoned for corruption in 1712. In the early years of the Hanoverian dynasty, he was not in favour but his reputation revived when he took leading responsibility in restoring confidence in Britain's developing financial system after the stock market collapse known as the South Sea Bubble (1720). He became First Lord of the Treasury in 1721 and, in effect, the nation's first 'prime minister'. He was attacked by his many opponents for his excessive power and always denied that he was 'sole and prime minister', seeing the term as one of criticism. His long tenure of power was characterised by highly skilled parliamentary management and financial policies which revealed his great shrewdness and business acumen. He was frequently criticised by opponents for corruption. However, retaining the confidence of both George I and

LEFT Erik the Red sets sail for Greenland
RIGHT York and Lancaster declare their rival claims to the throne

George II (and particularly the second George's wife, Caroline of Asbach-Brandenburg), he was able to ride out several storms. He was brought down in 1742 during the early stages of a war which he had striven for many years to avoid. He amassed huge wealth during his period in office, including a collection of art treasures so admired that it was eventually bought by Catherine the Great of Russia.

➤ *George I*

WALTON, WILLIAM (1902–83)

English composer. Walton has become one of the best-known composers of the twentieth century, mainly through his composition of music for films, most notably Lawrence Olivier's *Henry V.*

WARBECK, PERKIN (1474–99)

Pretender to the throne. In 1494, Warbeck impersonated the murdered Richard, Duke of York, posing as Richard IV. A merchant's assistant, Warbeck was born in Tournai in Picardy, France and toured Europe, gaining support in his bid for the English crown. He prepared to invade England, but Henry VII pre-empted him by detaining most of the English nobles who supported him. Warbeck enlisted the help of King James IV of Scotland but his invasion of the north of England in 1496 was a fiasco. Warbeck was captured and imprisoned in 1497. Later charged with treason, he was executed in 1499.

➤ *Henry VII, Lambert Simnel, Tudor Dynasty*

WARS OF THE ROSES (1455–85)

Struggle for the English throne between the Yorkists and Lancastrians. The Houses of York (White Rose) and Lancaster (Red Rose) were both descendants of Edward III. The Lancastrians had been in power since 1399 but civil disorder, heavy taxes and losses during the Hundred Years' War, and the temporary insanity of Henry VI, brought Richard, Duke of York, to prominence. The Yorkists won the first battle at St Albans (22 May 1455) but were beaten at Ludford Bridge (12 October). After their victory at Northampton (10 July 1460), Henry was forced to name Richard as his successor. Henry's wife, Margaret of Anjou, now disinherited, beat the Yorkists at Wakefield on 30 December and again at St Albans on 17 February 1461. Richard's son Edward, defeated the Lancastrians at Mortimer's Cross on 2 February 1461, was proclaimed Edward IV on 4 March and beat Margaret again at Towton on 29 March. The Lancastrians fled the country and Edward did not face another rebellion until 1469 when he again drove them out of England. In September 1470 Margaret, with the support of the French, restored Henry VI and Edward fled. Allying with Charles the Bold, Duke of Burgundy, he returned in 1471 and beat the Lancastrians at Barnet (14 April) and Tewkesbury (4 May). After Edward died (1483) Richard III seized power and the Yorkists turned to support Henry Tudor, a Lancastrian. He beat Richard at Bosworth (22 August 1485) and ended the wars by marrying Elizabeth of York in 1486.

➤ *Battle of Bosworth, Lancastrian Dynasty, Yorkist Dynasty*

WATERLOO, BATTLE OF (1815)

End of the Napoleonic Wars (18 June 1815). Two months after escaping from Elba, Napoleon mobilised 360,000 men and moved them towards the Franco-Belgian border, intent on destroying the Prussian army (16,000) and the Anglo-Dutch (93,000) while they were still separated. Crossing the border on 15 June he fought an inconclusive battle against the Prussians. The following day French General Ney attacked Wellington's Anglo-Dutch army at Quatre-Bras. Intent on stopping the Anglo-Dutch retreat to Brussels, Napoleon attacked Wellington. Stubborn resistance and the Prussian arrival in the afternoon sealed Napoleon's fate. French casualties were around 40,000, Anglo-Dutch 15,000, Prussians 7,000. Napoleon's downfall was complete.

➤ *Napoleonic Wars, Duke of Wellington*

WELFARE STATE (1945)

In 1942 the Beveridge Report on social security first planted the seed for the idea of a welfare state in Britain. The report committed the wartime coalition government to providing full employment, a free national health service and a social security system in post-war Britain. The Labour government, 1945–51, put the welfare state into effect as far as was practicable. The notion of the welfare state remains an ideal and has been eroded since by changes in political attitudes. Nevertheless it remains a fundamental characteristic of British society. The welfare state concept has been adopted by several other nations.

WELLINGTON, DUKE OF, ARTHUR WELLESLEY (1769–1852)

British General and prime minister. Commissioned into the British army (1787), he became an Irish MP (1790). In 1796, as a Colonel, he went to India and took part in several battles, including Assaye (1803) against the Marathas. He returned to England (1805), was knighted and became a British MP. During 1805–1807 he fought against France in Hanover and Denmark and commanded the British forces in Portugal (1810). During the Penninsular War (1808 – 1814) he beat the French at Talavera (1809), Salamanca (1812), Vitoria (1813) and Toulouse (1814). He was made first Duke of Wellington (1814). In June 1815 he decisively defeated Napoleon at Waterloo and was given a cabinet post in 1818.

He became Commander in Chief of the British Army in 1827 and prime minister in 1828. He resigned in 1830 but was reinstated in 1834, made Foreign Minister 1834–1835 and Commander in Chief again in 1842.

Napoleonic Wars, Battle of Waterloo

WELSH ASSEMBLY

Political body created in 1998 which allows a limited form of self-rule in Wales. It comprises 60 members and has the highest number of women members of Parliament outside Sweden and Norway. It controls a Budget of £7bn but it has no tax-raising powers. The current first secretary is Rhodri Morgan and the assembly is housed in Cardiff. Labour are the majority party with 28 of the 60 seats.

Devolution, Scottish Assembly

WESLEY, JOHN AND CHARLES (1729)

Founders of Methodism. John, an Anglican priest, returned to Oxford and joined his brother Charles' Holy Club, pejoratively called the 'Methodists', due to their methodical approach to the Bible and worship. John preached widely and in 1743 he published *Rules* for the Methodist society. Charles published 4,500 hymns, some of which Handel put to music, but at heart he remained an Anglican, uncomfortable with John's radical ordination of preachers.

Anglicanism, George Frederick Handel, Methodism

WESSEX, KINGDOM OF

Province of ancient Britain. Anglo-Saxon Britain was initially divided into seven kingdoms, known as the Heptarchy. The kingdom of the West Saxons was known as Wessex. Legend has it that Cerdic founded Wessex in *c.* AD 500. Wessex corresponded with the modern counties of Hampshire, Dorset, Wiltshire, Berkshire, Somerset and Devon. In around AD 829 Wessex became the supreme Anglo-Saxon kingdom under

ABOVE John Wesley preaching from his father's tomb

Egbert as overlord or Bretwalda. The most famous king of Wessex was Alfred the Great (*c.* 847–*c.* 899). He became king in AD 871. Alfred created the first English navy to help fend of invasions from his arch enemies the Danes.

Anglo-Saxons

WESTMINSTER ABBEY (c. 10TH CENTURY)

Historic religious building. Reputedly there has been a place of worship here since the 700s. William I was crowned in Westminster Abbey, setting a precedent for future monarchs. This royal connection saved the building from destruction during the Dissolution of the Monasteries (the religious order settled here was dissolved). In the Civil War the abbey housed Cromwell's soldiers, and was partially destroyed. Christopher Wren assisted with its restoration. The abbey contains many illustrious memorials, including Isaac Newton and David Livingstone. The area known as Poets' Corner contains many graves of, or memorials to, great writers, these include Charles Dickens and William Shakespeare.

Dissolution of the Monasteries, William I, Christopher Wren

THE WHIG PARTY

Important political grouping in the seventeenth, eighteenth and early nineteenth centuries. It eventually developed into the Liberal Party of the nineteenth century. The name Whig emerged in the late 1670s to describe those members of parliament who wished to keep James, Duke of York, from succeeding to the throne on the death of his elder brother, Charles II. They failed in this objective but recovered their position in the late 1680s as leading supporters of the Glorious Revolution of 1688, which ended the reign of James II. They were intermittently powerful in the reigns of William III and Anne before they became dominant under the Hanoverian monarchy which began in 1714. They always professed to support the political liberties of Englismen and religious toleration and looked back for inspiration to the Glorious Revolution since it witnessed the emergence of a 'balanced constitution' and strict limits to the powers of the monarchy. In the eighteenth century, rival groups of Whig politicians, headed by immensely wealthy aristocratic politicians, vied for power. Out of power for almost fifty years after 1783, they returned in 1830 to pass the first parliamentary reform Act under Earl Grey in 1832.

William Pitt the Elder, William Pitt the Younger.

WHITBY, SYNOD OF (AD 663–64)

Council of the Anglo-Saxon church to discuss Roman or Celtic usage in Britain. Northumbria was originally converted by the Celts, but by AD 662 the Roman church had influence there. Hilda hosted the synod at her abbey of Whitby and with bishops Colman and Cedd she led the Celtic church; Bishop Wilfrid led the Roman church. A key issue was the date of Easter and Wilfrid won the argument. Due to the outcome of the synod the English church became more closely linked with Rome.

Celtic Christianity, Hilda, Oswy, Roman Christianity

WHITE SHIP (1120)

Vessel carrying Henry I's son William from France to England in 1120. It foundered in the English Channel and William and many of his friends were drowned, leaving Henry without a male heir. This tragedy forced Henry to obtain the alliegance of his barons for his daughter, the Empress Matilda, as his successor. They concurred, but later reneged, prompting the civil war between Matilda and her cousin Stephen, who usurped the throne in 1135.

➡ ***Henry I, Empress Matilda, King Stephen***

WILBERFORCE, WILLIAM (1759–1833)

British philanthropist. William Wilberforce entered British Parliament in 1780. He had philanthropic sympathies and began to develop reformist ideas on slavery. In 1807 his bill for the abolition of slavery was passed. Slavery was ubiquitous in the British Empire and its practice generated a great deal of profit, so Wilberforce had his work cut out convincing others that slavery should be outlawed. In the year of his death though, slavery was abolished throughout the empire.

➡ ***Abolitionists***

WILDE, OSCAR (1854–1901)

Irish writer and exponent of aestheticism, who lived in England. Wilde wrote one novel, *The Picture of Dorian Gray*; plays, including *The Importance of Being Earnest* and *An Ideal Husband*; poems and children's stories. His plays, ostensibly drawing-room comedies, dealt with the prejudices of Victorian England. He was married to Constance and they had two sons. In 1895 he was accused of homosexuality – then a criminal offence – by the 8th Marquess of Queensberry (father of his lover, Lord Alfred Douglas). Wilde was imprisoned with hard labour. On his release, he fled England for Paris, where he died. He was granted a posthumous pardon in the 1990s.

WILLIAM I (1028–87)

King of England (1066–87). Known as William the Conqueror or William the Bastard because of his illegitimate birth. William, first king of the Norman dynasty, had already proved his military prowess and his ruthlessness in wars in Normandy before he seized power in England in 1066. As a young duke with many enemies, William had led a dangerous life, escaping assassination on several occasions. As king, he therefore determined to impose his authority on his new realm. Not all of England accepted him as king and in 1067, he began a systematic conquest to control the population. He built 78 castles including the Tower of London and appointed Normans to powerful positions, giving them large estates taken from the Anglo-Saxon aristocracy. William faced several rebellions, but suppressed them with considerable force. The traditionally restless north of England was virtually laid waste by William's armies and its inhabitants were ruthlessly killed or terrorised. Even twenty years later, when the Domesday Book was compiled, land in the north was still designated as *wasta*, or waste. By 1074, when the Saxon claimant to the throne Edgar the Atheling submitted to William, Norman power in England was complete. King William was greatly hated by the English for his cruelty, his heavy taxation and the virtual slavery of the feudal system which he imposed on them. William spent a large part of his reign in Normandy defending his duchy from the French. He died there after a riding accident which occurred while he was besieging the town of Mantes.

➡ ***Feudal System, Harold II, Battle of Hastings, Norman Dynasty, Tower of London***

WILLIAM II (c. 1057-1100)

King of England (1087–1100). Third son of William I. Nicknamed 'Rufus' because of his red hair. William II was a strong, capable king, who tamed the Welsh princes and controlled the Scots in the north. He was, however, detested by churchmen for his avarice and godlessness. After Lanfranc, Archbishop of Canterbury, died in 1089, William failed to appoint a successor and meanwhile appropriated the Canterbury revenues. William made Anselm archbishop in 1092, when he thought he was dying, but he so mistreated the archbishop that he left England in 1097. William died while out hunting in the New Forest, mysteriously shot by an arrow.

➠ ***Saint Anselm, Henry I, William I***

WILLIAM III (1650–1702)

Joint monarch of England with his wife Queen Mary II (1689-1702). Originally Prince of Orange in Holland. William married Mary, daughter and heir of the Catholic James II in 1677. In 1688, to prevent King James from re-Catholicising England, seven English peers invited William to invade England. James fled to France. Parliament considered that he had abdicated, but MPs were worried that if his daughter Mary became reigning queen, she could have been considered a usurper. William for his part, had no intention of becoming a King Consort. He had his own uses for England and its resources, as financial aid in his fight to keep Louis XIV of France from invading Holland. William therefore insisted on becoming king and in 1689, he was offered the throne jointly with Mary. They became England's only dual monarchy as William III and Mary II.

Parliament, however, imposed restrictions on their powers through the introduction of constitutional monarchy. The exiled James was still regarded as king in Ireland, but his attempt to win back his crown was stifled by his defeat at the Battle of the Boyne in 1690. The Scots were also curbed by William's forces, though this involved a tragedy. The recalcitrant Scots Highlanders were given until 1 January 1792 to swear alliegance to King William, but Alexander McIan MacDonald of Glencoe was inadvertently late in doing so. The result was a fearful massacre at Glencoe in which nearly forty members of the clan were killed, including MacDonald. Queen Mary suffered a succession of miscarriages and stillbirths and she and her husband remained childless. Mary died of smallpox in 1694, to the deep grief of her husband. However, with the agreement of Princess Anne, Mary's sister and the next direct heir to the throne, William remained king until his death after a fall from his horse in 1702.

➠ ***Queen Anne, Battle of the Boyne, Constitutional Monarchy, James II, Mary II, Parliament***

ABOVE RIGHT William IV, the sailor king

LEFT Oscar Wilde

WILLIAM IV (1765–1837)

King of England (1830–37). Son of George III. William IV was so delighted to become king, on the death of his brother George IV in 1830, that he drove round London personally greeting his new subjects. In his youth, William had served in the Royal Navy and commanded ships. He was made a Rear Admiral in 1789, the same year he was created Duke of Clarence. In 1811, William became Admiral of the Fleet. William married Adelaide of Saxe-Meiningen in 1818 after the death of Princess Charlotte, George IV's daughter, had removed the last heir to the throne in her generation. For the sake of this marriage, William had to leave his longstanding mistress, Mrs Dorothea Jordan and their ten children. Sadly, the two daughters of William and Adelaide, who were devoted to each other, died in infancy and William's heir was his niece, Victoria. William was 65 when he became king and his great ambition was to live long enough for Victoria to reach her majority at age 18. This would rob her mother, the Duchess of Kent, whom William detested, of the chance to become Victoria's regent. William achieved his ambition in 1837 by a mere four weeks. The most important political events of William IV's reign were the passing of the Great Reform Act of 1832 which completely transformed the make-up of Parliament, and of two major pieces of legislation in 1833, the Factory Act banning child labour and the Abolition Act which abolished slavery in British colonies.

➠ ***Abolitionists, Queen Adelaide, George IV, Great Reform Act, Queen Victoria, William Wilberforce***

WILLIAM, PRINCE (b. 1982)

Elder son of Charles, Prince of Wales. Second heir to the throne after his father. Prince William made his first official public appearance when he accompanied his parents on their tour of Australia in 1983. Despite intense public interest, the media granted Prince William an unusual degree of privacy, for a member of the Royal Family, during his schooldays. During his 'gap' year before university, William travelled on adventure expeditions to South America and Africa.

Charles, Prince of Wales, Diana, Princess of Wales, House of Windsor

WILLIAMS, RALPH VAUGHAN (1872–1958)

Composer whose music is described as quintessentially 'English'. Vaughan Williams studied in Cambridge, Berlin and Paris (with Ravel). He travelled round Britain recording traditional songs and carols. In World War I he volunteered for the Field Ambulance Service, after which he became Professor of Composition at the Royal College of Music. His works were diverse and include symphonies, hymns and music for the ballet and opera; they include *The Sea*, *London* and *Pastoral*. In 1938 he was awarded the Order of Merit.

World War I

WILSON, HAROLD (1916–95)

British prime minister (1964–70, 1974–76). Wilson helped to shape British politics in the 1960s and 1970s. He was first elected as an MP in 1945 and succeeded Hugh Gaitskell as leader of the Labour Party in 1963 while it was still in opposition. He first became prime minister in October 1964. Famous for smoking a pipe, Wilson was again elected in 1974, ousting his great Tory rival Ted Heath. But he resigned only two years into his second term as prime minister for reasons that have never been properly explained. Later in life he suffered from Parkinson's disease.

WILTON DIPTYCH (c. 1400)

Panels show saints commending the patron, Richard II, to the Virgin and Christ Child. The diptych demonstrates typical agendas of the time; propaganda and insurance for the patron's soul. It also depicts the flag of St George and is memorable for its gold background and host of blue-clad angels. The painting is now displayed in the National Gallery, London.

Edward the Confessor, St George, Reformation, Richard II

WINCHESTER CATHEDRAL

Longest cathedral in Britain, at 169 m (556 ft). In the seventh century the West Saxon episcopal see moved to Winchester and the cathedral consequently houses Alfred the Great's bones. Building began in the latter part of the eleventh century and during William of Wykeham's lifetime the fourteenth-century perpendicular nave was built. Winchester not only had a religious role: Alfred the Great encouraged education there and it developed as a seat of royal government.

Alfred the Great

WINDSOR CASTLE (1066)

The monarch's official residence in Windsor, South-East England. The original castle at Windsor was made of earth and was not a permanent structure.It was built by William I to guard the main route to London. The first stone castle, built on the same site, was erected during the reign of Henry II. It was added to through the reigns of several successive monarchs, including the construction of the impressive St George's Chapel. Among the monarchs buried at the castle are Charles I, Queen Victoria and Prince Albert and Edward VII. The castle stands near the River Thames, surrounded by spectacular grounds. Nearby is Windsor

Great Park, with its resident deer. Over the bridge from the castle is one of England's most famous schools, Eton College. In 1992 Windsor Castle was damaged in a fire. The restoration cost £37,000,000 and took five years to complete. Today the castle is both a royal home and a popular visitor attraction.

Prince Albert, Ascot, Charles I, Edward VII, Henry II, Queen Victoria, William I

WINDSOR, HOUSE OF

The royal House of Windsor is not a dynasty in the true sense, that is, it was not a new family only distantly related to the previous dynasty, as happened, for example, when the Stuarts succeeded the Tudors in 1603. The monarchs of the House of Windsor – George V, Edward VIII, George VI and Elizabeth II – were direct descendants of the Hanoverian dynasty which inherited the throne when the Elector of Hanover became King George I in 1714. The dynasty's name was changed in 1901, to 'Saxe-Coburg-Gotha', a German state where Queen Victoria's husband, Prince Albert, was born. Edward VII, son and heir of Queen Victoria and Prince Albert, was the first king of the House of Saxe-Coburg-Gotha.

In 1910, his son George V came to the throne as the second king of this House, but in 1917, he altered its name to Windsor. He did so because of the British hatred of Germany and its Kaiser, Wilhelm II, that developed during World War I. This hatred was so pronounced that shops with German names on their fascias had their windows broken. Families with German names, many of them German-Jewish immigrants, were attacked. Anti-German feeling went so far that dachshunds, the long-bodied German dogs, were kicked in the streets. The problem for the Royal Family, whose major members were thoroughly anglicised by this time, was not only because of the name Saxe-Coburg-Gotha or their descent from the Hanoverian monarchs. In the nineteenth century, several children of Queen Victoria and Prince Albert married German husbands or wives, a fact that gave rise to a great deal of popular protest at the time. Consequently, by 1916, the Royal Family had many relatives, the descendants of these marriages, who bore German titles. One of them was Prince Louis of Battenberg, Admiral and First Sea Lord in the First World War: despite many years of faithful service to the Royal Navy, he was forced to resign because of his German name and connections. Anti-German feeling was a severe embarrassment to George V, who not only ordered the change of name to Windsor but told his royal relatives to drop their German titles and take new, English ones. The family of Prince Louis of Battenberg, for example, translated their name directly into English and called themselves Mountbatten.

BELOW George V and Queen Mary

Prince Albert, Edward VII, Edward VIII, Elizabeth II, George V, George VI, Hanoverian Dynasty, Queen Victoria, World War I

WITAN, THE

Council for Anglo-Saxon kings which is seen as a precursor of the modern Parliament. The council, established in the ninth century, gave advice to the king on matters of state. Its members included bishops and major landowners. One of its major roles was to become a check and balance on the power of the monarch. It also proceeded with government business during times when there were no kings.

➜ *Anglo-Saxons, Canute*

WOODVILLE, ELIZABETH

Queen Consort of Edward IV. Edward married the beautiful widow Elizabeth Woodville in 1464. The marriage was disliked by the Yorkist nobility because Elizabeth was a commoner and came from a Lancastrian family. As queen, Elizabeth increased her unpopularity by her avarice in gaining noble titles and important offices for her family. Edward and Elizabeth had seven surviving children. Both they and their mother were in great danger after the sudden death of Edward IV in 1483, when his brother, Richard of Gloucester, usurped the throne. Elizabeth fled for sanctuary with her younger children to Westminster Abbey. For reasons unknown, she gave them into Richard's care. Subsequently, after Richard's downfall in 1485, the former queen's daughter, Elizabeth, married King Henry VII. Elizabeth Woodville appears to have indulged in treasonable activities, for in 1487 she was disgraced and forced to enter a convent where she died five years later.

➜ ***Edward IV, Edward V, Princes in the Tower, Richard III, Tower of London***

WORDSWORTH, WILLIAM (1770–1850)

English poet; leading figure of the Romantic movement. Wordsworth was born in the Lake District, where he spent the majority of his life. His love for nature and the natural world is the most prominent feature in his works, which includes such classics as 'The Prelude' and 'Daffodils'. This almost obsessional love of nature has led to his being described as a pantheist. Wordsworth's unmarried sister, Dorothy, was his lifelong companion, even following his marriage to Mary Hutchison (1802). Dorothy's journals are believed by many scholars to have inspired some of William's best works. The Wordsworths are strongly associated with their great friend, Coleridge.

➜ ***Samuel Taylor Coleridge***

WORLD WAR I (1914–18)

Worldwide conflict claiming 30 million casualties. There are many reasons why World War I broke out against the allies and the central powers of Germany, Austro-Hungary and the Ottoman Empire. The main act was the assassination of Austrian Archduke Francis Ferdinand (28 June 1914) by Serbian nationalists. Germany supported demands to suppress Serbian militants. Despite negotiations Austria declared war on Serbia (July 28). European powers mobilised their armies.

On August 1, Germany declared war on Russia and marched into Luxembourg. On August 3 they declared war on France, forcing Britain to declare war on them (August 4). The British Expeditionary Force (BEF) under the French began landing at Le Havre (August 7). The Russians invaded from the east on August 13 and threw the Austrians into confusion. Three attempted Austrian invasions of Serbia in August, September and November failed. The Germans continued through Belgium, defeating the French and Belgians at Charleroi (August 22) and the BEF at Mons (August 23–24). Hindenburg defeated the Russians at Tannenberg (August 26–29) and Mazurian Lakes (September 9–14). German advances on the western front were checked at Marne (September 5–9). On the eastern front they continued to make ground against the Russians. At Ypres (October 30–November 24) the BEF held against the Germans but an allied offensive in December failed. The Gallipoli Campaign failed to knock the Turks out of the war. On the western front throughout 1915 both the Germans and allies failed to make headway despite huge casualties. On May 23, Italy declared war on Austro-Hungary and in

RIGHT Members of the 9th Battalion, Yorkshire Regiment cut German wire in preparation for an attack on enemy trenches.

September British and French offensives faltered. German attacks at Verdun began 21 February 1916, continuing for a year but gaining little ground.

In May 1916 the British fleet defeated the Germans at Jutland and in June the Russians launched a new offensive. Throughout July and November the Battle of the Somme raged, seeing the first use of tanks. The British advanced from Egypt and in three battles occupied Palestine and later Mesopotamia. The US declared war on Germany on 6 April 1917 after submarine attacks on their ships. New allied offensives in April and May gained some ground. In October the American Expeditionary Force arrived but in November the Russians began negotiations for an armistice. In 1918 the German spring offensive gained 40 miles; a second 15 miles. A third was stopped by US troops. In August the allied offensive saw victories against the Germans at Amiens, Arras and the Somme. The last allied offensive broke the Hindenburg line and armistice talks began 28 September. The Austro-Hungarians signed an armistice 3 November 1918 and following the collapse of the German government and mutinies the Emperor abdicated. The Germans signed the armistice on 11 November 1918. The Treaty of Versailles imposed harsh terms on the Germans.

➠ ***BEF, Dardanelles Campaign, Gallipoli, Kitchener's Army, Battle of the Somme, Battles of Ypres***

WORLD WAR II (1939–45)

Worldwide conflict between the allies and axis powers. Hitler came to power in Germany (1933) and began re-arming. In March 1938 he annexed Austria and in September took Sudetenland from Czechoslovakia. On 1 September, Germany invaded Poland; two days later Britain and France declared war on them. Poland was beaten by 22 September and on 30 November the Russians invaded Finland. In April 1940 the Germans invaded Denmark and Norway and launched their offensive against the Netherlands, Luxembourg, France and Belgium (10 May). The Netherlands were conquered (14 May) and Belgium surrendered (28 May). The BEF and French forces evacuated from Dunkirk on 4 June. By 22 June France had sued for peace, overrun by the Germans. In August, whilst the Italians had started their offensive in Africa, Britain was winning the Battle of Britain. Italian invasion of Egypt (September) was met with a counter-offensive that swept the Italians back into Libya.

Axis forces turned to the Balkans; Yugoslavia surrendered (17 April 1941), Athens was captured (27 April) and Crete (31 May). German submarines were sinking hundreds of allied ships but the US lend-lease programme provided the allies with urgent munitions. Under Rommel, the German offensive in North Africa was launched (April 1941), driving the British back to Egypt. On 22 June Germany invaded the USSR, rapidly advancing towards Leningrad, Moscow and Kiev. By December the Russians had counter-attacked and the offensive was halted. In North Africa the British had launched a counter-offensive driving the Germans back. A Russian winter offensive forced the Germans to withdraw west.

On 7 December the Japanese attacked the US Pearl Harbor, forcing America to declare war on them and their allies Germany and Italy. The Japanese overran British, French and American colonies in the east and threatened India. In 1942 the Japanese were defeated at Midway and America now went on the offensive. The German's June offensive in the east gained ground but the USSR began counter-attacks. In the Far East America had regained Japanese conquests and in Africa the Battles of El Alamein drove the Germans back into Libya. US forces landed in Algeria (8 November), capturing thousands of Germans at Stalingrad on the Russian front (2 February 1943). By May the Germans had been cleared from Africa. The allies invaded Sicily (10 July) and the new Russian offensive pushed westward. The Americans had captured more Japanese-held islands and in September the allies invaded the Italian mainland; Italy surrendered on September 3. On 6 June 1944 the allies landed in France whilst the Russians overran Romania (24 August), Bulgaria (8 September) and Yugoslavia (20 October). By 25 August the allies were in Paris and reached the German border by 11 September. A last German counter-attack in the west failed and, with Russia advancing from the east, the allies launched their last offensive culminating in the Russian capture of Berlin (2 May). Hitler had committed suicide. Japan now faced the full might of the allies but it took two atomic bombs to force their surrender (14 August).

➠ ***Winston Churchill, D-Day, Dunkirk***

ABOVE Fitting gas masks
RIGHT Rommel with troops in North Africa
FAR RIGHT German infantry during attack

THE BATTLE OF BRITAIN

THE Battle of Britain was the German air campaign intended as a prelude to invasion. It began on 10 July 1940 and continued until October. Hitler ordered Goering's Luftwaffe to seize control of the Channel and destroy the Royal Air Force. He had 3,000 aircraft at his disposal against about 600 RAF fighters.

In early August the attacks centred on the Channel ports and airfields. On 15 August 1940 German aircraft hit targets further north. In the crucial two-week period from 24 August to 6 September the RAF lost 25 per cent of its pilots and the Germans twice as many. On 7 September the Germans launched the first of their daylight air raids, but huge losses forced a switch to night attacks. By 12 October, with losses mounting, Hitler abandoned Operation Sealion, his invasion plan, and the hitherto-invincible German armed forces suffered its first defeat. The battle gave rise to Churchill's famous words about the Royal Air Force: 'Never in the field of human conflict was so much owed by so many to so few.'

WREN, CHRISTOPHER (1632–1723)

English architect in the time of Charles II. As well as being one of England's most revered architects, Wren was also Professor of Astronomy at Oxford University and one of the founders of the Royal Society. Perhaps best known for St Paul's Cathedral, he designed many other famous buildings, including Kensington Palace, the Admiralty building in Whitehall, Chelsea Hospital, the Royal Observatory at Greenwich and parts of Hampton Court Palace. Despite his illustrious career, Wren became an architect relatively late in life, in 1663. His very first job was commissioned by his uncle (the Bishop of Ely). The commission was to design the Pembroke College Chapel at Cambridge University. St Paul's Cathedral was part of a grand scheme to rebuild the City of London in the aftermath of the Great Fire of London. Due to lack of funds for Wren's expensive plans, the original plan was only partially completed.

➠ ***Cambridge University, Charles II, Great Fire of London, Hampton Court Palace, St Paul's Cathedral***

WYCLIF, JOHN (*c.* 1330–84)

Forebear of the Protestant Reformation. Ordained a clergyman, Wyclif was a controversial yet popular figure. He advocated preaching and the rejection of worldly goods and corruption: views that became the backbone of the Lollards. Arrested in 1377 for the political slant of his religious views, Wyclif nevertheless supported the Peasants' Revolt in 1381, and consequently much of his work was condemned. Less conscientiously, he practised absenteeism, a corruption he opposed, from his parish of Westbury-on-Trym.

➠ ***Peasants' Revolt, Protestant Reformation***

YALTA CONFERENCE (1945)

Allied conference on military and political strategy. US President Franklin Roosevelt, British prime minister Churchill and Russian Premier Stalin agreed to 'destroy German militarism and Nazism and to ensure that Germany will never again be able to disturb the peace of the world'. They agreed to partition Germany; how Europe would appear after the war and how to collect reparations. This high point of allied unity was aimed to deal with a number of political problems.

➠ ***Winston Churchill, World War II***

YEOMEN OF THE GUARD

Royal bodyguard specially formed for the coronation of the first Tudor king, Henry VII in 1485. The Yeomen of the Guard still exist today and still wear their Tudor uniforms. Their duties included searching the cellars of Parliament for possible assassins before the state opening by the monarch.

➠ ***Henry VII, Parliament, Tudor Dynasty***

YORK, HOUSE OF

Branch of the Plantagenet (Angevin) dynasty which challenged the right to the throne of the House of Lancaster, another branch of the same dynasty. The basis of the Yorkist claim was that their ancestor, Lionel, Duke of Clarence had been an older son of King Edward III than John of Gaunt, Duke of Lancaster from whom the Lancastrians were descended. Richard, Duke of York, great-grandson of Lionel claimed the throne from the Lancastrian King Henry VI, great-grandson of John of Gaunt. The challenge precipitated the civil Wars of the Roses, but the Duke of York was killed at the battle of Wakefield in 1460. The Yorkist cause was taken up by his son, who deposed Henry VI in 1461 and became the first Yorkist monarch as King Edward IV. In 1470, his erstwhile supporter Richard Neville, Earl of Warwick joined forces with Margaret, Henry VI's queen and invaded England to restore Henry to the throne. Edward fled to Europe, but returned in 1471. He defeated Warwick at the battle of Barnet and defeated Queen Margaret's army at Tewkesbury, where her son, Henry VI's heir, was killed. Henry was again deposed and Edward IV resumed his reign. On his death, in 1483, his successor was his 12-year old son, King Edward V. Edward's uncle, Richard, Duke of Gloucester, took charge of the child king and established himself as Protector of England. Though a faithful supporter of his brother, Edward IV, throughout his reign, Richard now usurped the throne. He claimed that his brother and Queen Elizabeth Woodville had not been legally married, since

Edward had been betrothed to another woman when they wed in 1464. This made King Edward V illegitimate and so not fit to succeed to the throne. The young king and his brother Richard, Duke of York disappeared while in the Tower of London and were never seen alive again. Richard was crowned King Richard III in Westminster Abbey on 6 July 1483. He was the third and last Yorkist king, reigning for two years until he was defeated and killed at the battle of Bosworth in 1485.

➠ ***Battle of Bosworth, Edward IV, Edward V, Henry VI, John of Gaunt, House of Lancaster, Richard III, Wars of the Roses***

YORKTOWN, BATTLE OF (1781)

The last of the campaigns of the American Revolution. After General Cornwallis had failed to subjugate Carolina he then moved his troops north to occupy Yorktown and fortify it against the rebels. A rebel army, 8,000 strong, under General Lafayette besieged the force whilst a French fleet under de Grasse blockaded the harbour. Under continual bombardment the British held out, hoping for reinforcements from New York where Clinton was refitting his troops. Lafayette was reinforced by Washington and Rochambeaux who had marched south. Cornwallis was forced to surrender on 19 October, thus securing for the rebels American independence.

➠ ***American Revolution, Charles Cornwallis***

YPRES, BATTLES OF (1914–1918)

Four battles in Belgium during World War I. The first battle was the last major one of 1914. The Germans attacked the BEF and advanced several miles, but were halted by French and Belgian reinforcements. The British counter-attacked and the Germans launched another assault in rain and snow. About 80 percent of the BEF died. The second battle is notable for being the first time the Germans used chlorine gas (24 April 1915). The Germans attacked the British salient but the front was held with the introduction of Canadian reserves. The third battle, also known as Passchendaele, opened with a ten-day artillery bombardment by the British, including

LEFT Big Three Conference, Yalta
TOP RIGHT The Battlefield of Ypres

Australians and Canadians, advancing two to five miles. By the end of the five months' fighting, allied losses were approaching 300,000, the costliest of all British offensives. The last battle saw significant German advances, being unable to break the Ypres salient despite heavy fighting.

➠ ***World War I***

ZULU WAR (1879)

British expansion in Africa. In December 1878 Sir Henry Vartle Frere, the British High Commissioner in South Africa, had decided that the strong and independent Zulu kingdom to the north represented a threat to British expansion in the region. He demanded that the Zulu king, Cetshwayo, disband his army and submit his country to British guidance. Under Lord Chelmsford three British columns entered Zululand in January 1879. On 22 January the centre column was attacked and virtually wiped out by the Zulus at Isandlwana. Zulu warriors then crossed into Natal but were beaten off by a company of British regulars at Rorke's Drift. The two remaining columns were left exposed and simply had to dig in and wait. British reinforcements were quickly sent to the area to relieve the two other columns. The Zulus were defeated at Khambula and kwaGingindlovu and a column under Sir Evelyn Wood had almost been wiped out at Hlobane on March 28. On 1 June Louis Napoleon, Prince Imperial of France, was killed in a skirmish. The British continued to advance towards Ulundi, the Zulu capital, where, on 4 July the Zulus were again defeated and the capital burned. Cetshwayo was captured and sent into exile.

➠ ***Battle of Rorke's Drift***

CHRONOLOGIES

CULTURE

2600 BC Avebury stone circle constructed
AD 735 Death of the Venerable Bede
1400 Death of Geoffrey Chaucer
1484 College of Arms established
1491 Death of printer William Caxton
1533 Henry VIII employs Hans Holbein as his court painter
1536 Henry VIII seizes the area of Hyde Park to use as a hunting ground
1613 Inigo Jones is appointed as James I's surveyor of works
1625 Death of Orlando Gibbons
1633 Work begins on Buckingham Palace
1637 Death of playwright Ben Jonson
1668 John Dryden becomes the first poet laureate

1674 Death of John Milton
1687 Isaac Newton publishes *Mathematical Principles of Natural Philosophy*
1705 Work begins on the construction of Blenheim Palace
1711 First race meeting at Ascot
1755 Samuel Johnson published his *Dictionary*
1759 First botanic gardens laid out at Kew
1762 Robert Adam becomes George III's architect
1764 Death of William Hogarth
1783 Death of Lancelot 'Capability' Brown
1786 Robert Burns publishes his first volume of poetry

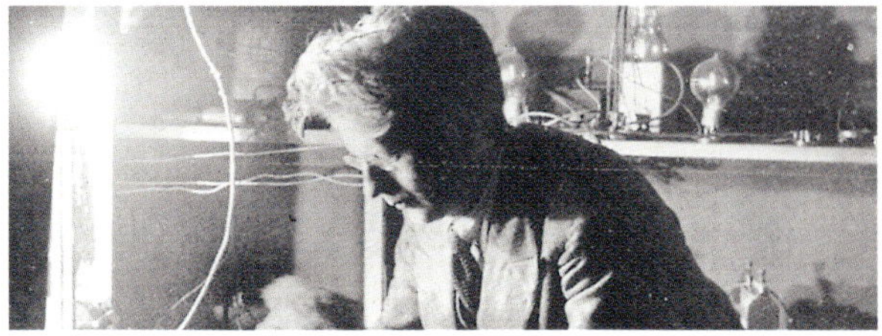

1798 Wordsworth and Coleridge publish *Lyrical Ballads*
1812 Lord Byron publishes *Childe Harold's Pilgrimage*
1815 Work begins on the Royal Pavilion at Brighton, commissioned by the Prince Regent
1848 Pre-Raphaelite movement begins
1851 Crystal Palace built to house the Great Exhibition
1852 Queen Victoria buys the land on which she builds Balmoral Castle
1870 Death of Charles Dickens
1887 Arts and Crafts Exhibition Society founded
1895 The Proms are held in the Royal Albert Hall
1896 Death of William Morris
1915 Death of Rupert Brooke
1926 John Logie Baird gives first demonstration of television
1927 British Broadcasting Corporation founded
1963 The Beatles have their first Number One hit with 'Please Please Me'
1970 First Glastonbury Festival
1972 John Betjemen becomes poet laureate
1976 Death of Benjamin Britten
2000 Millennium Dome opened

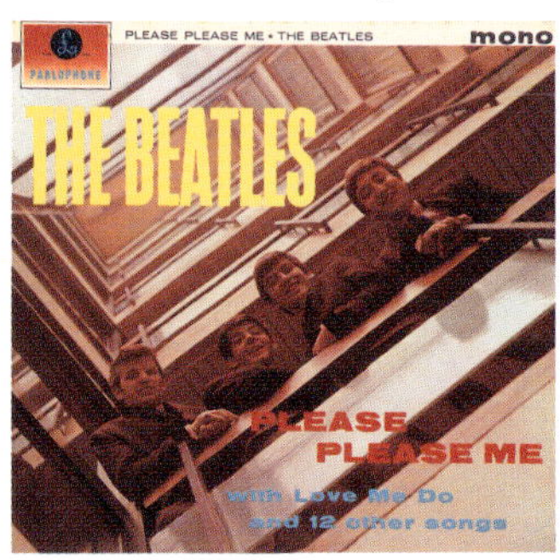

INDUSTRY

AD 122 Hadrian's Wall built
AD 142 Antonine Wall built
1540s Debasement of the Coinage
1600 East India Company established
1603 First Enclosure Act introduced
1693 Britain's first national debt
1694 Bank of England founded
1701 Jethro Tull invents the seed drill, sparking the Agricultural Revolution
1762 Work begins on the Bridgewater Canal
1768 Richard Arkwright invents the spinning frame
1800 Utopian community set up at New Lanark
1802 First Factory Act introduced
1821 Michael Faraday begins his experiments with electromagnetism
1846 Prime minister Robert Peel repeals the Corn Laws, controlling the import and export of corn and other cereals in Britain

1876 Alexander Graham bell demonstrates his new invention: the telephone
1906 Construction of *HMS Dreadnought*
1926 General Strike
1936 John Maynard Keynes publishes *General Theory of Employment, Interest and Money*
1976 First flight of Concorde
1994 Channel Tunnel opened

POLITICS

AD 991 Peace with the Danes is bought with the Danegeld
1258 Provisions of Oxford
1259 Treaty of Paris
1295 Edward I forms the Model Parliament
1400 Owen Glendower begins a revolt against Henry IV in Wales
1520 Field of the Cloth of Gold between Henry VIII and Francis I of France
1525 Cardinal Wolsey re-established the Council of the North
1535 Thomas More executed
1540 Thomas Cromwell executed on charges of treason
1586 Babington Plot to assassinate Elizabeth 1
1601 Elizabeth I gives her 'Golden Speech' to Parliament
1605 Gunpowder Plot
1608 Robert Cecil becomes lord treasurer
1621 Francis Bacon impeached on charges of corruption
1629 Charles I dissolves Parliament and begins the Eleven Years' Tyranny
1640 Long Parliament convened
1641 Long Parliament dissolves the Council of the North
1647 Rise of the Levellers
1648 Pride's Purge
1653 The Barebones Parliament convenes

1658 Death of Oliver Cromwell
1661 Cavalier Parliament affirms the Restoration of the monarchy
1670 Treaty of Dover
1679 First Exclusion Bill introduced
1685 Monmouth's rebellion
1686 Bloody Assizes set up to try those involved in Monmouth's rebellion
1689 Grand Alliance in Europe
1697 First Civil List Act passed
1707 Act of Union passed uniting England and Scotland
1732 Lord Frederick North becomes prime minister
1743 Henry Pelham becomes prime minister
1766 William Pitt the Elder becomes prime minister
1767 Duke of Grafton becomes prime minister
1771 Warren Hastings becomes governor of Bengal
1783 William Pitt the Younger becomes prime minister
1783 Britain recognises the independence of its former colonies in North America
1807 Duke of Portland becomes prime minister
1812 Lord Liverpool becomes prime minister
1820 Cato Street conspiracy
1822 Viscount Castlereagh commits suicide
1827 George Canning becomes prime minister
1828 Daniel O'Connell elected as MP for County Clare
1830s Rise of the Conservative Party
1832 Great Reform Act introduced
1834 Robert Peel becomes prime minister
1834 Viscount Melbourne becomes prime minister
1852 Lord Aberdeen becomes prime minister
1868 William Gladstone becomes prime minister
1868 Benjamin Disraeli becomes prime minister
1900 Labour Party is formed

1902 Arthur Balfour becomes prime minister

1904 Britain and France sign the Entente Cordiale
1908 Herbert Henry Asquith becomes prime minister
1911 Andrew Bonar Law is elected leader of the Conservative Party
1916 David Lloyd George becomes prime minister
1916 Easter Rising in Dublin
1917 Balfour issues his Declaration in favour of a home for Jews in Palestine; Cooperative Party formed
1919 IRA formed to fight for an independent Irish state
1921 James Craig becomes first prime minister of Ireland
1922 Death of Irish nationalist leader Michael Collins; Irish Free State Agreement Act passed
1924 Ramsay MacDonald becomes prime minister
1931 Statute of Westminster recognises the British Commonwealth of Nations
1932 Clement Attlee becomes prime minister
1937 Eámon De Valera begins his first term as prime minister of Ireland
1940 Winston Churchill becomes prime minister
1948 Mahatma Gandhi is assassinated
1949 NATO is formed
1952 Winston Churchill begins second office as prime minister
1955 Anthony Eden becomes prime minister
1957 Harold Macmillan becomes prime minister
1963 Alec Douglas-Home becomes prime minister
1970 Edward Heath becomes prime minister
1972 13 unarmed protestors are killed on Bloody Sunday
1976 James Callaghan becomes prime minister
1985 Anglo-Irish Agreement signed

1990 John Major takes over from Margaret Thatcher as prime minister
1993 European Union comes into force
1997 Tony Blair becomes prime minister after Labour win a landslide victory in the general election
1998 Scotland and Wales vote for their own Assemblies; Good Friday Agreement in Northern Ireland

RELIGION

AD 313 Constantine converted to Christianity
AD 400 Ninian established the first church in Scotland
AD 597 Augustine converts 1,000 pagan Britons to Christianity
AD 600 Death of St David
AD 651 Death of St Aidan
AD 657 Hilda founds the abbey at Whitby
1070 Lanfranc becomes first Norman primate
1095 First Crusade begins
1098 Cistercian Order founded
1154 Nicholas Breakspear becomes Pope Adrian IV
1170 Thomas Becket slain in Canterbury Cathedral
1189 Third Crusade begins
1198 Fourth Crusade begins
1215 Dominican Order founded
1240 Death of St Edmund
1373 Julian of Norwich receives her vision
1532 Henry VIII breaks with Rome to gain his divorce from Catherine of Aragon

1534 Society of Jesus (Jesuits) founded
1536 Dissolution of the Monasteries begins Pilgrimage of Grace
1544 David Beaton created papal legate and effectively becomes ruler of Scotland
1545 Council of Trent is convened
1572 Death of John Knox
1603 Millenary Petition signed by 1,000 ministers to effect Church of England reform
1611 King James Bible published
1638 Scottish Presbyterians sign the National Covenant
1661 First of the Clarendon Codes introduced
1662 First Declaration of Indulgence announced
1689 Act of Toleration passed
1780 Anti-Catholic Gordon Riots
1833 Rise of the Oxford Movement
1843 Free Church of Scotland established
1871 The abolition of Test Acts end the struggle for Catholic emancipation

ROYALTY

AD 61 Death of Boudicca, queen of the Iceni
AD 871 Alfred the Great becomes king of Wessex
AD 899 Death of Alfred the Great
AD 939 Edmund I becomes king of England
AD 942 Malcolm I becomes king of the Scots
AD 955 Edwy becomes king of England
AD 975 Edward the Martyr becomes king of England
AD 978 Ethelred the Unready becomes king of England
1013 Sweyn Forkbeard is acknowledged king of England
1016 Edmund II ascends the throne of England
1034 Duncan I becomes king of Scotland
1035 Harold I becomes king of England
1042 Edward the Confessor becomes king of England
1058 Malcolm III becomes king of Scotland
1093 Donald III seizes the throne of Scotland; Duncan II briefly usurps the throne
1100 Henry I becomes king of England
1107 Alexander I becomes king of Scotland
1124 David I becomes king of Scotland
1153 Malcolm IV becomes king of Scotland
1154 Henry II becomes king of England
1190 Alleged tomb of King Arthur discovered at Glastonbury Abbey
1199 John becomes king of England
1216 Henry III becomes king of England
1272 Edward I becomes king of England
1307 Edward II becomes king of England
1312 Nobles murder Edward II's favourite Piers Gaveston

1327 Edward III becomes king of England
1329 David II becomes king of Scotland
1376 Death of Edward, the Black Prince
1399 Henry IV becomes king of England
1406 James I becomes king of Scotland
1413 Henry V becomes king of England
1422 Henry VI becomes king of England
1461 Edward IV becomes king of England
1470 Edward IV is deposed and Henry VI restored to the throne
1471 Henry VI is once again replaced by Edward IV

1483 Edward V is taken to the Tower of London to await his coronation; it never takes place, Richard III assumes the throne
1485 Henry Tudor becomes Henry VII
1509 Henry VIII marries Catherine of Aragon
1513 James V becomes king of Scotland
1536 Anne Boleyn is executed at the Tower of London
1542 Mary becomes Queen of Scots
1547 Edward VI becomes king following the death of Henry VIII
1553 Mary I becomes queen of England
1558 Elizabeth I becomes queen of England
1565 Mary, Queen of Scots marries Lord Darnley
1567 James VI becomes king of Scotland
1603 James VI of Scotland becomes James I of England

1625 Charles I becomes king of England
1649 Charles I is executed and the country becomes a commonwealth under the leadership of Oliver Cromwell
1660 Charles II is restored to the throne
1685 James II becomes king of England
1689 Constitutional monarchy introduced with the accession of William and Mary
1701 Act of Settlement ensures the succession of the Electors of Hanover
1702 Anne becomes queen of England
1714 George I becomes king of England
1727 George II becomes king of England
1795 The future George IV marries Princess Caroline of Brunswick
1861 Death of Prince Albert
1876 Queen Victoria is created Empress of India
1901 Edward VII becomes king
1936 Edward VIII abdicates
1948 Birth of Prince Charles
1952 Elizabeth II becomes queen of England
1979 Earl Mountbatten murdered by the IRA
1981 Marriage of Prince Charles and Lady Diana Spencer
1997 Diana, Princess of Wales, is killed in a car crash in Paris

SOCIETY

2700 BC Beaker people in British Isles
55 BC Julius Caesar makes his first visit to the island of Britain
50 BC Commius, leader of the Atrebates, flees to Britain after fighting the Romans
AD 43 Emperor Claudius leads the Roman Conquest of Britain; Roman spa town established at Bath
AD 60 Boudicca leads a revolt against the Romans
AD 757 Offa's Dyke built
AD 825 Wessex becomes the leading province of ancient Britain, under the 'bretwalda'
AD 891 *Anglo-Saxon Chronicle* begun
1070 Hereward the Wake leads a revolt against the Normans in Cambridgeshire
1086 Domesday survey of England begun
1284 Peterhouse College, Cambridge founded
1344 Edward III established the Order of the Garter
1348 The Black Death ravages England
1381 Peasants' revolt
1497 John Cabot becomes the first man to reach mainland America, under English patronage
1577 Francis Drake sets off around the world
1601 First Poor Law Act passed
1620 The Pilgrim fathers set sail for the New World
1665 Great plague ravages England
1666 Great Fire of London
1772 John Harrison's H4 is designed

1773 Boston Tea Party starts a revolution against British rule in North America
1787 Abolition society formed
1789 Jeremy Bentham publishes his *Principles of Morals and Legislation*
1791 Thomas Paine publishes *The Rights of Man*
1811 Rise of the Luddites
1817 Elizabeth Fry forms a society to improve conditions for female prisoners
1819 Peterloo massacre
1829 Metropolitan Police established by Robert Peel
1838 Rise of Chartism in Britain
1849 Harrods is opened
1856 David Livingstone discovers Victoria falls
1858 Fenian movement established in America
1859 Charles Darwin publishes *On the Origin of Species by Process of Natural Selection*
1863 Work begins on the London Underground
1870 First Education Act passed
1884 Greenwich Mean Time adopted
1905 Emmeline Pankhurst launches the suffragettes movement
1929 Beginning of the Depression
1948 National Helath Service brought into operation
1953 Francis Crick and James Watson unravel the mystery of DNA
1966 Aberfan disaster leaves 116 children dead
1980s Corn circles appear throughout the UK
1988 Lockerbie bombing

WAR

1066 Battle of Hastings
1214 Battle of Bouvines
1215 King John is forced to sign the Magna Carta
1263 Barons' Wars break out between Henry III and his nobles
1265 Battle of Evesham
1298 Battle of Falkirk
1314 Battle of Bannockburn
1320 Declaration of Arbroath asserts Scottish independence
1333 Battle of Halidon Hill and Siege of Berwick
1346 Battle of Crécy
1356 Battle of Poitiers
1357 First treaty of Berwick
1415 Battle of Agincourt
1485 Battle of Bosworth brings the Wars of the Roses to an end
1513 Battle of Flodden
1638 Start of the Bishops' Wars between Charles I and Scottish Presbyterians
1642 Battle of Edgehill begins the English Civil War
1644 Battle of Marston Moor
1645 Battle of Naseby
1649 Siege of Drogheda
1650 Battle of Dunbar

1652 First Anglo-Dutch War begins
1664 Second Anglo-Dutch War begins
1672 Third Anglo-Dutch War begins
1688 Outbreak of the Nine Years' War
1689 Siege of Londonderry
1690 Battle of the Boyne
1704 Battle of Blenheim
1715 Jacobite Rebellion
1739 Battle of Jenkins' Ear
1740 War of Austrian Succession begins
1743 Battle of Dettingen
1746 Black Hole of Calcutta; Battle of Culloden
1748 Treaty of Aix-la-Chapelle ends the War of the Austrian Succession
1757 Battle of Plassey
1763 Treaty of Paris ends the Seven Years' War

1775 Battle of Bunker Hill
1780 Fourth Anglo-Dutch War begins
1781 Cornwallis surrenders after Battle of Yorktown in American Revolution
1803 Outbreak of the Napoleonic Wars
1805 Battle of Trafalgar
1815 Battle of Waterloo
1839 First Afghan War begins
1853 Crimean War breaks out
1854 Battle of Balaclava and Charge of the Light Brigade
1878 Second Afghan War
1899 Beginning of the Boer War
1902 Treaty of Vereeninging ends the Boer War
1914 World War I breaks out
1915 Unsuccessful campaign in the Dardanelles

1917 Third Battle of Ypres (Passchendaele)
1918 Armistice ends World War I
1919 Third Afghan War
1939 Conscription Act introduced
1940 Blitz, Battle of Britain, Evacuation of Dunkirk
1941 Japanese attack on Pearl Harbor brings US into the war
1944 D-Day landings; Battle of Arnhem
1982 Falklands War
1990 Gulf War

GLOSSARY

ABSOLUTE MONARCHY
Rule by a king or queen whereby they are not subject to the laws of government or Parliament.

AFRIKAANER
Native of South Africa descended from predominantly Dutch heritage. Afrikaans were also referred to as Boars or Voertrekkers.

AGNOSTICISM
Belief that the existence of God is indeterminable, but one which does not exclude belief in other spiritual existence.

ALLIES
Term commonly used to describe the countries opposing the Central Powers during World War I: Great Britain, France and Russia. A term also used in World War II.

ANABAPTISTS
Members of Protestant movements, generally from the sixteenth century, who rejected child baptism in favour of adult baptism.

ANARCHY
Political theory that advocates a society run without coersive authority from government, religion or education, that would impose limits on the freedom of the individual.

ANGLICANISM
Belief in the Christian teachings and doctrine of the Church of England, as opposed to that of the Roman Catholic Church.

BRONZE AGE
Period of history characterized by the use of early metals such as copper and its alloys. The Bronze Age is commonly dated at around 3000–2000 BC, although it began at different times around the world.

CAPITALISM
Economic system of private rather than state ownership, as a means to employ people and produce food and goods.

CENTRAL POWERS
Term used to describe the nations of central Europe that formed various alliances between 1882 and 1945. Originally they comprised Germany, Austria-Hungary and Italy. During World War I, Italy was absent, but rejoined for World War II. Austria became a member, independent of Hungary, in 1918.

CIVIL WAR
War between peoples of the same nation, usually proving socially and economically devastating for the country concerned.

COLONIALISM
Political policy by which one country subjugates another to its own rule, with the aim of creating an empire. This can be by economic, religious or military means.

CONSERVATION
Preservation, protection and efficient management of all natural resources, including that of living organisms. The sustainable use by a country of its natural resources has long been recognised as essential for economic growth.

CONSTITUTION
Fundamental principles on which a state is governed; may be written or based on precedent, but should embody the rights of the individual.

CONSTITUTIONAL MONARCHY
Rule by a king or queen in which their powers are limited by means of a democratic political system.

CRO-MAGNON
Early type of Stone Age *Homo sapien* who lived in Europe during Paleolithic times.

DARK AGES
Period in Europe from the fifth to eleventh centuries, noted for its lack of enlightenment in thought or government, law and order.

DEMOCRACY
System of government for the people, by the people, normally through election. The word derives from the Greek words *demos* ('community') and *kratos* ('power').

DISESTABLISHMENT
Situation in which the Church of England is denied constitutional involvement in Parliament and no longer holds the position of a national institution.

DIVINE RIGHT OF KINGS
Christian political belief that the monarch is God's representative on Earth and is subject to no man's will or laws. Rebellion against the monarch was therefore rebellion against God and thus blasphemous.

ECUMENICISM
Religious theory that argues for the mass unity of all denominations of Christianity around the world.

FIN DE SIÈCLE
Prevailing artistic mood at the close of the nineteenth century – one both of optimism and decadence.

GAUL
Area covering largely what is present-day France during the period of the Roman Empire. It stretched into what is now northern Italy and the Netherlands.

GUILDS
Trade associations in which members share the same skill, such as silvermaking, in order to maintain craft standards and protect business.

HERETICS
Those who held beliefs contrary to the teachings of the established church; heretics were frequently burnt at the stake if they would not recant.

HUMANITARIANISM
Theory that places importance on the interests of humanity as opposed to personal or national interests. Most recently humanitarianism has manifested itself in environmental policies and aid for the Third World.

ICE AGE
Periods of time, lasting millions of years, when the Earth, its oceans and atmosphere experience a significant drop in temperature causing the formation of large ice masses. The most recent ice age began about two million years ago.

IMPERIALISM
Practice of any one state to influence or conquer another in order to expand its own wealth, levels of power and dominions.

IRON AGE
Period of history characterised by the use of iron, a development of the bronze previously used. The Iron Age is usually dated at around 1000–500 BC.

JACOBITE
Follower of James II or his descendants, wishing to restore the Stuarts to the throne after the Glorious Revolution.

JUTES
Germanic peoples who originated in Jutland but later settled in the territory of the Franks. They came to occupy Kent in around AD 450 under Hengist and Horsa and conquered the Isle of Wight.

LIBERALISM
Theory that places importance on an individual's civil or political rights, particularly their freedom of speech and expression.

MAYPOLES
Poles painted with spiral stripes and decked with flowers; danced around on May Day to celebrate the coming Spring.

MESOLITHIC
Name given to the Middle period of the Stone Age, normally taken to begin when the Ice Age finally receded and Earth's climate took on its present-day status. The Mesolithic era is normally dated from around 10,000 years ago.

MODERNISM
Early twentieth-century approach to the arts that explored Freud's ideas on human consciousness through abstract artistic techniques.

NATIONALISM
Pride in, and a sense of belonging to, a nation. In extreme forms nationalism can lead to hatred of other nations and peoples, such as in Nazi Germany.

NEANDERTHAL
Type of primitive Stone Age man, who hunted and gathered in Europe during the Paleolithic era.

NEOLITHIC
Name given to the final part of the Stone Age, after the Mesolithic period, normally dated from around 8000–3000 BC. The Neolithic era is characterised by the development of agriculture.

OLD ENGLISH
Earliest English, spoken by Anglo-Saxons from their first settlements in the fifth to twelfth centuries.

PACIFISM
Belief in the immorality of war; that it cannot be in any way justified. During World Wars I and II pacifism became increasingly widespread, with those refusing to fight on grounds of pacifism called conscientious objectors.

PAGANISM
Name given to anyone who followed a religion other than Christianity. First used in the fourteenth century, pagans suffered years of persecution once Christianity was established.

PATRIOTISM
Historically a devotion to and desire to defend one's nation and way of life; patriotism can now have nationalistic connotations.

PICTS
Roman name given to Scottish tribes inhabiting Britain before the Celts. The Picts united with Scotland's Celts in AD 844.

PREHISTORY
Period of history that covers the time since life first formed on Earth (about 3.5 billion years ago) up until human beings began to keep records.

RACISM
Belief in the superiority of one race over another; often manifesting itself in social discrimination and giving rise to violence.

REPUBLICANISM
Support for a system where heads of state are not monarchs; only once realised in England under Oliver Cromwell, who was named 'Lord Protector'.

ROMANTICISM
Late eighteenth to early nineteenth-century Classical artistic movement in Europe, emphasising individual imagination, inspired by revolution and social changes.

SECULARISM
Belief that rejects religion, particularly in political or civil matters, and embraces worldly and material rather than sacred things.

SOCIALISM
Political ideal that opposes the theory of class and private ownership. Such ideas can be traced back to Ancient Greece and beyond, but became popular only with the industrial revolution and large urban populations.

STONE AGE
The earliest period of human history. As its name suggests the Stone Age was characterized by the use of stone tools and implements. The Stone Age encompasses the periods of history known as Paleolithic, Mesolithic and Neolithic.

SUFFRAGE
Term used to identify which citizens are eligible to vote in elections. The UK has universal adult suffrage (over 18 years old) with a few exceptions. Universal suffrage is a key tenet of modern democracy.

TORYISM
Political ideology of Conservative values. From 1680 to modern day, Toryism has been traditionally supported by landed classes and latterly the middle classes.

UTILITARIANISM
Ethical thinking outlined by Jeremy Bentham and John Stuart Mill maintaining that actions are morally right if leading to happiness.

UTOPIANISM
Idea that an ideal society is possible where systems are set in place for humans to live in co-operative communities.

BIBLIOGRAPHY

Addington, L. H., *The Patterns of War Since the Eighteenth Century*, Indianapolis, 1984
Alford, B. W. E., *Britain in the World Economy Since 1880*, Harlow, 1996
Arnold, C. J., An *Archeology of the early Anglo-Saxon Kingdoms*, London, 1998
Ball, S. J., *The Cold War: An International History*, 1947–1991, London, 1998
Banks, A., *A Military Atlas of the First World War*, London, 1975
Bennett, M., *The Civil Wars In Britain and Ireland, 1638–1651*, Oxford, 1997
Black, C. F., Greengrass, M., Howarth, D. et al, *Cultural Atlas of the Renaissance,* Oxford, 1993

Blackburn, Simon, *Oxford Concise Dictionary of Philosophy,* Oxford University Press, Oxford, 1996
Blair, P. H., *Roman Britain and Early England, 55 BC–AD 871*, 1963
Blanning, T. C. W. (ed.), *The Oxford Illustrated History of Modern Europe*, Oxford University Press, Oxford, 1996
Bohlander, R. E., *World Explorers and Discoverers*, New York, 1992
Bowker, John (ed.), *The Oxford Dictionary of World Religions,* Oxford University Press, Oxford, 1997
Bruce, George, *Collins Dictionary of Wars,* London, 1995
Calvocoressi, Peter, *World Politics Since 1945*, New York, 1991
Chacoliades, Militiades, *International Economics*, New York and London, 1990
Chandler, David, *The Dictionary of Battles*, London, 1987
Chapman, Stanley, *Merchant Enterprise in Britain from the Industrial Revolution to World War One*, Cambridge, 1992
Cootes, R. J., *Britain Since 1700*, London, 1968
Corrie, L. W., *Life in Britain*, London, 1980
Cross, F. L., *The Oxford Dictionary of the Christian Church,* Oxford University Press, Oxford, 1978
Cunliffe, Barry (Foreword), *The Cassell Atlas of World History,* London, 1997
Dalton, P., *Conquest, Anarchy & Lordship, Yorkshire, 1066–1154*, Cambridge, 1994
Darby H. C. (ed.), *A New Historical Geography of England*, Cambridge, 1973
Darvill, T., *Prehistoric Britain*, London, 1987
Daunton, M. J., *Progress and Poverty: An Economic and Social History of Britain, 1700–1850*, Oxford, 1995
Deane, P., *The First Industrial Revolution*, Cambridge, 1965
Delaney, Frank, *A Walk in the Dark Ages*, London, 1994
Douglas, J. D. (ed.), *The New International Dictionary of the Christian Church*, Paternoster Press, 1978
Du Boulery, F. R. H., *An Age of Reason*, London, 1970
Edmund, G. E., *Land and Society,* London, 1994
Eliade, Mircea, *A History of Religious Ideas*, Chicago, 1984
Evans, Eric (ed.), *The Illustrated Guide to British History,* Dempsey Parr, Bath, 1999
Evans, Eric, *The Complete A–Z Nineteenth and Twentieth Century British History Handbook*, London, 1998
Featherstone, Donald, *Colonial Small Wars*, David and Charles Publishing, London
Fieldhouse, D. K., *The Colonial Empires*, London, 1966
Foreman-Peck, James and Millward, Robert, *Public and Private Ownership of British Industry 1820–1990*, Oxford, 1994

Fraser, Antonia (ed.), *The Lives of the Kings & Queens of England*, Weidenfeld and Nicholson, London, 1993
Friend, W. H. C., *The Rise of Christianity, London*, 1984
Fussell, P., *The Great War and Modern Memory*, London, 1975
Gardiner, Judith, *The History Today Who's Who in British History*, Collins and Brown, London, 2000
Gilbert, Martin, *First World War*, HarperCollins, London, 1994
Gilbert, Martin, *Second World War*, London, 1989
Gilbert, Martin, *The Dent Atlas of British History*, London, 1993
Goodman, A., *The Wars of the Roses, Military Activity and English Society, 1452–1497*, London, 1981
Goodman, M., *The Roman World*, 44 BC–AD 180, London, 1997
Graham-Campbell, J. (ed.), *Atlas of the Viking World*, Oxford, 1994
Greene, D. M., *Greene's Biographical Encyclopedia of Composers*, London, 1996
Haigh, Christopher (ed.), *The Cambridge Historical Encyclopedia of Great Britain and Ireland*, Cambridge, 1996
Hanbury-Tenison, R. (ed.), *The Oxford Book of Exploration*, Oxford, 1993
Hart, L., *The History of the Second World War*, London, 1970
Haswell, Jock, *The Battle for Empire*, Cassell, London, 1976
Hayes, M. and Smalley, K. (eds), *Work, Employment & Development*, London, 1990
Heath, Ian, *Armies of the Dark Ages*, War Games Research Group, 1980
Herrin, J., *The Formation of Christendom*, Oxford, 1987
Hillier, Bevis, *The Style of the Century*, London, 1983
Hinnells, John (ed.), *Who's Who of Religions*, Penguin Books, London, 1996
Hobsbawm, E. J., *The Penguin Economic History of Britain, Volume 3: Industry and Empire*, London, 1990
Hobsbawn, E. J., *Industry and Empire*, London, 1990
Hobsbawn, E. J., *The Age of Extremes, 1919–1991*, London, 1994
Holmes, George (ed.), *The Oxford Illustrated History of Medieval Europe*, Oxford University Press, Oxford, 1988
Hughes, Robert, *The Shock of the New*, London, 1991
Janson, H .W., *History of Art*, London, 1991
Jones, B. & Mattingly, D., *An Atlas of Roman Britain*, Oxford, 1990
Keen, M., *The Pelican History of Medieval Europe*, London, 1968
Knowles, D., *The Monastic Order in England 940–1216*, Cambridge, 1963
Kussmaul, *A. A .,General View of the Rural Economy of England, 1538–1840*, Cambridge, 1990
Lanfton, J. & Morris, R. J. (eds), *Atlas of Industrialising Britain, 1780–1914*, London, 1986
Langmuir, Erika and Norbert, Lynton, *The Yale Dictionary of Art and Artists*, Yale University Press, 2000
Laybourn, Keith, *Britain on the Breadline*, Surrey, 1990
Lenman, B. P. (ed.), *Chambers Dictionary of World History*, Chambers, London, 2000
Ling, Trevor, *A History of Religion East and West*, London, 1977
Lloyd, T. O., *The British Empire, 1558–1995*, Oxford, 1996
Macfarlane, L. J., *The Theory and Practice of Human Rights*, London, 1985
Manners, John (ed.), *The Oxford Illustrated History of Christianity*, Oxford University Press, Oxford, 1990
Marshall, P. J. (ed.), *The Eighteenth Century: Oxford History of the British Empire, Vol. II*, Oxford, 1998
Mathias, Hefin, *Wales and Britain in the Early Medieval World c. 1000–c. 1500*, London, 1996
Mayr-Harting, H., *The Coming of Christianity to Anglo-Saxon England*, London, 1972

McHenry, Robert (ed.), *Webster's New Biographical Dictionary*, Miriam Webster, Inc., 1988
McManners, John, *The Oxford History of Christianity*, Oxford, 1993
Messadie, Gerald, *Great Modern Inventions*, Edinburgh, 1991
Messenger, Charles, *The Century of Warfare: Worldwide Conflict from 1900 to the Present Day*, London, 1995
Morgan, Kenneth O. (ed.), *The Oxford Illustrated History of Britain*, Oxford, 1997
Morillo, S., *Warfare Under the Anglo-Norman Kings, 1066–1135*, Woodbridge, 1994
Newman, P., *A Companion to the English Civil Wars*, Oxford, 1990
Norwich, John Julius (ed.), *The Oxford Illustrated Encyclopedia of the Arts*, Oxford University Press, Oxford, 1984
Ousby, Ian (ed.), *The Cambridge Guide to Literature in English*, Cambridge University Press, London, 1989
Pakenham, T., *The Scramble for Africa, 1876–1912*, London, 1991
Parker, G. (ed.), *The Times Atlas of World History* (4th ed.), London, 1996
Pollard, A. J., *The Wars of the Roses*, London, 1988
Pope, R. (ed.), *Atlas of British Social and Economic History Since c. 1700*, London, 1990

Porter, A. N., *Atlas of British Overseas Expansion*, London, 1991
Pugh, Martin, *The Making of Modern British Politics*, Oxford, 1982
Quennell, Q. and C. H. B., *A History of Everyday Things 1066–1799*, London, 1931
Quirke, S. & Spencer, J., *The British Museum Book of Ancient Egypt*, London, 1992
Radway, R., *Britain, 1900–1951*, London, 1997
Reay, Barry, *Popular Cultures in England 1550–1750*, London, 1998
Roberts, J. M., *The Penguin History of Europe*, Penguin Books, London, 1996
Rolleston, T. W., *Celtic*, London, 1995
Ross, Josephine, *Kings and Queens of Britain*, London, 1982
Salway, P., *Roman Britain*, Oxford, 1981
Sauvain, Philip A., *British Economic and Social History*, 1987
Savage, A. (trans.), *The Anglo-Saxon Chronicles*, London, 1982
Smout, T. C., *A History of the Scottish Peoples*, London, 1969
Solomon, Robert C. and Higgins, Kathleen M., *A Short History of Philosophy*, Oxford, 1996
Taylor, A. J. P., *English History, 1914–1945*, Oxford, 1965
Taylor, A. J. P., *From the Boer War to the Cold War*, London, 1995
Thomas, H., *The Slave Trade: The History of the Atlantic Slave Trade,1440–1870*, New York, 1997
Tomlinson, Jim, *Public Policy and the Economy Since 1900*, New York, 1990
Treasure, Geoffrey, *Who's Who in British History*, London, 1997
Tucker, S. C., *The Great War*, London, 1998
Walsh, B., *British Economic & Social History*, London, 1997
Weller, P. (ed.), *Religions in the U.K. A Multi-faith Directory*, University of Derby, 1997
Wood, Jack, *Union for Recovery the Failure and Rise of British Industry*, Wembley, 1986
Woolf, Stewart (ed.), *Nationalism in Europe*, London, 1996
Young, John, W., *Britain and the World in the Twentieth Century*, London, 1997

AUTHOR BIOGRAPHIES

ERIC EVANS
General Editor

Eric Evans is Professor of Social History at the University of Lancaster. He has edited and contributed to numerous studies on the history of the British Isles, as well as writing many of his own titles, including *The Birth of Modern Britain* and *The Complete A–Z 19th and 20th Century British History Handbook.*

GERARD CHESHIRE
Industry and Society

Gerard Cheshire is a prolific writer. He has written and contributed to many books on a wide range of subjects, including science, social history and technology as well as magazine articles and partworks.

DAVID HARDING
Politics

David Harding is an experienced journalist. His specialist subject is political history and current affairs, but he also writes on subjects as diverse as sport and war.

LUCINDA HAWKSLEY
Culture

Lucinda Hawksley is a freelance writer and editor. She studied art history and has published several books on art, including *Pre-Raphaelites.*

BRENDA RALPH LEWIS
Royalty

Brenda Ralph Lewis has been writing on historical subjects for 35 years, specialising in the history of the British royal family. She has written or contributed to nearly 100 books on the subject and also writes BBC television programmes.

JON SUTHERLAND
War

Jon Sutherland is an experienced writer and lecturer in business studies. He has written and contributed to over 100 books and encyclopedias on a wide range of subjects. His specialist area is military history.

HELEN TOVEY
Religion

Helen Tovey completed a degree in History at the University of Exeter. Since then she has been working as a writer and editor, specialising in British and European social history, religion, art and architecture.

PICTURE CREDITS

The Art Archive Limited
13, The Art Archive/Musee de Versailles/Dagli Orti, 17(t) The Art Archive/Biblioteca Nazionale Turin/Dagli Orti,(b) David Shepherd OBE FRSA FRGS/Parachute Regiment_19 (c)The Art Archive/ Museo Civico Cremona/ Dagli Orti (A), 24(l) The Art Archive/ Canterbury Cathedral/ Dagli Orti, (r) The Art Archive/ British Library, 29(c) The Art Archive/Civiche Race d'Arte Pavia Italy/Dagli Orti, 34 The Art Archive/Eileen Tweedy, 35 The Art Archive/Lords Gallery/Eileen Tweedy, 39 The Art Archive/Civiche Race d'Arte Moderna Pavia/ Dagli Orti (A), 40 The Art Archive/Jan Vinchon Numismatist Paris/Dagli Orti (A), 41(tl) Art Archive/Bibliotheque Universitaire Geneva/Dagli Orti, 42(r) The Art Archive/British Library (bl) The Art Archive/Dagli Orti (A), 44(l) The Art Archive/Musee de Versailles/Dagli Orti, 45 The Art Archive/British Library, 46 The Art Archive/British Museum, 47(tl) The Art Archive/Eileen Tweedy, 49(t) The Art Archive/National Gallery London, (b) The Art Archive/British Library, 50(b) The Art Archive/Musee des Beaux Arts Orleans/Dagli Orti (A), 53(tr) The Art Archive (bl) The Art Archive/Eileen Tweedy, 54(cr) The Art Archive/India Office Library, (b) The Art Archive/Ironbridge Gorge Museum, 55 The Art Archive/Private Collection/John Webb, 56(bl) The Art Archive/British Museum/Eileen Tweedy, 58(br) The Art Archive/Chateau de Blerancourt/Dagli Orti, 60(l) The Art Archive/British Library (r)The Art Archive/Royal Leicestershire Regiment/Eileen Tweedy, 61 The Art Archive/Pitti Palace Florence/Dagli Orti, 62(c) The Art Archive/ Museum of London/ Eileen Tweedy, 65(tl) The Art Archive/ Imperial War Museum [WM], 66 The Art Archive/Science Museum London, 69 The Art Archive/Dickens House London/Dagli Orti (A), 70 The Art Archive/Public Record Office London, 72 The Art Archive/Musee de Versailles/Dagli Orti (A), 73(r) The Art Archive/British Library, 75(tl) The Art Archive/Private Collection, 76 The Art Archive/British Library, 80(br) The Art Archive/Terence Cuneo, 82 The Art Archive/Musee de Versailles/Dagli Orti, 83 The Art Archive/Co of Merchants, City of Edinburgh, 91(all) The Art Archive/Royal Institution/Eileen Tweedy, 92(b) The Art Archive/Musee de Versailles/Dagli Orti, 95(b) The Art Archive/Musee de Versailles/Dagli Orti, 97 The Art Archive/British Museum/Eileen Tweedy, 99(t) The Art Archive/Cavalry Museum Pinerolo/Dagli Orti, 104(t) The Art Archive/Musee de L'Armee Paris/Dagli Orti, 106(l) The Art Archive/Miramare Museum Trieste/Dagli Orti, 110 The Art Archive, 112(t) The Art Archive/British Library (b)The Art Archive/Bibliotheque Nationale Paris, 113 The Art Archive, 114(bl) and 115 The Art Archive/Windsor Castle, 116(r) The Art Archive/ Galleria degli Uffizi Florence, 121(br) The Art Archive/London Museum/Eileen Tweedy, 122(l) The Art Archive/Eileen Tweedy, 123 The Art Archive/Tate Gallery London, 130(t) The Art Archive/Eileen Tweedy, 132(tl) The Art Archive/Imperial War Museum/Eileen Tweedy, 138 The Art Archive/Cromwell Museum, 139(l) The Art Archive/Eileen Tweedy, 146(l) The Art Archive/Eileen Tweedy (r) The Art Archive/Museo Tosio martinengo Brescia/Dagli Orti (A), 153(b) The Art Archive/Imperial War Museum [WM], 155(tr) The Art Archive/Museo del Prado Madrid/Dagli Orti, 158(r) The Art Archive/British Library, 159 The Art Archive/Musee de Versailles/Dagli Orti, 160(all) The Art Archive/Bibliotheque Nationale Paris, 161 The Art Archive/Private Collection/Eileen Tweedy, 164(b), The Art Archive/Imperial War Museum [WM], 169(t) The Art Archive/Museum of London, (b)The Art Archive/National Army Museum London/Eileen Tweedy, 170(all)The Art Archive/National Army Museum London/Eileen Tweedy, 175(t) The Art Archive/Musee des Artes Africains et Oceaniens/Dagli Orti, 176(l) The Art Archive/Eileen Tweedy, 179 The Art Archive/Dagli Orti, 180(tl) The Art Archive/Pitti Palace Florence/Dagli Orti (A), 181 The Art Archive/Musee du Louvre Paris/Dagli Orti (A), 182(cr and br) The Art Archive, 183 The Art Archive/British Museum/Eileen Tweedy, 185(t) The Art Archive/Eileen Tweedy, 186(r) The Art Archive/Museo Tridentino Arte Sacra Trento/Dagli Orti, 187 The Art Archive/National Gallery London/Album/Joseph Martin, 192(r)The Art Archive/City Temple, London/Eileen Tweedy, 202 The Art Archive/Imperial War Museum, 203(t) The Art Archive/Imperial War Museum [WM]

Foundry Arts: 23

Impact
19 (b)Tony Page/Impact, 26 (r)Piers Cavendish/Impact, 32 Simon Shepheard/Impact, 50 (t)Mohamed Ansar/Impact, 57 Philippe Achache/Impact, 63 Peter Arkell/Impact, 88 Simon Shepheard/Impact, 90 (b)Tom Picton/Impact, 99(b)Nigel Davies/Impact, 102 Tony Page/Impact, 103(t)Debay/Ernoult/Impact, 104(b)David Freeman/Impact Photos 105 Aerial Portraits/Impact, 109 Brian Rybolt/Impact, 118 Philip Gordon/Impact, 119(b) Geraint Lewis/Impact, 128(bl) Christine Porter/Impact Photos, 132(r) Impact Photos, 137 John Arthur/Impact, 145(b)Alex Macnaughton/Impact, 151 Jacqui Spector/Impact, 167 Julian Calder/Impact, 172(t)Tony Page/Impact, 193 Mike McQueen/Impact, 196/197 Tony Page/Impact

Maritime Museum Picture Library: 108(br

Mary Evans Picture Library: 8, 9(all), 10, 11(l), 12(all), 14, 15(l), 18, 20(all), 21, 22(all), 25, 26(bl), 27, 28, 29(br), 30(all, l: Mary Evans/Edwin Wallace), 31, 33(all), 36, 37(all, centre: Mary Evans / Institute of Civil Engineers), 38, 41(bl), 44(r), 47(r), 48, 51, 52, 56(r), 58(tl: Mary Evans/Lucy Pringle), 59, 62(bl), 64, 65(br), 67(all), 68(tl), 71(all), 73(l), 74(all), 77(r), 79, 81 Mary Evans/National Portrait Gallery London, 84(all), 86, 87(all), 89, 90(t), 92(t), 93, 94(all), 95(t), 96(b), 98, 100(all), 101, 103(b), 106(r), 107(all), 108(t), 114(t), 117, 119(t), 120, 122(r), 124, 125, 127(all), 130(b), 131, 133, 134, 135, 136(r), 141, 142(t), 143, 144, 145(tr), 147, 148 Mary Evans/Edwin Wallace, 150, 152, 153(tl and tr), 154(all), 155(b), 156, 157(all), 158(l), 164(t) 165, 166(all, l; Mary Evans/ Institution of Civil Engineers), 171, 172(b), 173, 176(br), 177, 178, 180(tr), 185(b), 188(t), 190 Mary Evans/Edwin Wallace, 191(r), 192(l), 195(all), 198, 199, 200(r), 201, 203(br),

Topham Picturepoint:11(r), 15(r), 16, 41(r), 43, 68(br), 75(br), 77(l), 78, 80(t and br), 85(all), 96(tl and tr), 111(all), 114(br), 116(b), 121(bl), 126, 128(br), 129, 136(t), 139(t), 140, 142(b), 149, 162(all), 163, 168, 174, 175(b) 182(bl), 184, 186(t), 188(b), 189, 191(bl), 194, 196(t), 197(br), 200(l)

INDEX

Page references in bold indicate articles on the subject and italics refer to illustrations.